SORRY
I RUINED YOUR
CHILDHOOD

Andrews McMeel Publishing
a division of Andrews McMeel Universal
1130 Walnut Street, Kansas City, Missouri 64106

www.andrewsmcmeel.com

19 20 21 22 23 TEN 10 9 8 7 6 5 4 3 2 1

ISBN: 978-1-5248-5173-6

Library of Congress Control Number: 2019932739

Editor: Lucas Wetzel
Art Director: Spencer Williams
Production Editor: Amy Strassner
Production Manager: Tamara Haus

ATTENTION: SCHOOLS AND BUSINESSES
Andrews McMeel books are available at quantity discounts with bulk purchase for educational, business, or sales promotional use. For information, please e-mail the Andrews McMeel Publishing Special Sales Department: specialsales@amuniversal.com.

SORRY
I RUINED YOUR
CHILDHOOD

Berkeley Mews Comics

Ben Zaehringer

Andrews McMeel
PUBLISHING®

SORRY I RUINED YOUR ...

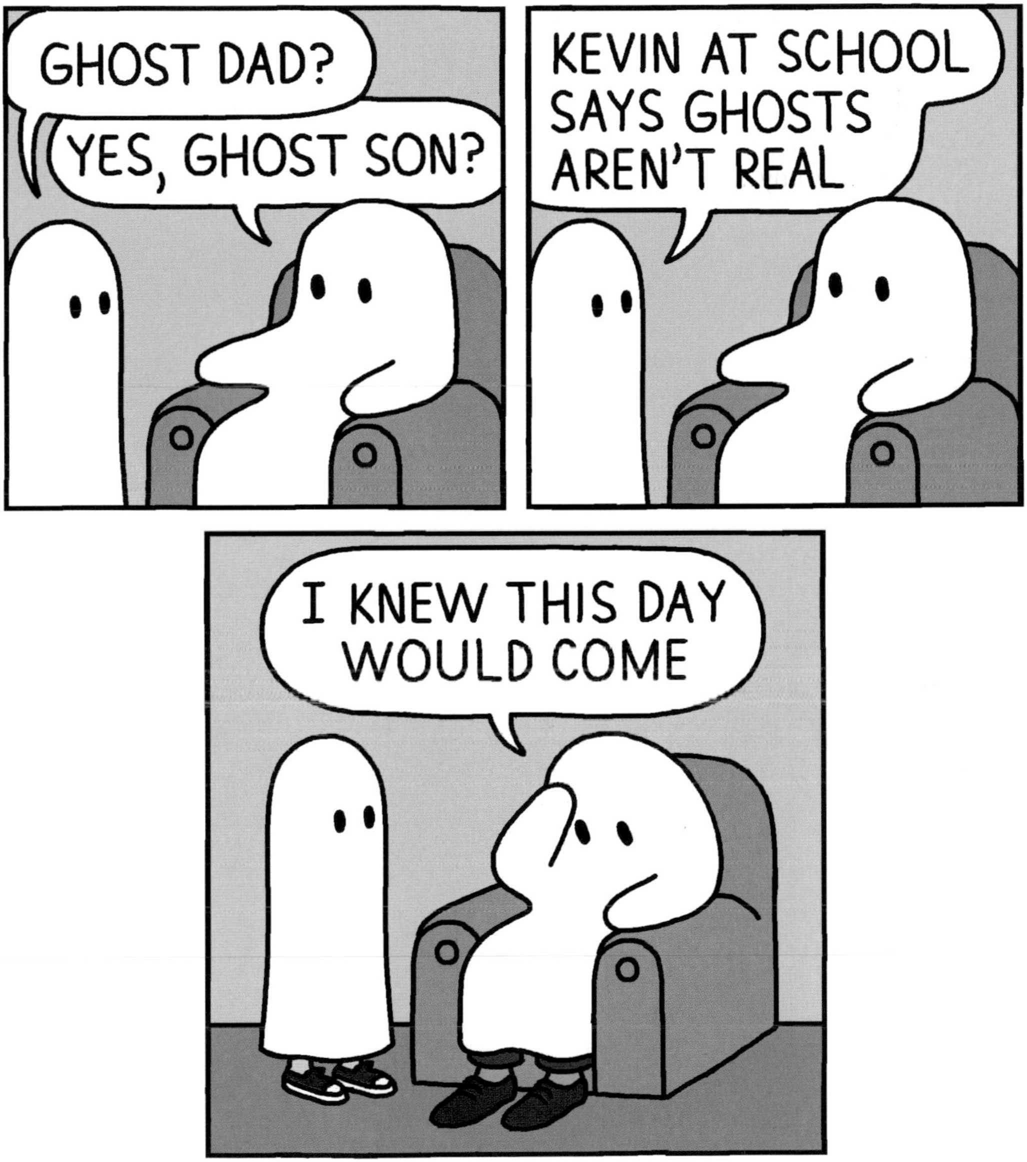
GHOST DAD?
YES, GHOST SON?
KEVIN AT SCHOOL SAYS GHOSTS AREN'T REAL
I KNEW THIS DAY WOULD COME

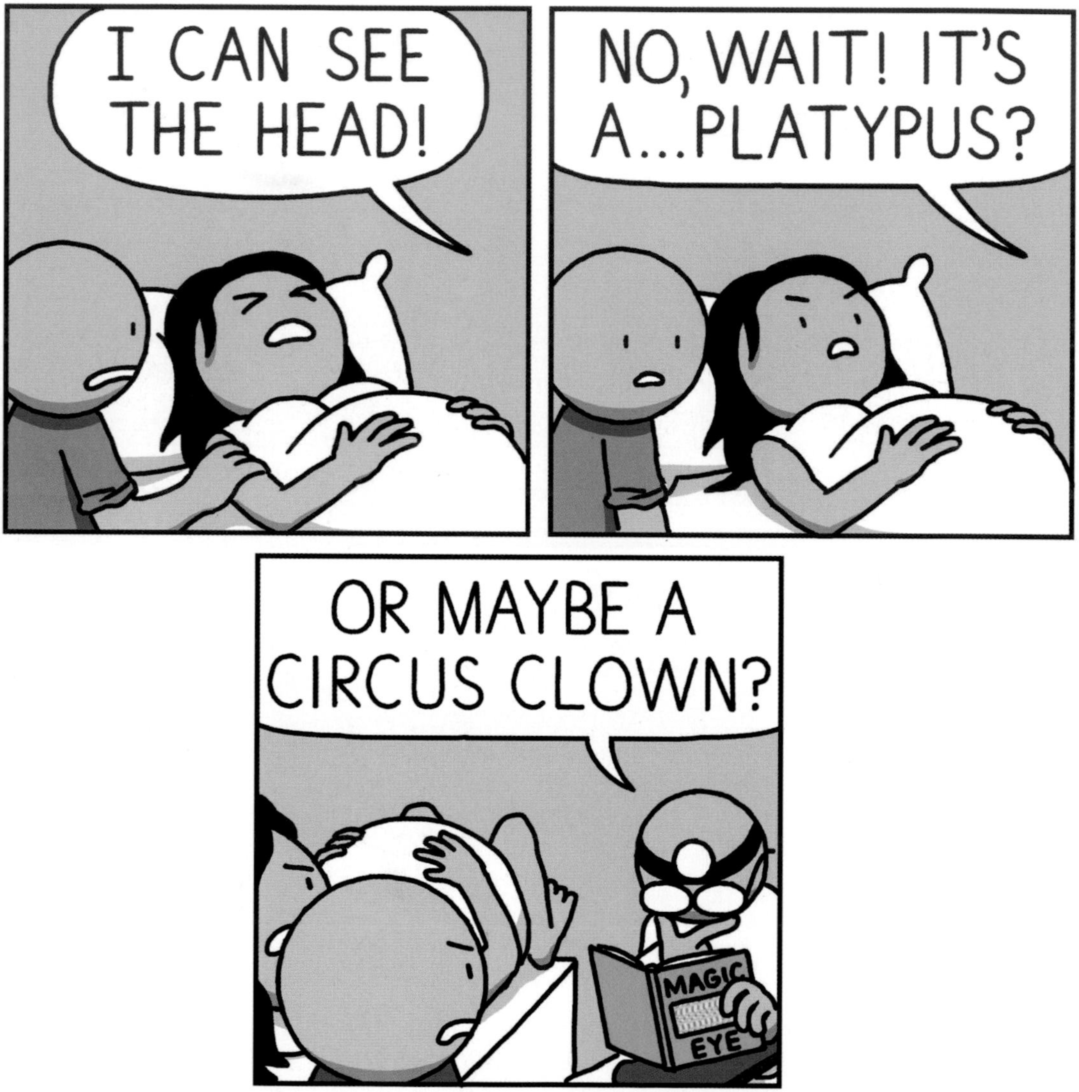
I CAN SEE THE HEAD!
NO, WAIT! IT'S A...PLATYPUS?
OR MAYBE A CIRCUS CLOWN?
MAGIC EYE

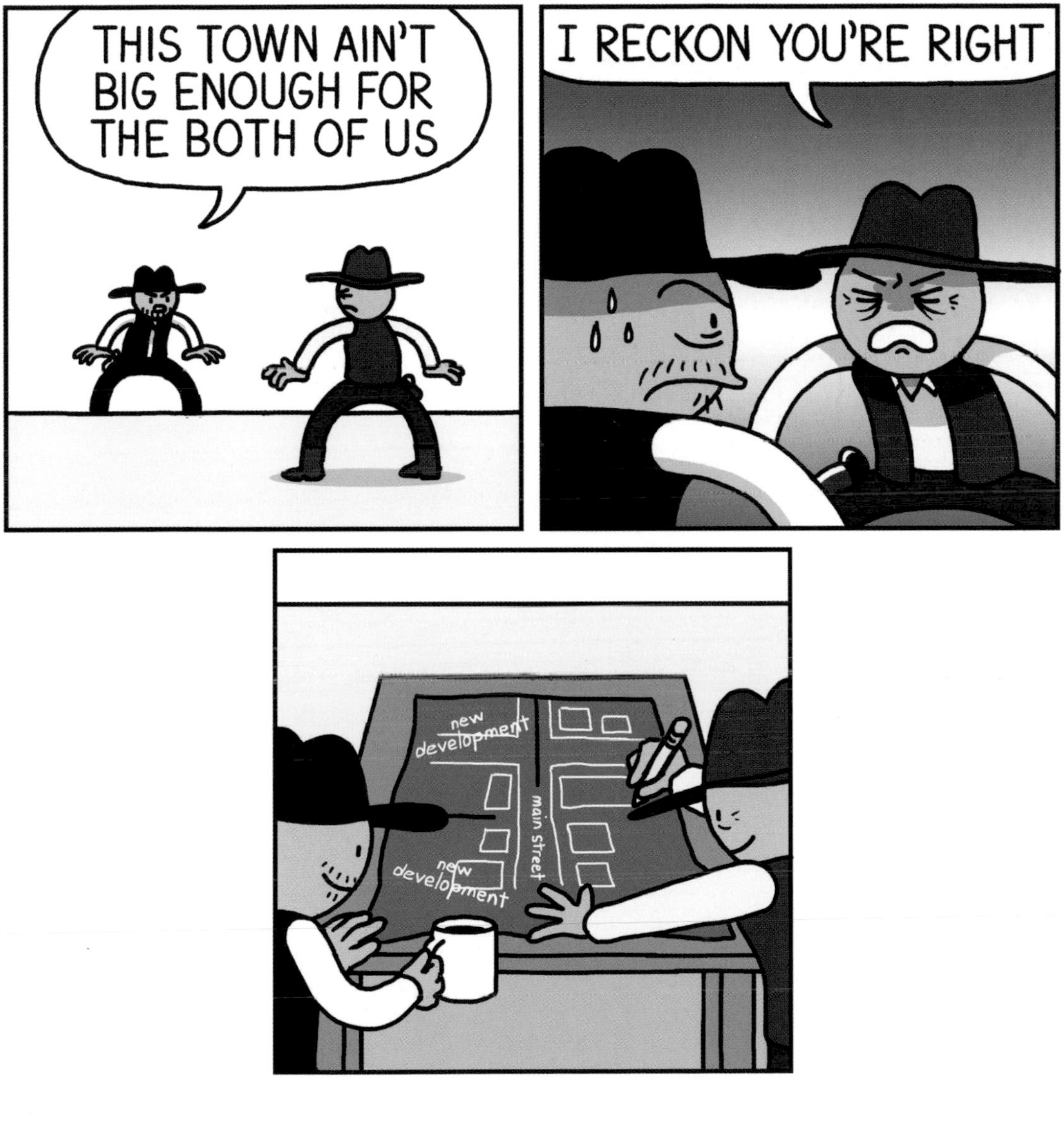
THIS TOWN AIN'T BIG ENOUGH FOR THE BOTH OF US
I RECKON YOU'RE RIGHT
new development
main street
new development

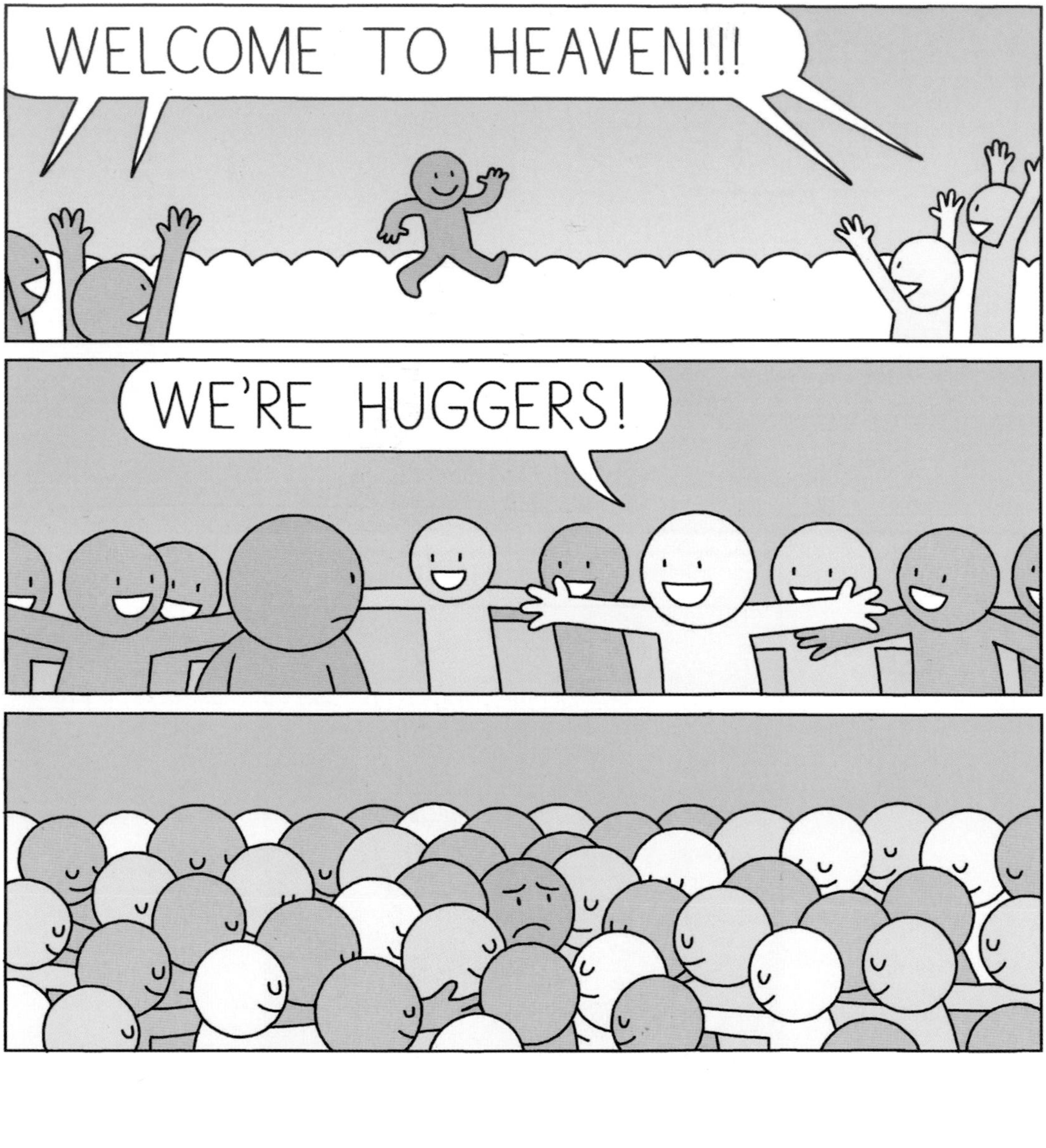
WELCOME TO HEAVEN!!!
WE'RE HUGGERS!

nintinder

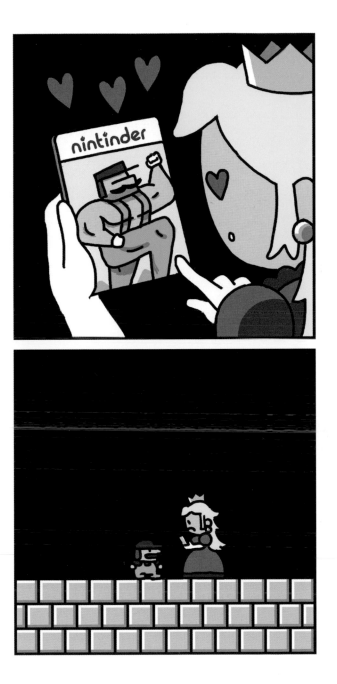

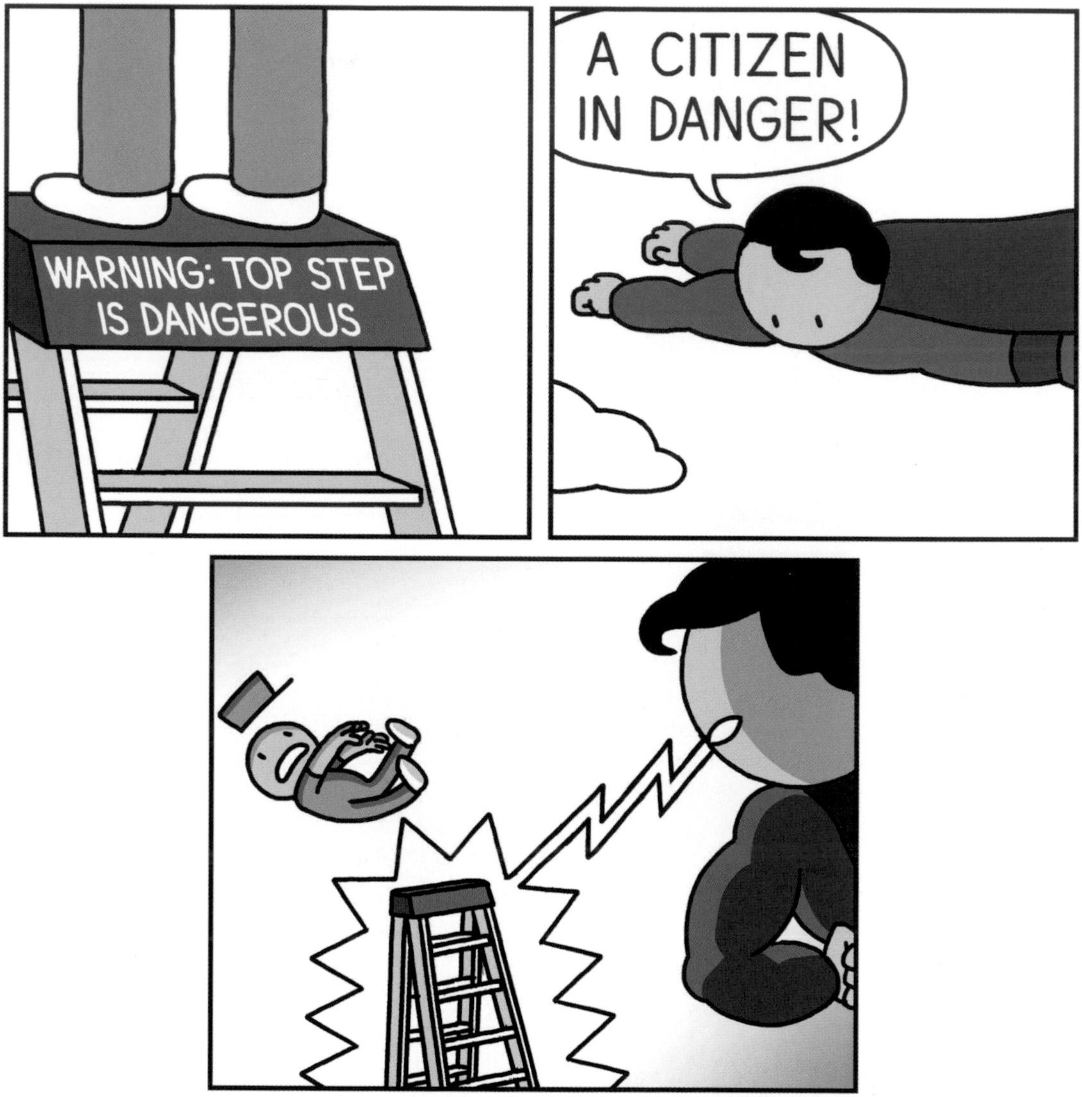
WARNING: TOP STEP IS DANGEROUS
A CITIZEN IN DANGER!

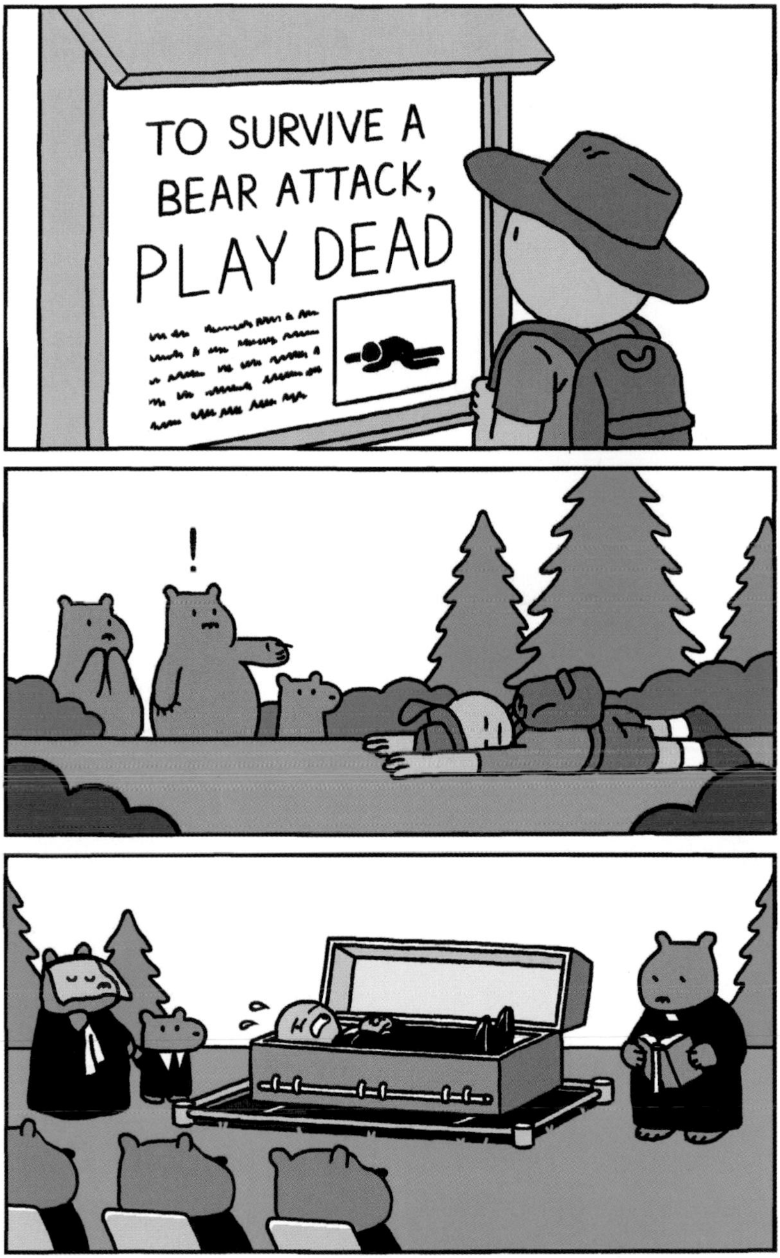
TO SURVIVE A BEAR ATTACK, PLAY DEAD
!

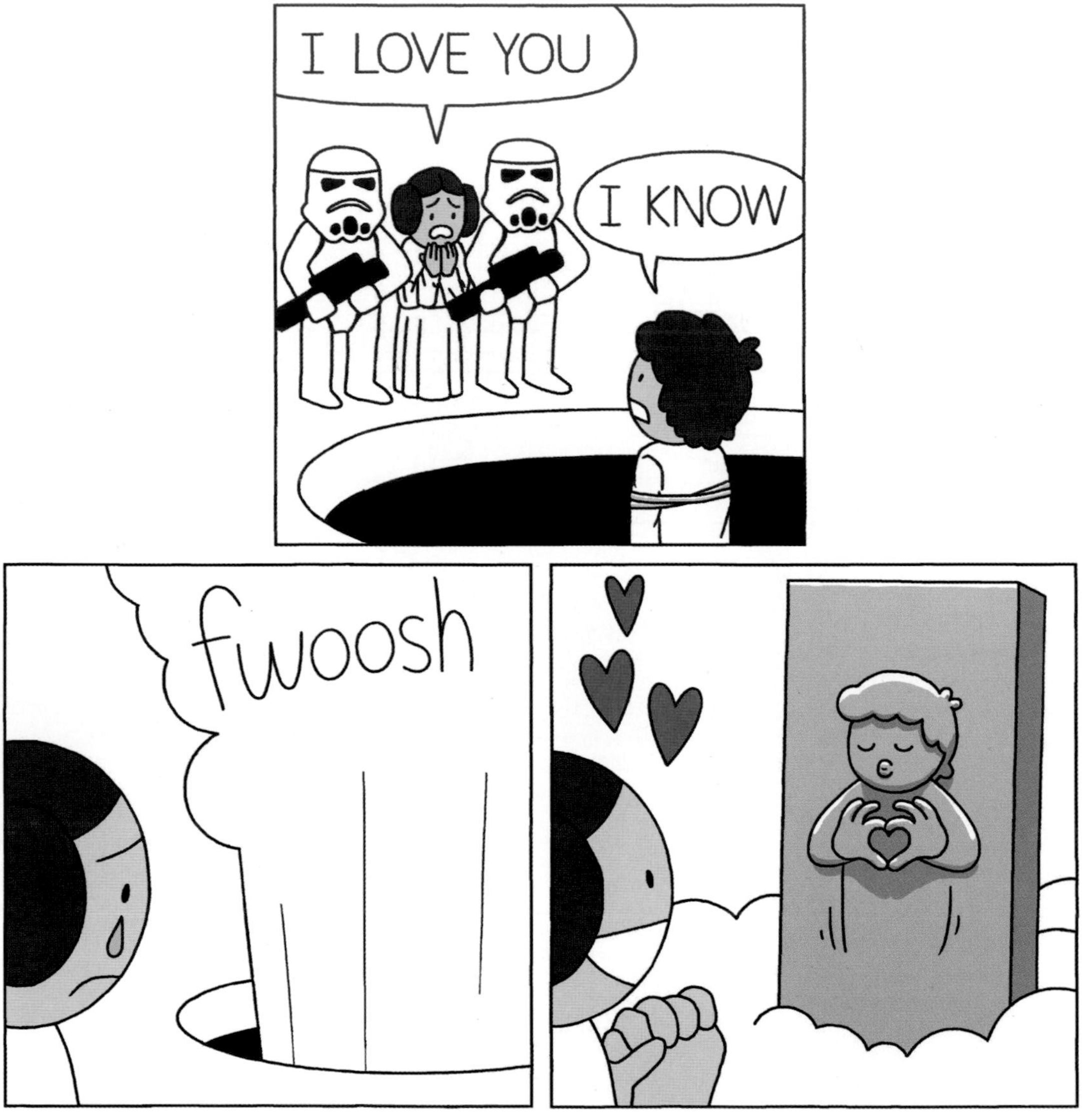
I LOVE YOU
I KNOW
fwoosh

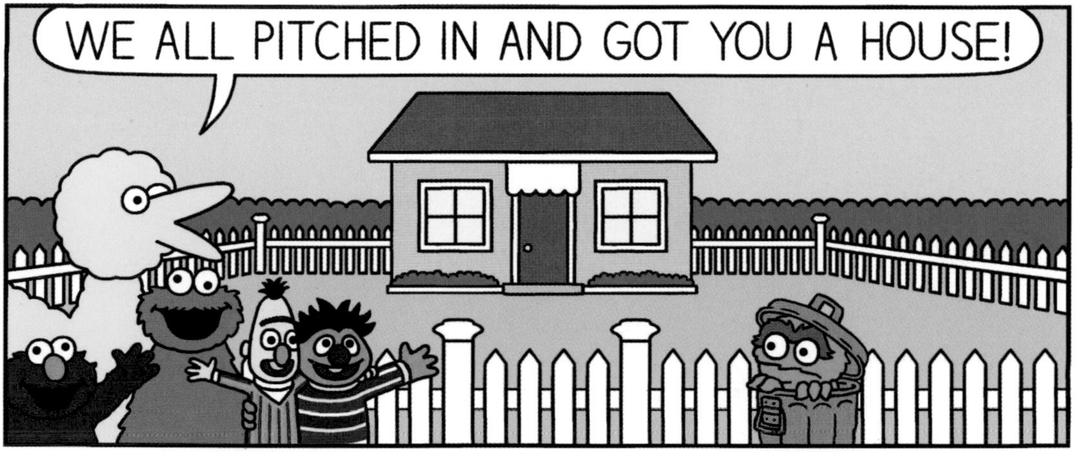
WE ALL PITCHED IN AND GOT YOU A HOUSE!

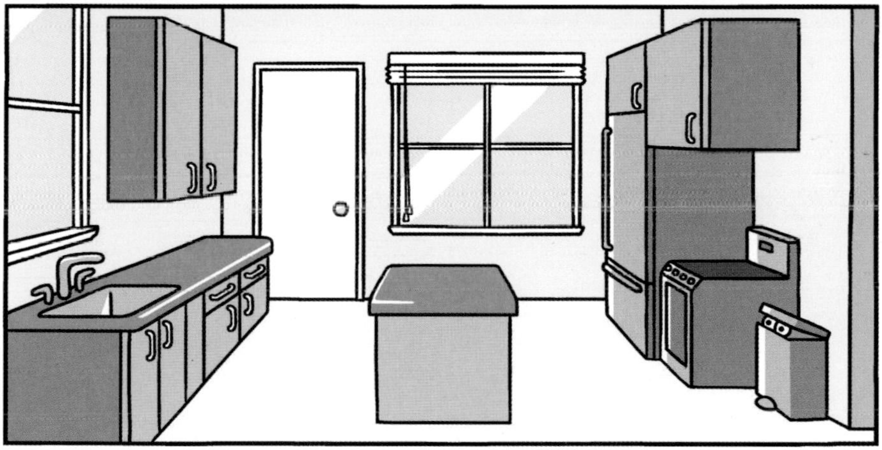

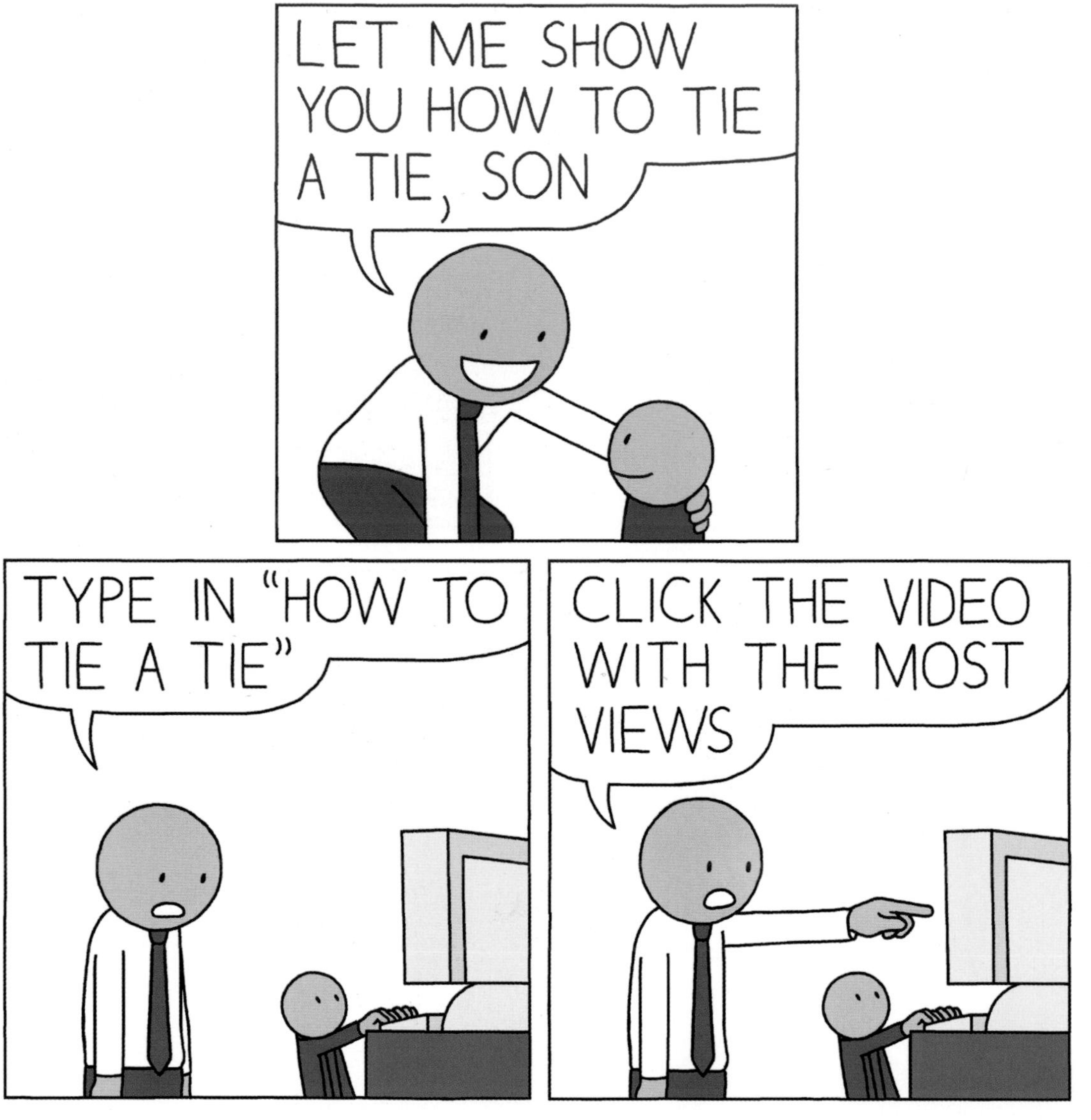
LET ME SHOW YOU HOW TO TIE A TIE, SON
TYPE IN "HOW TO TIE A TIE"
CLICK THE VIDEO WITH THE MOST VIEWS

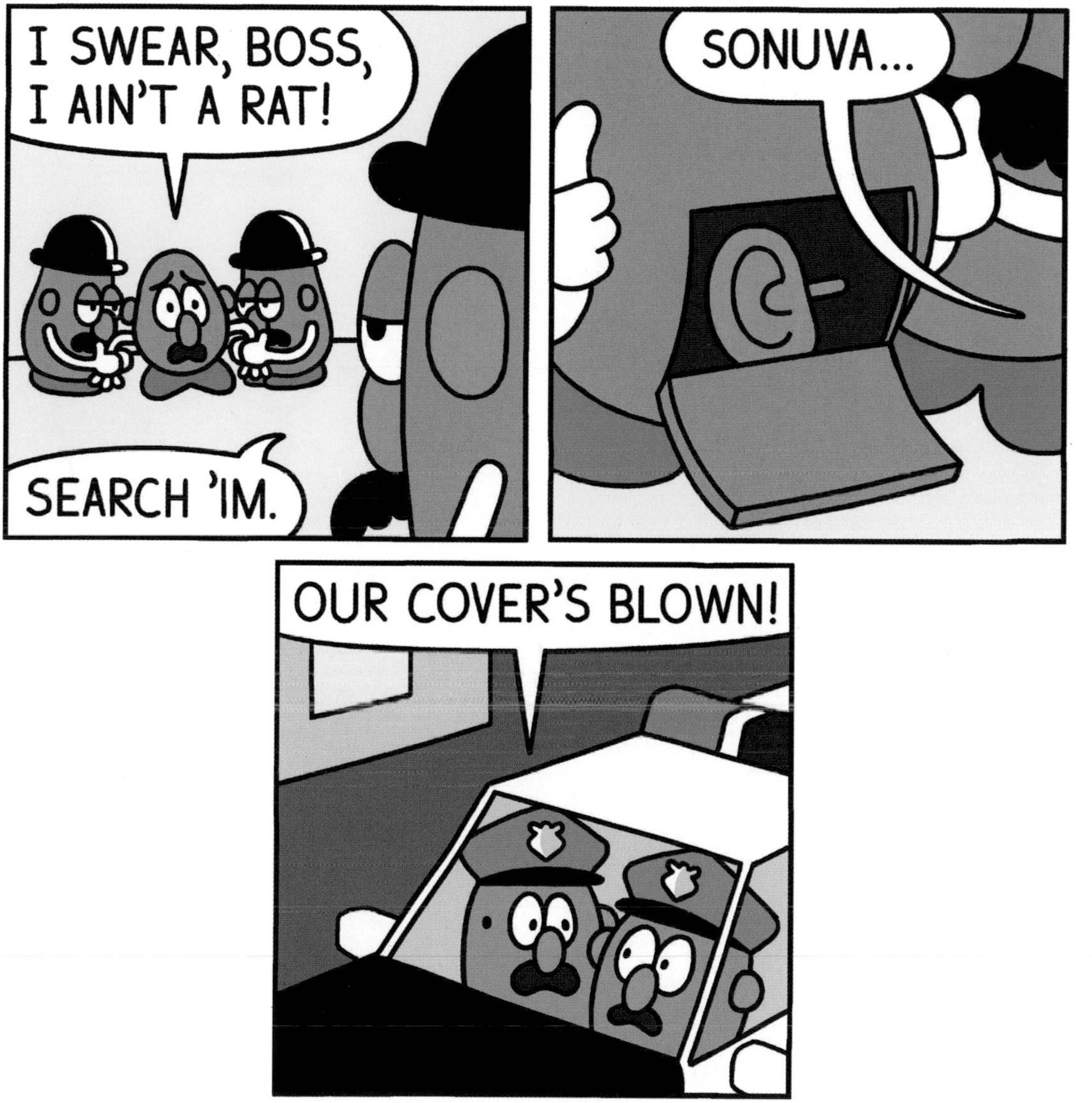
I SWEAR, BOSS, I AIN'T A RAT!
SEARCH 'IM.
SONUVA...
OUR COVER'S BLOWN!

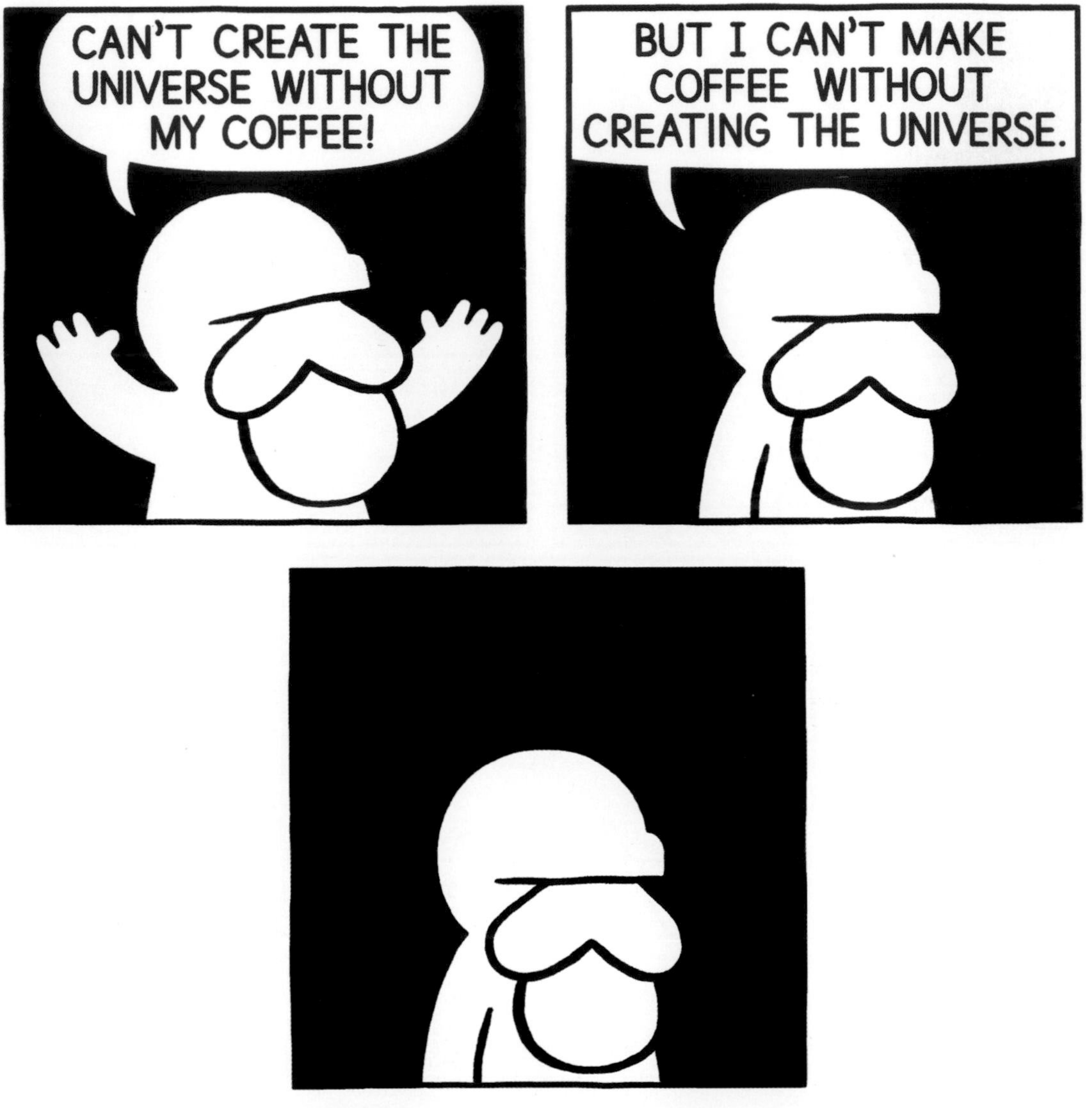
CAN'T CREATE THE UNIVERSE WITHOUT MY COFFEE!
BUT I CAN'T MAKE COFFEE WITHOUT CREATING THE UNIVERSE.

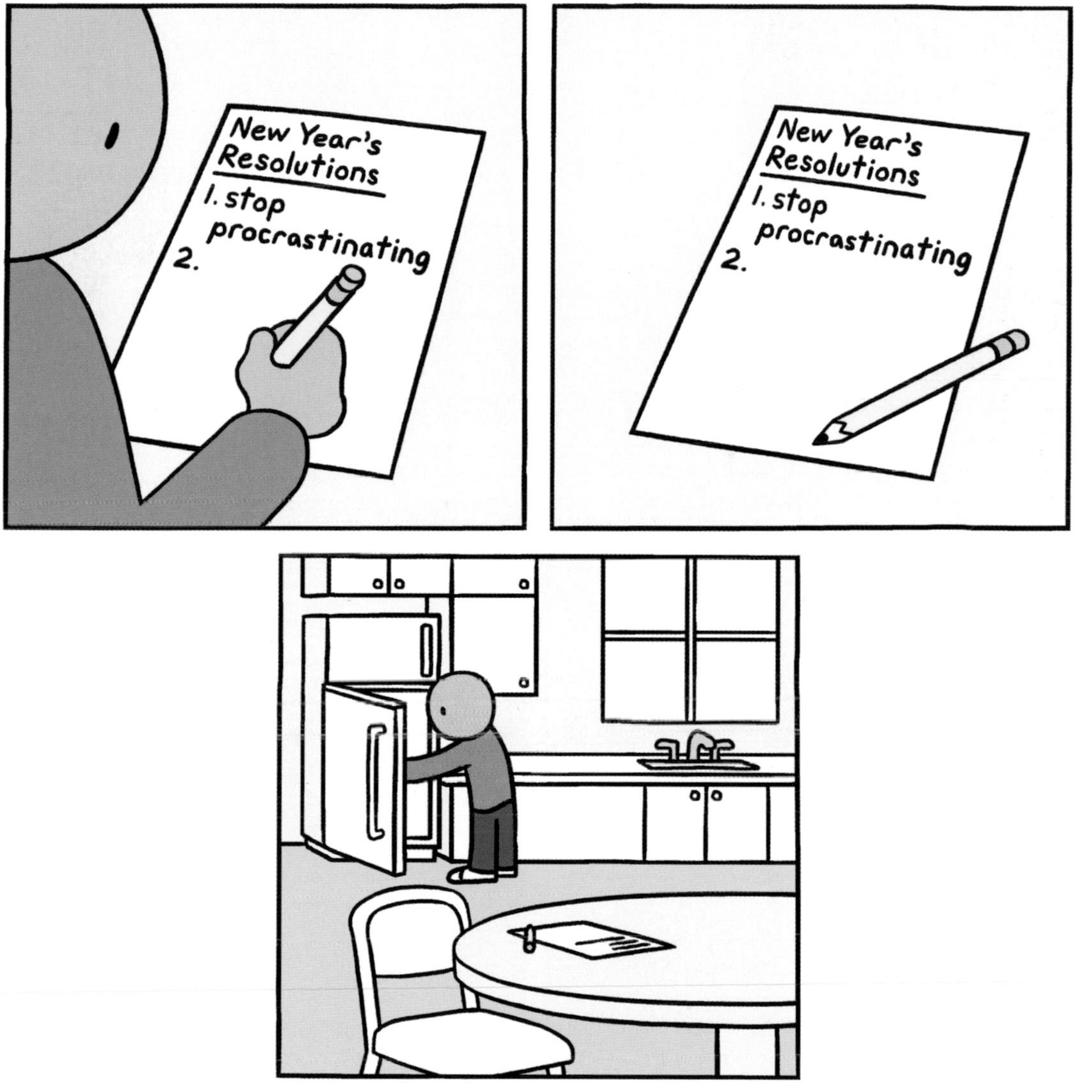
New Year's Resolutions
1. stop procrastinating
2.
New Year's Resolutions
1. stop procrastinating
2.

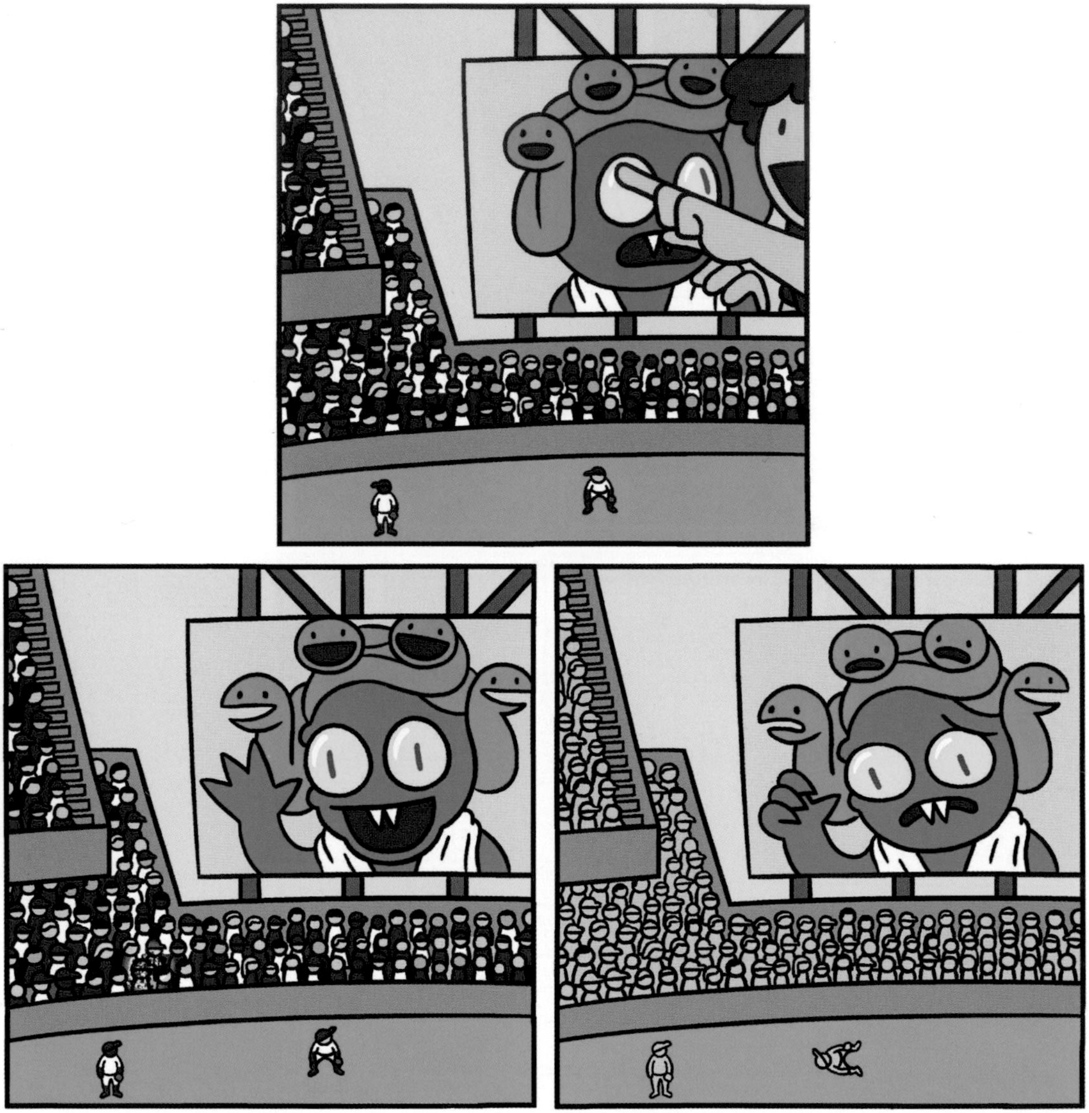

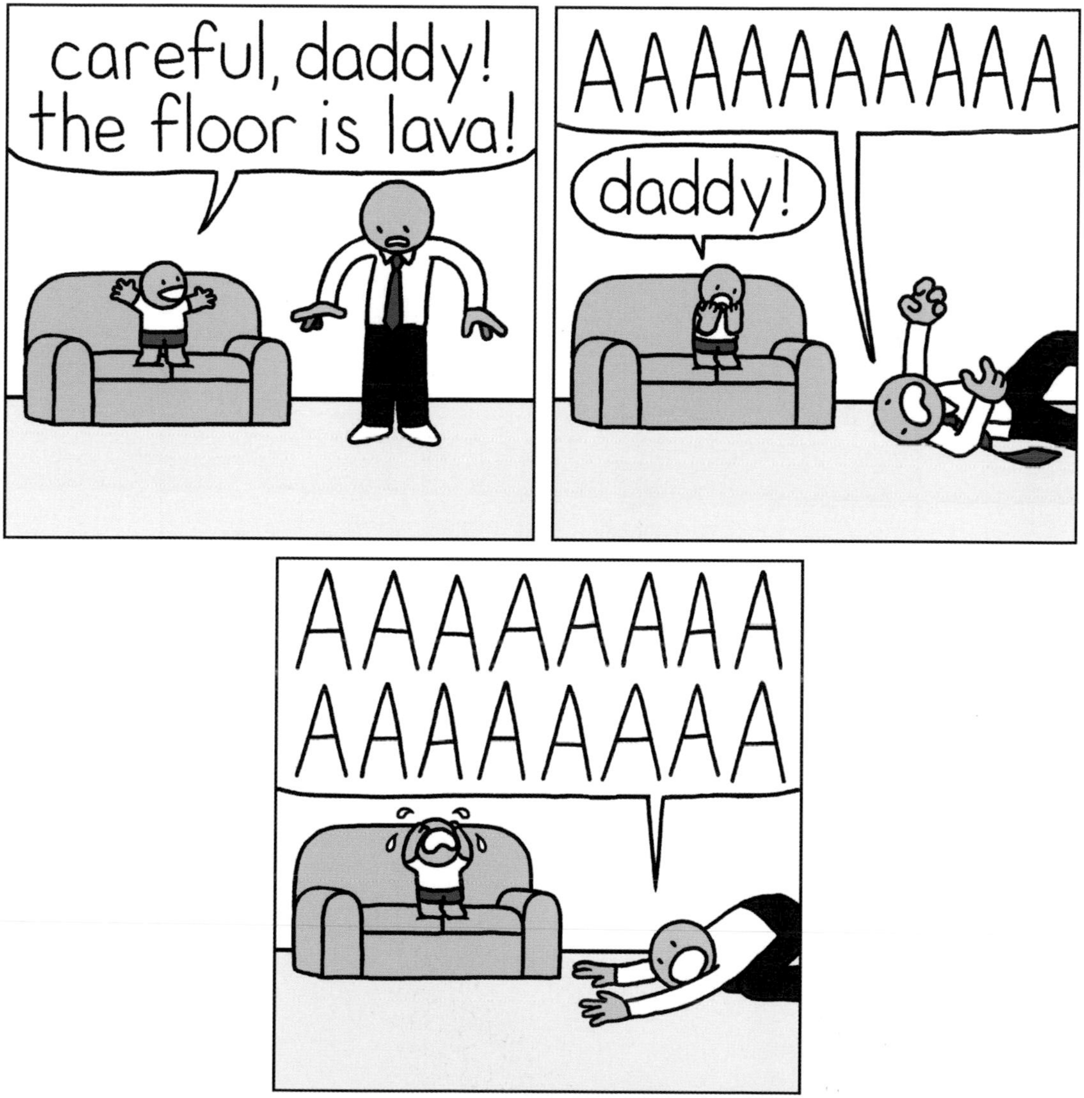
careful, daddy! the floor is lava!
AAAAAAAAAAA
daddy!
AAAAAAAA
AAAAAAAA

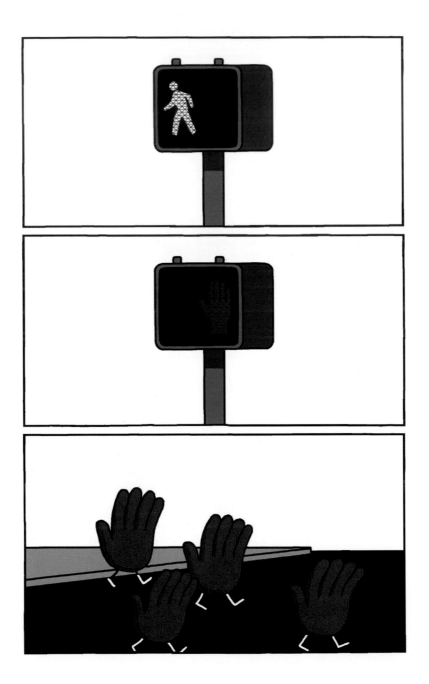

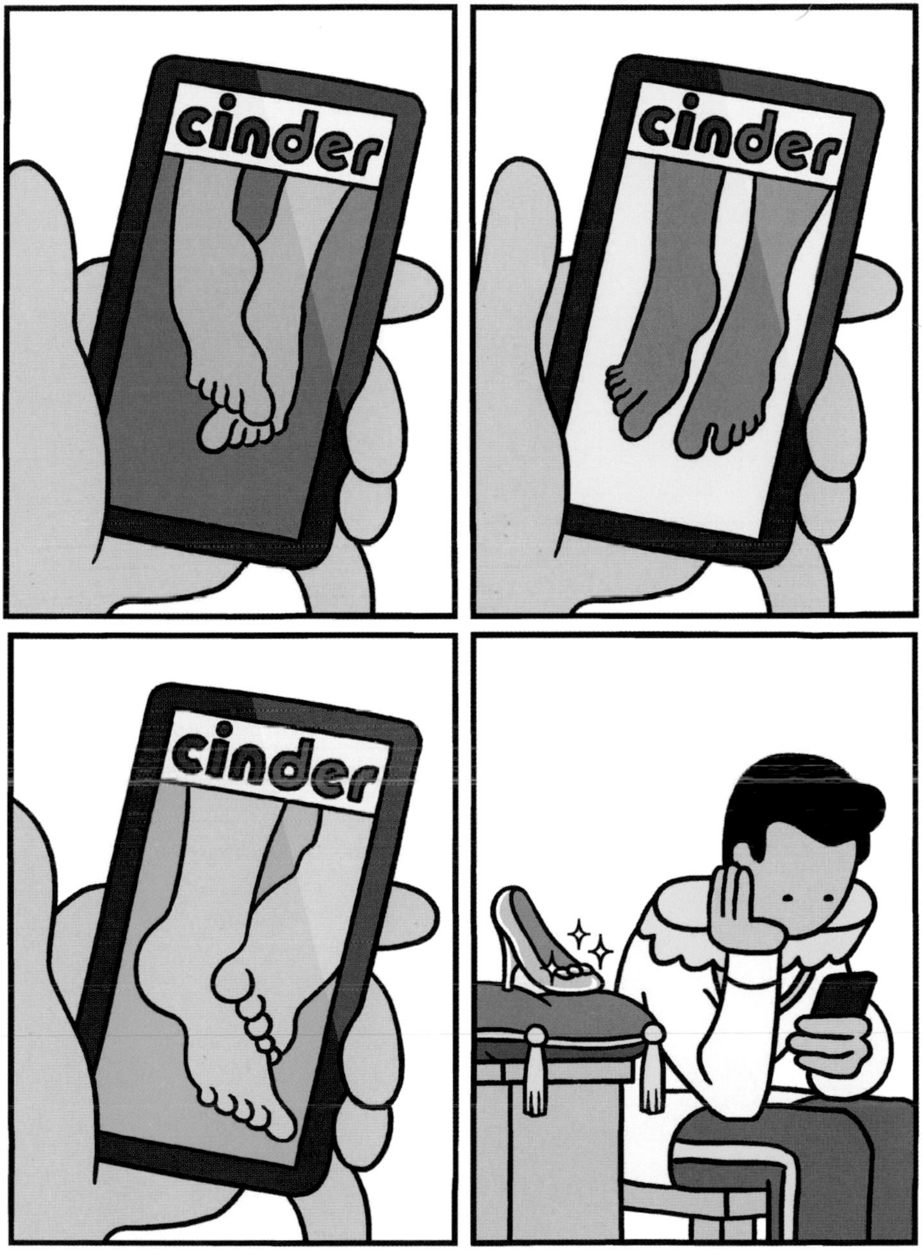
cinder
cinder
cinder

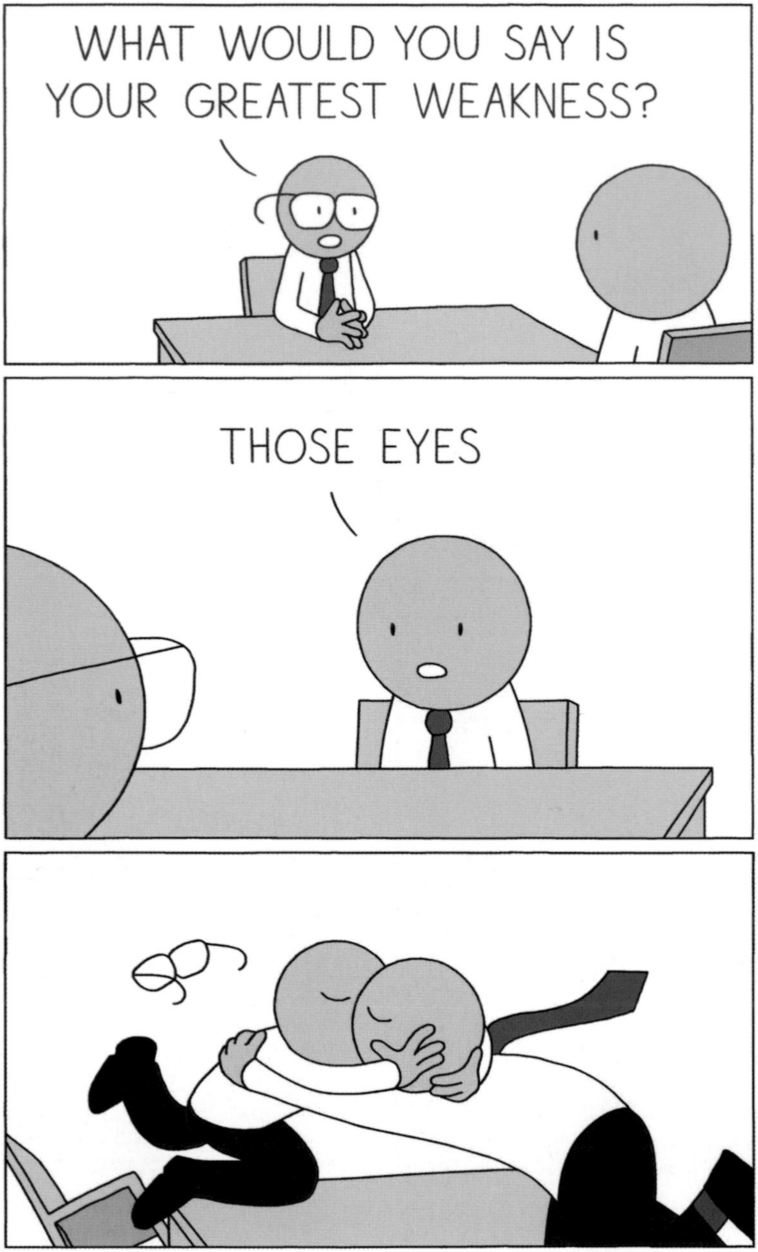
WHAT WOULD YOU SAY IS YOUR GREATEST WEAKNESS?
THOSE EYES

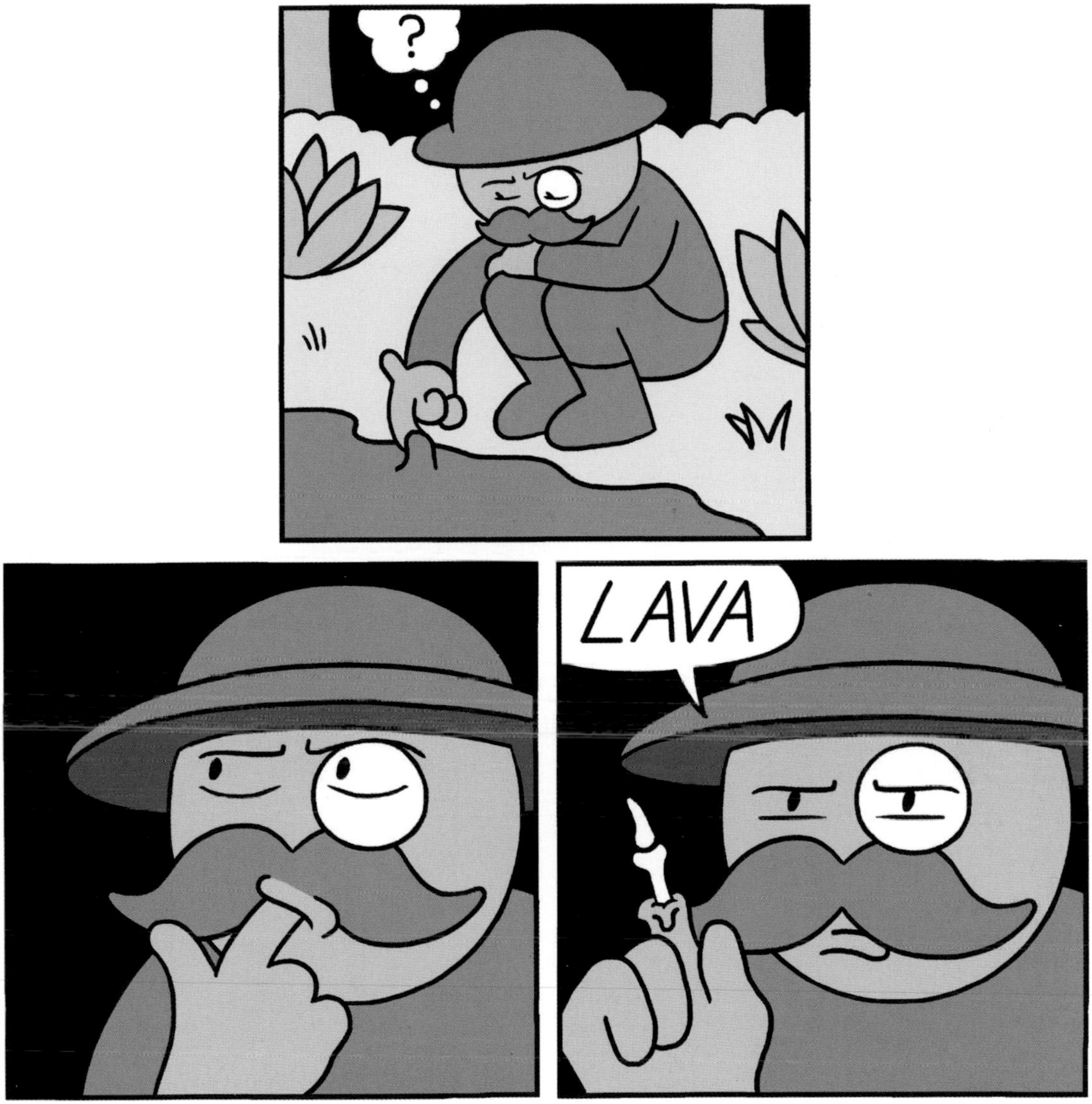
?
LAVA

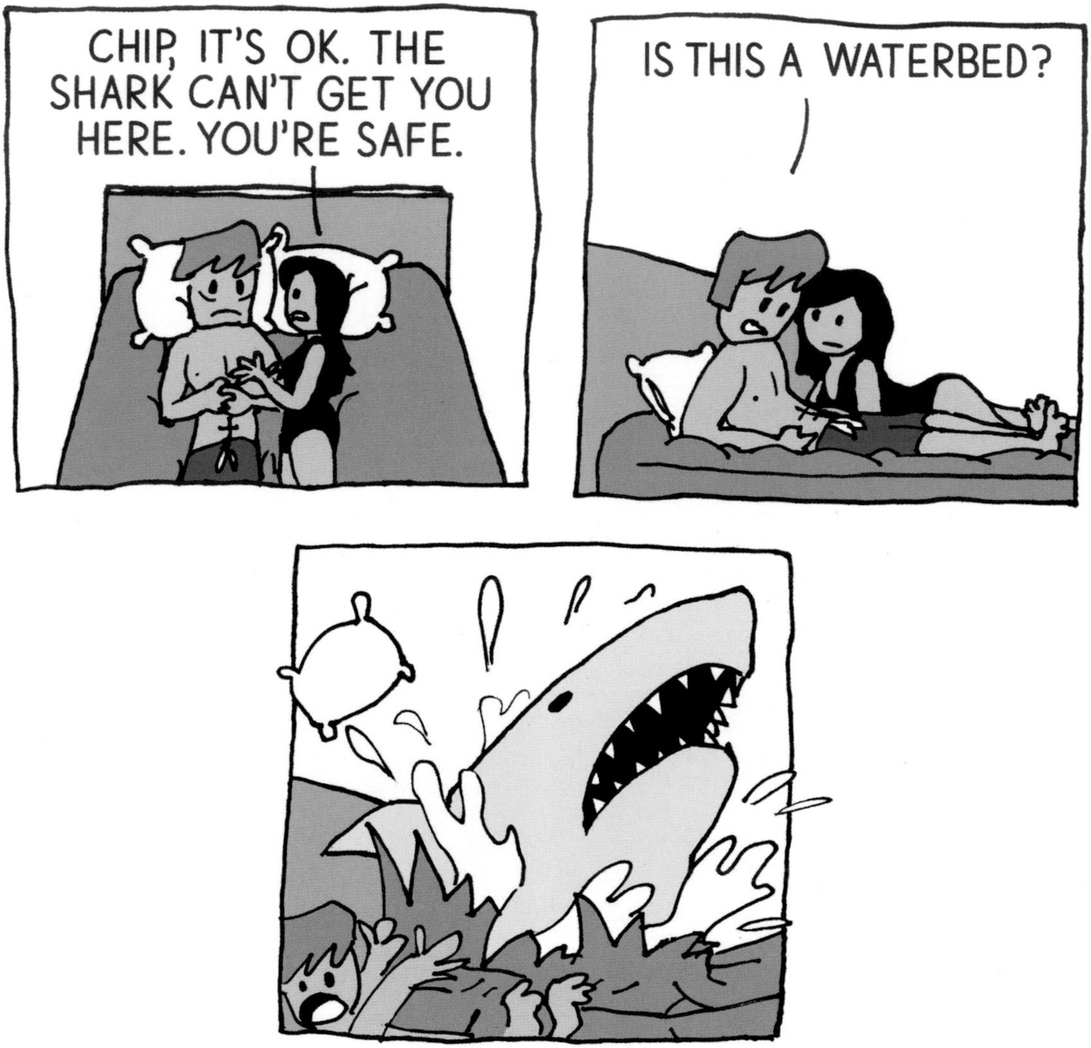
CHIP, IT'S OK. THE SHARK CAN'T GET YOU HERE. YOU'RE SAFE.
IS THIS A WATERBED?

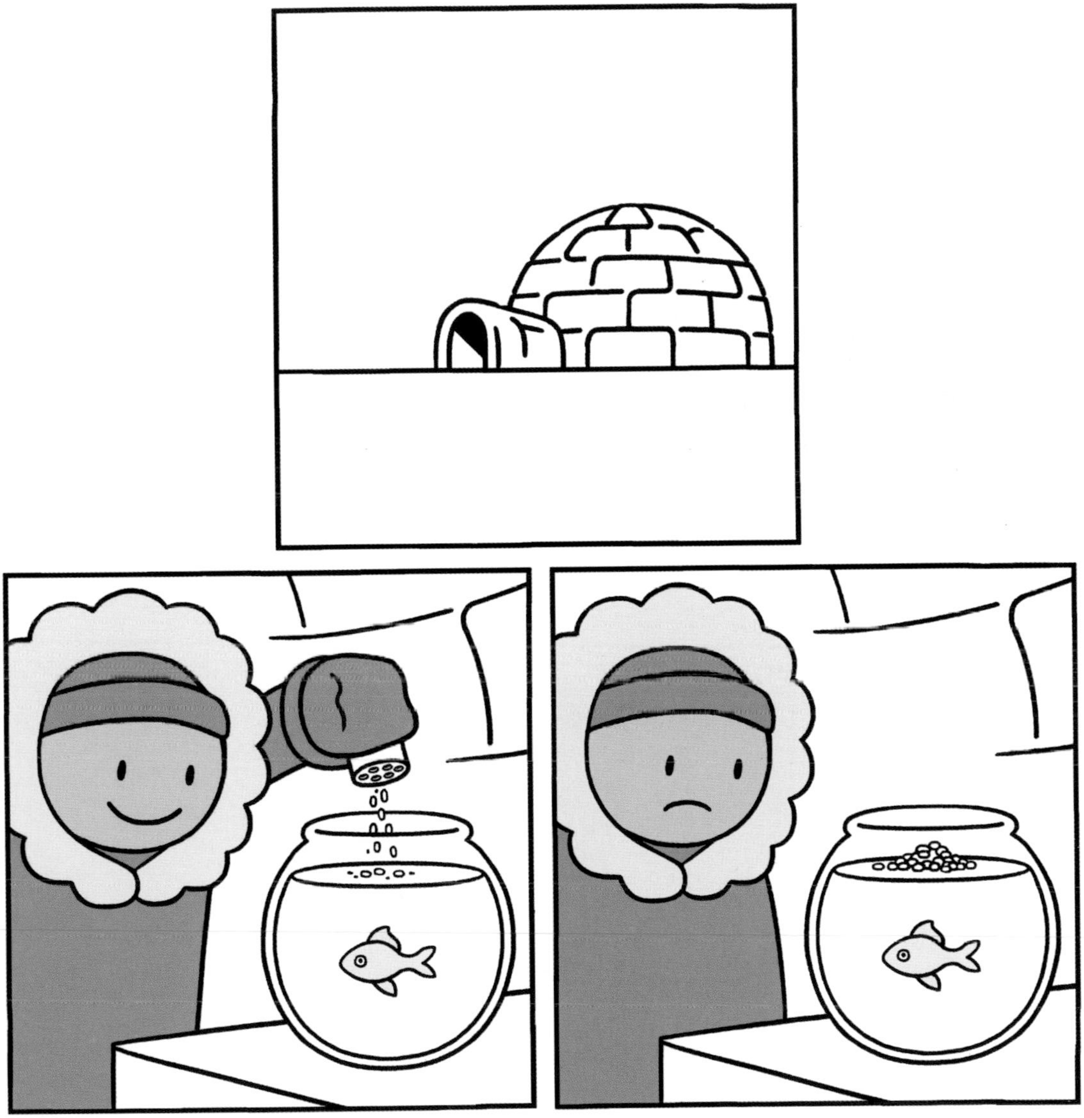

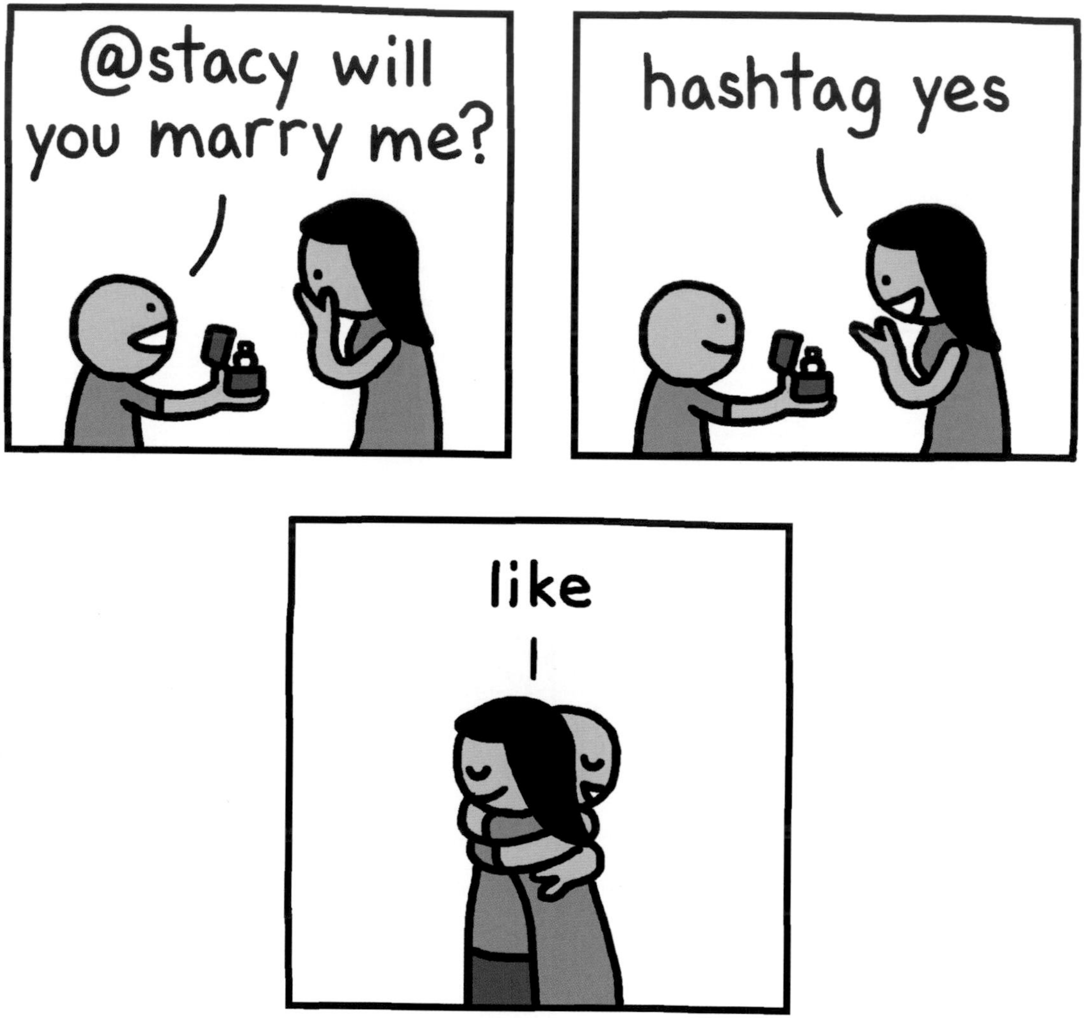
@stacy will you marry me?
hashtag yes
like

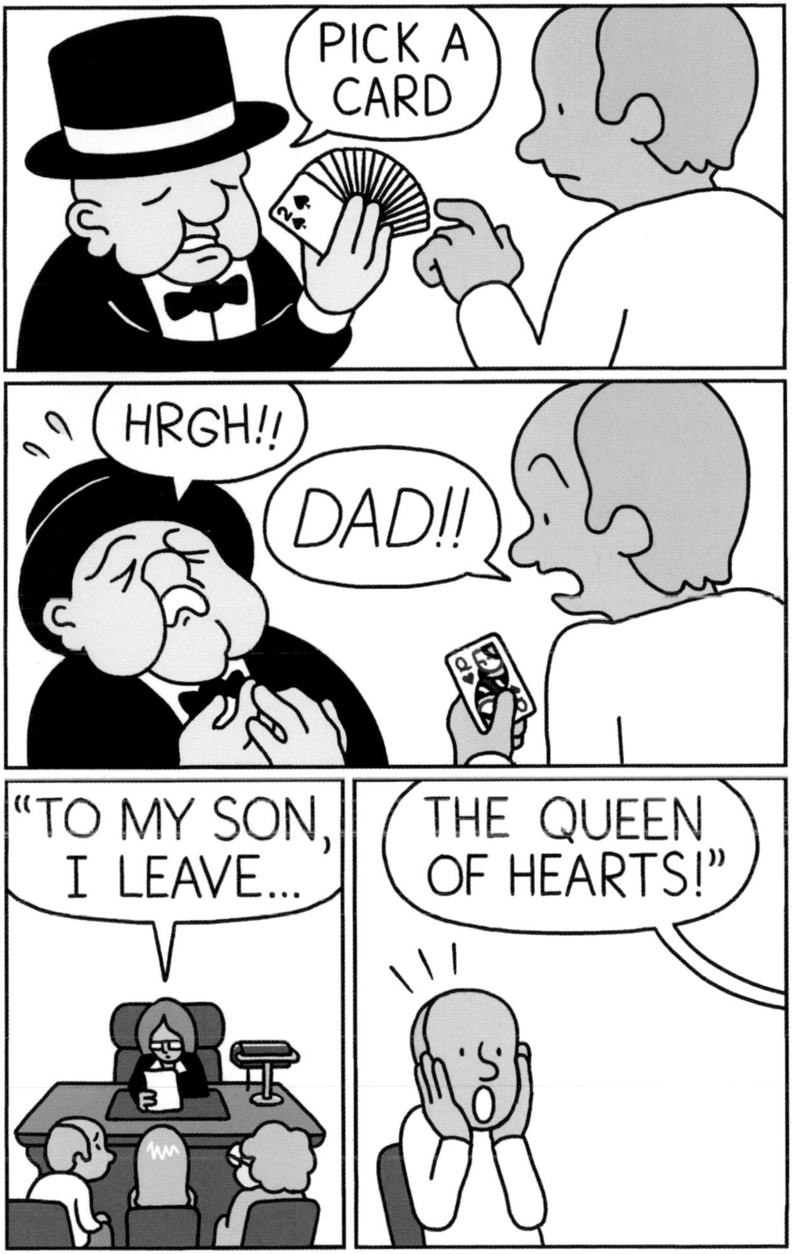
PICK A CARD
HRGH!!
DAD!!
"TO MY SON, I LEAVE...
THE QUEEN OF HEARTS!"

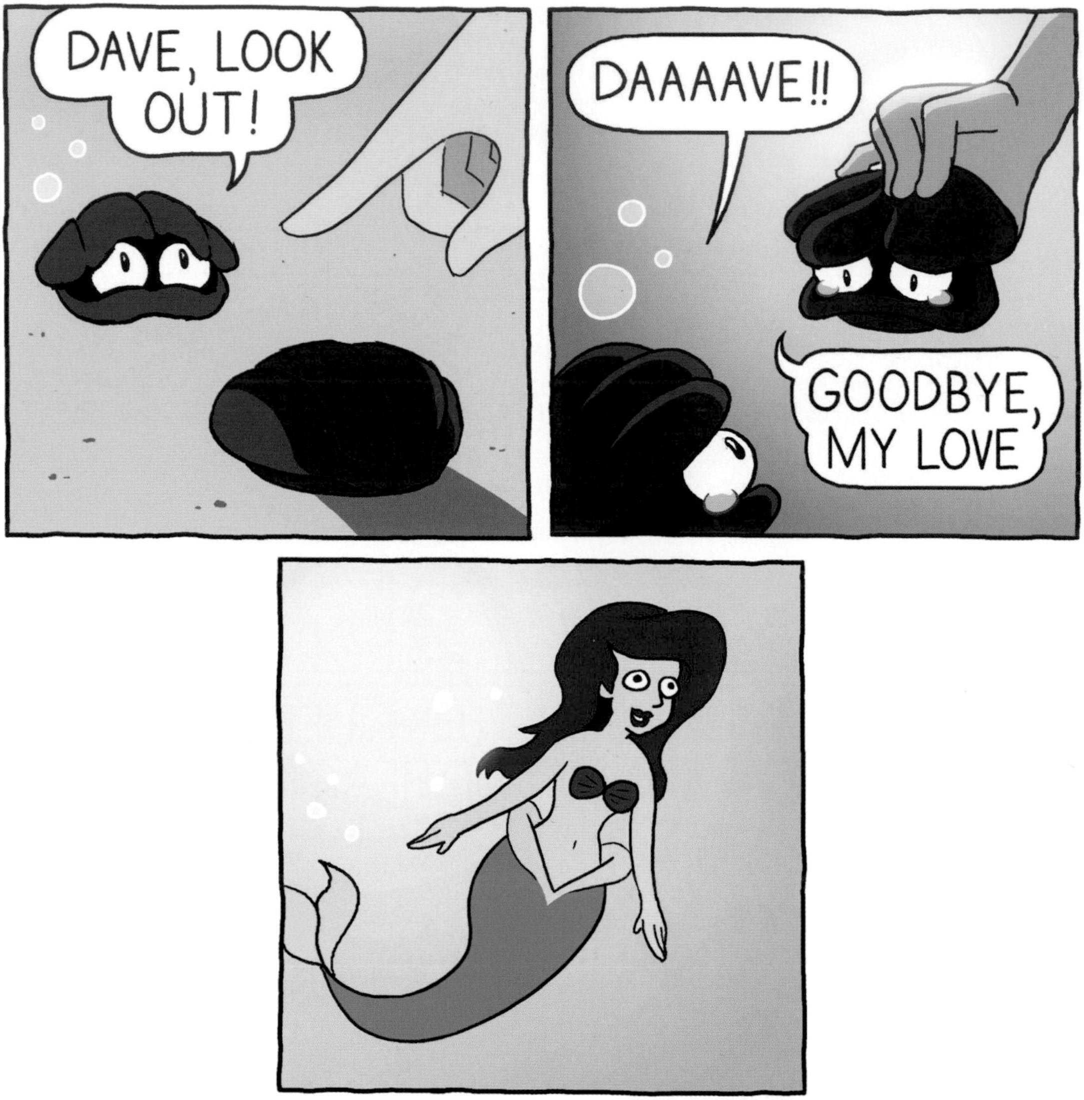
DAVE, LOOK OUT!
DAAAAVE!!
GOODBYE, MY LOVE

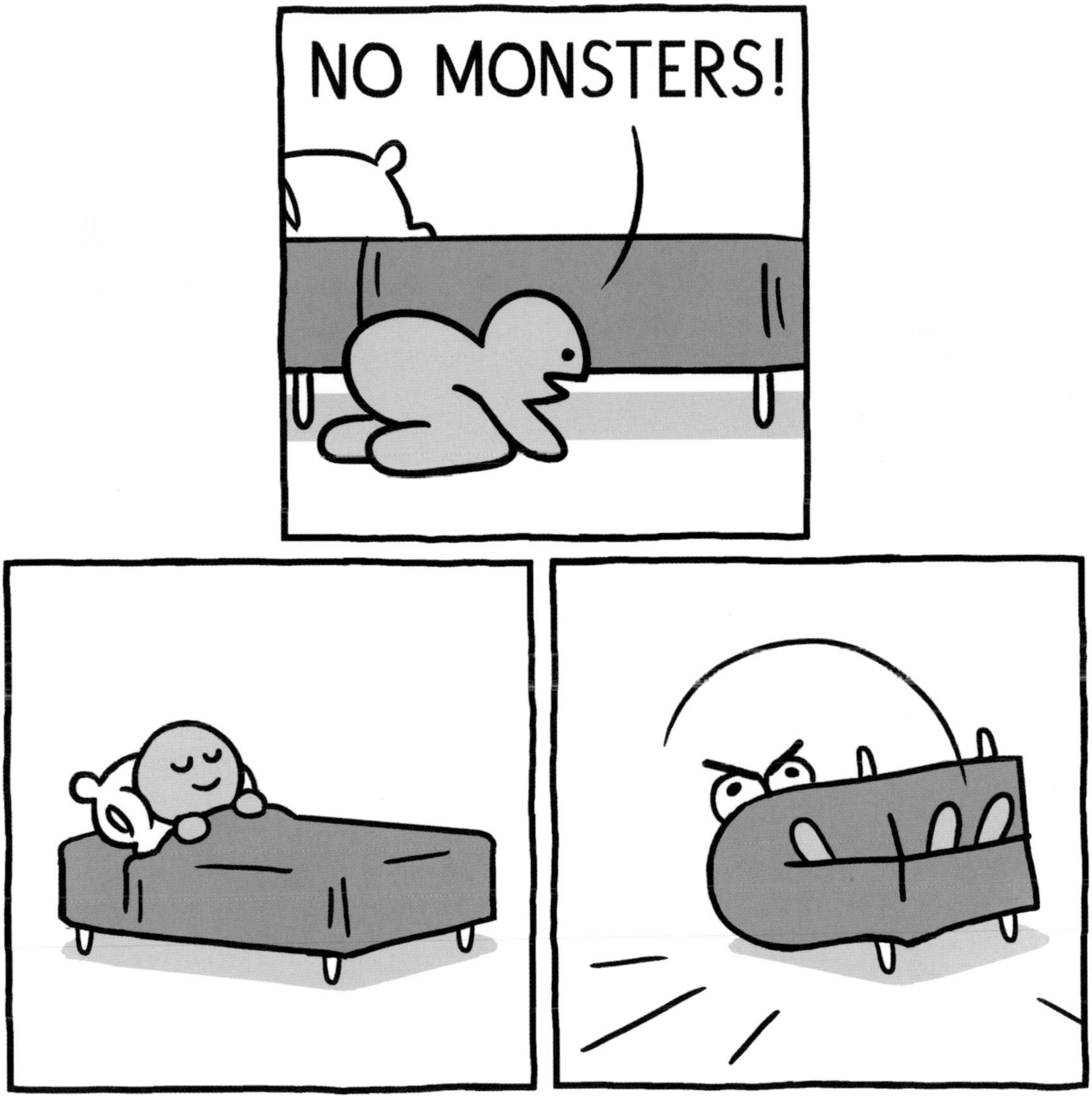
NO MONSTERS!

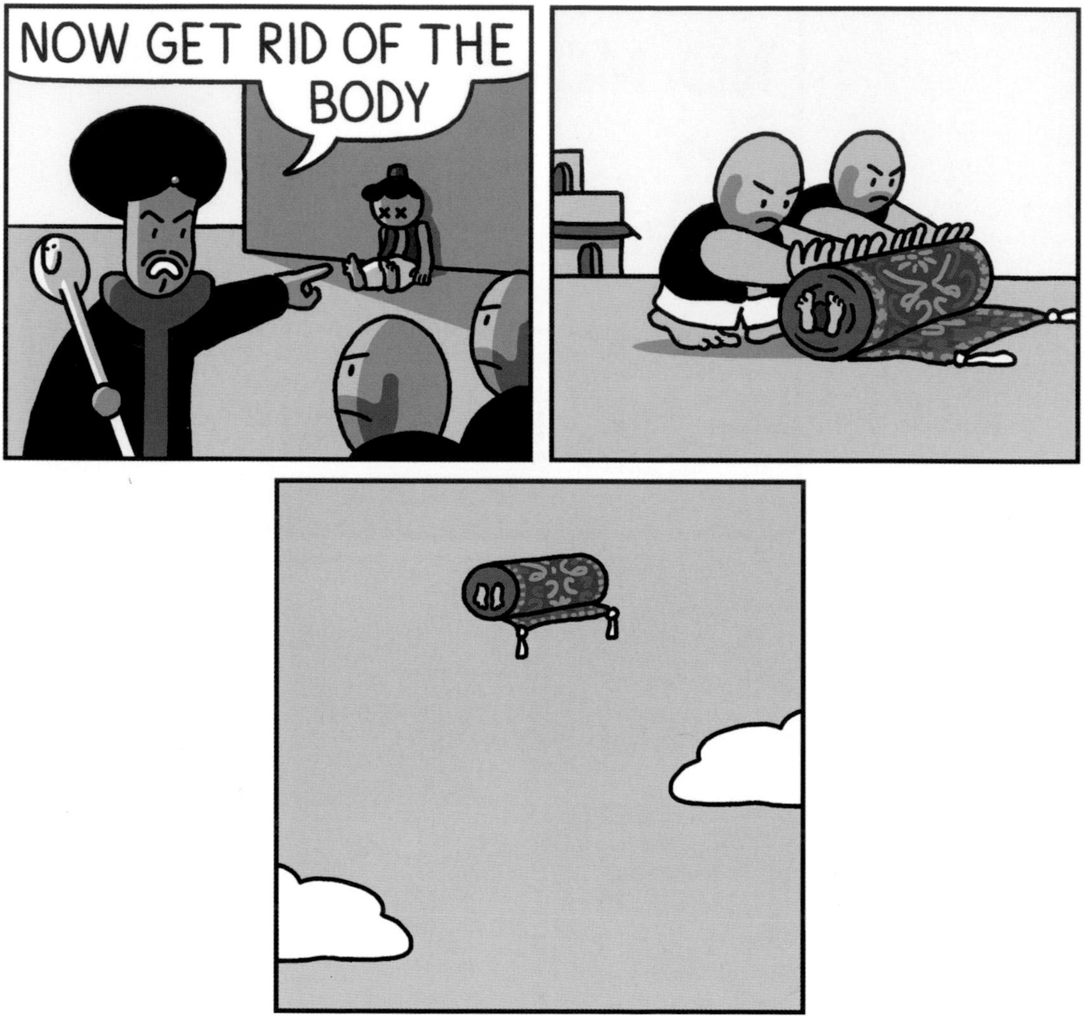
NOW GET RID OF THE BODY

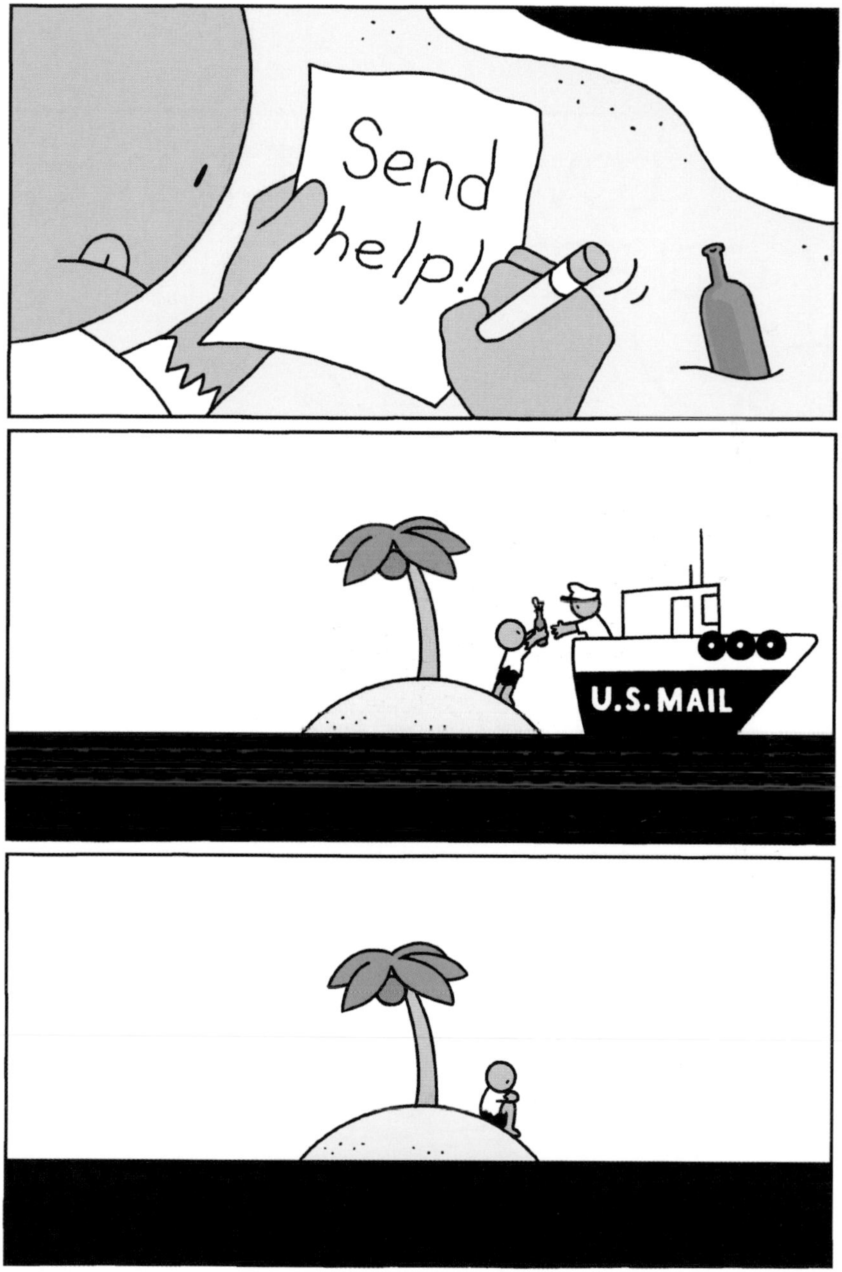
Send help!
U.S. MAIL

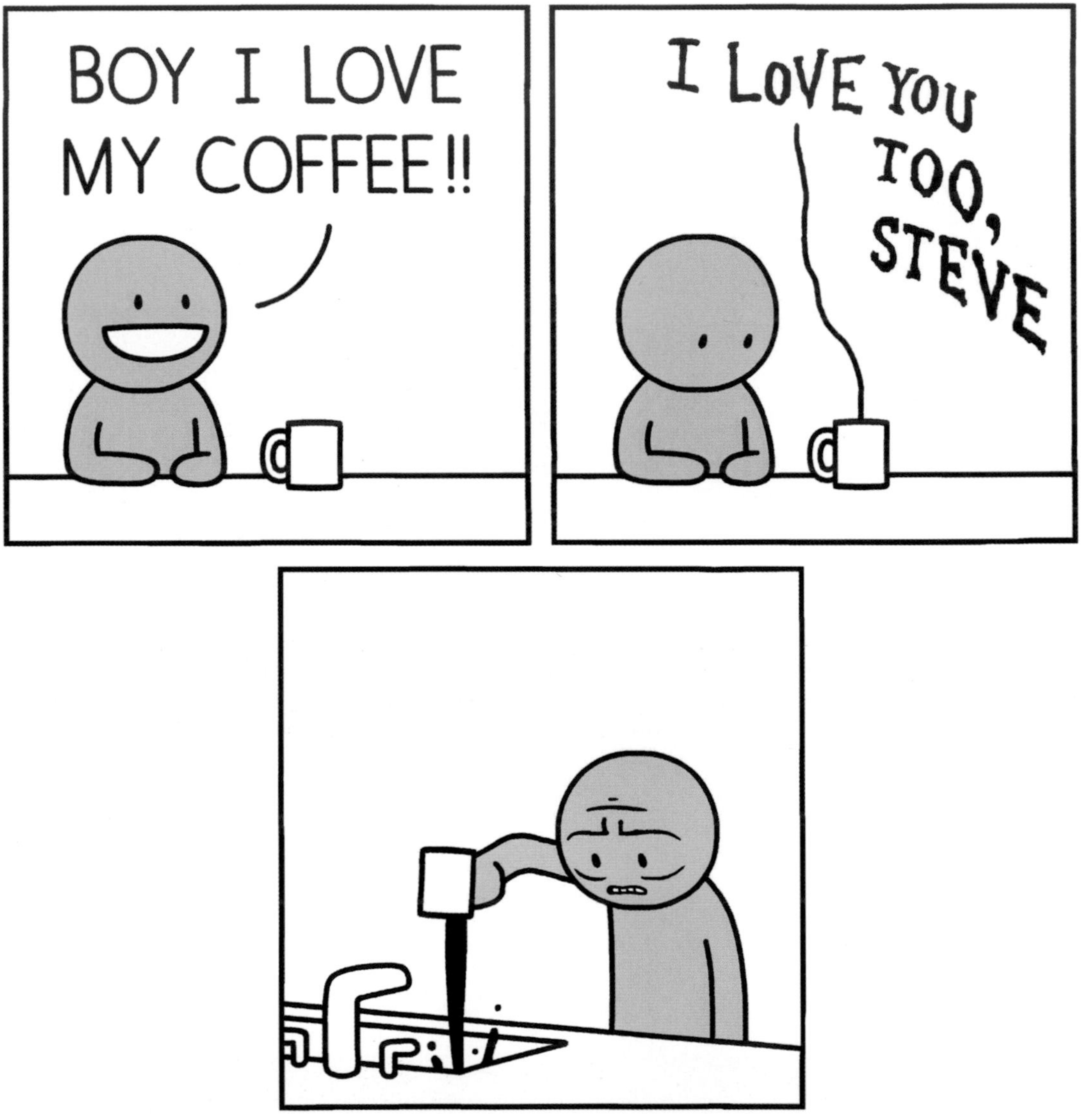
BOY I LOVE MY COFFEE!!
I LOVE YOU TOO, STEVE

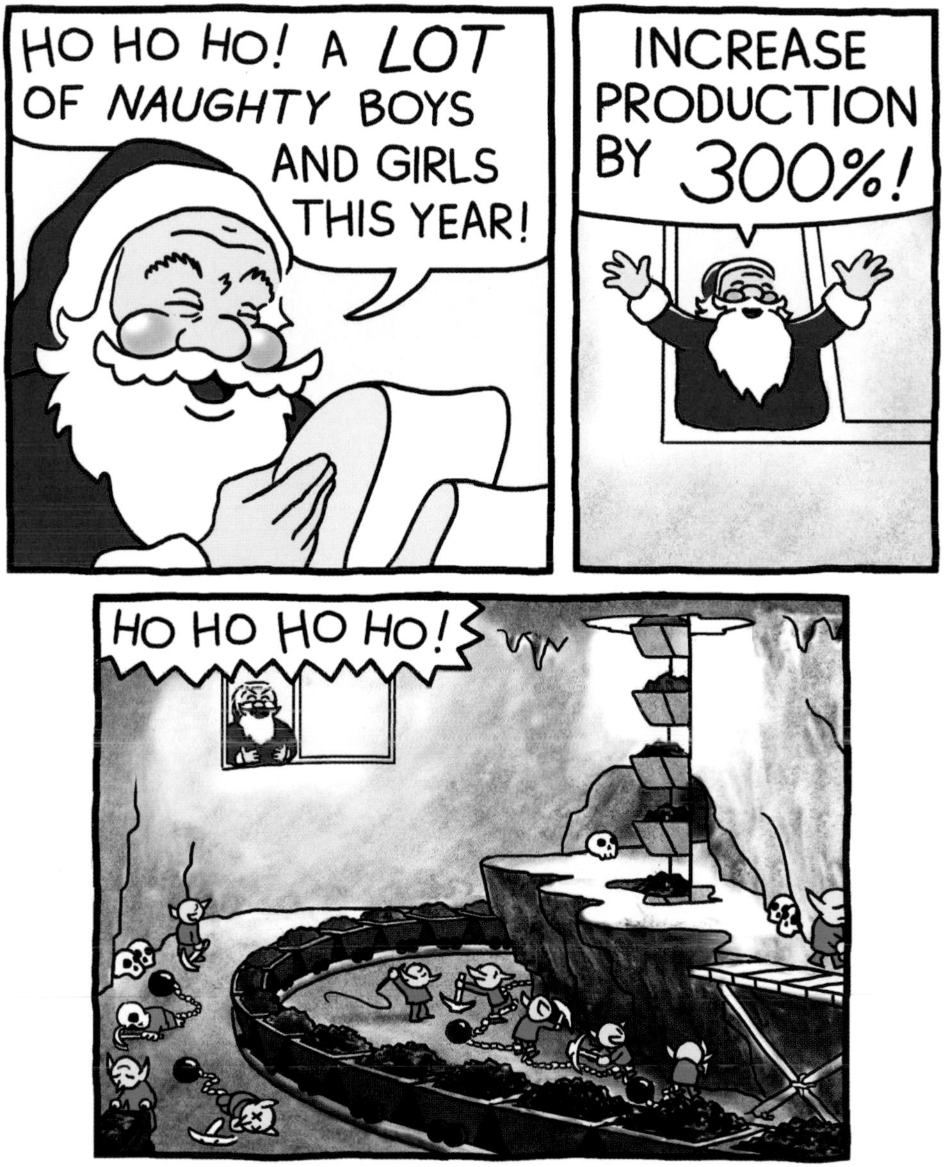
HO HO HO! A LOT OF NAUGHTY BOYS AND GIRLS THIS YEAR!
INCREASE PRODUCTION BY 300%!
HO HO HO HO!

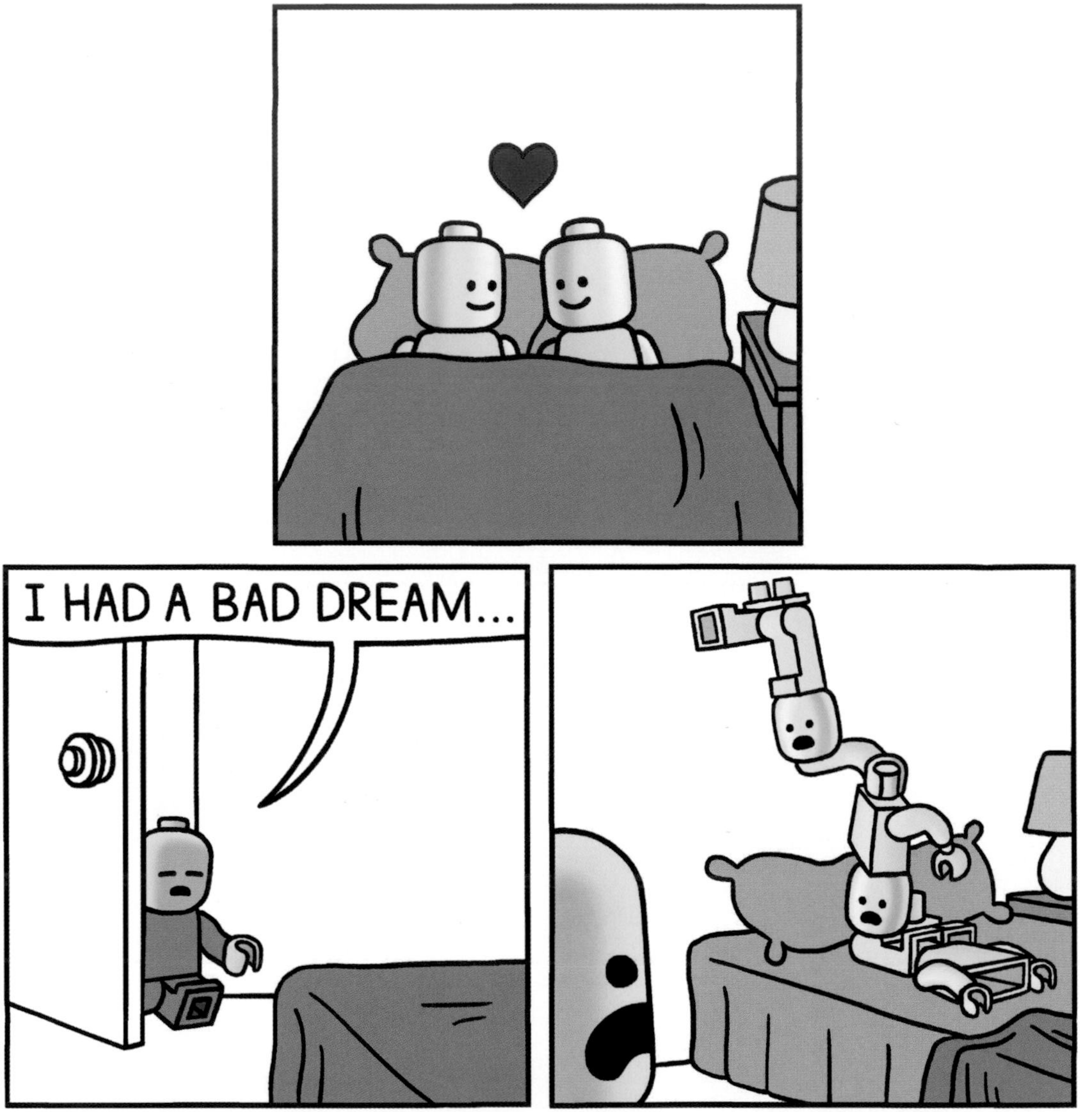
I HAD A BAD DREAM...

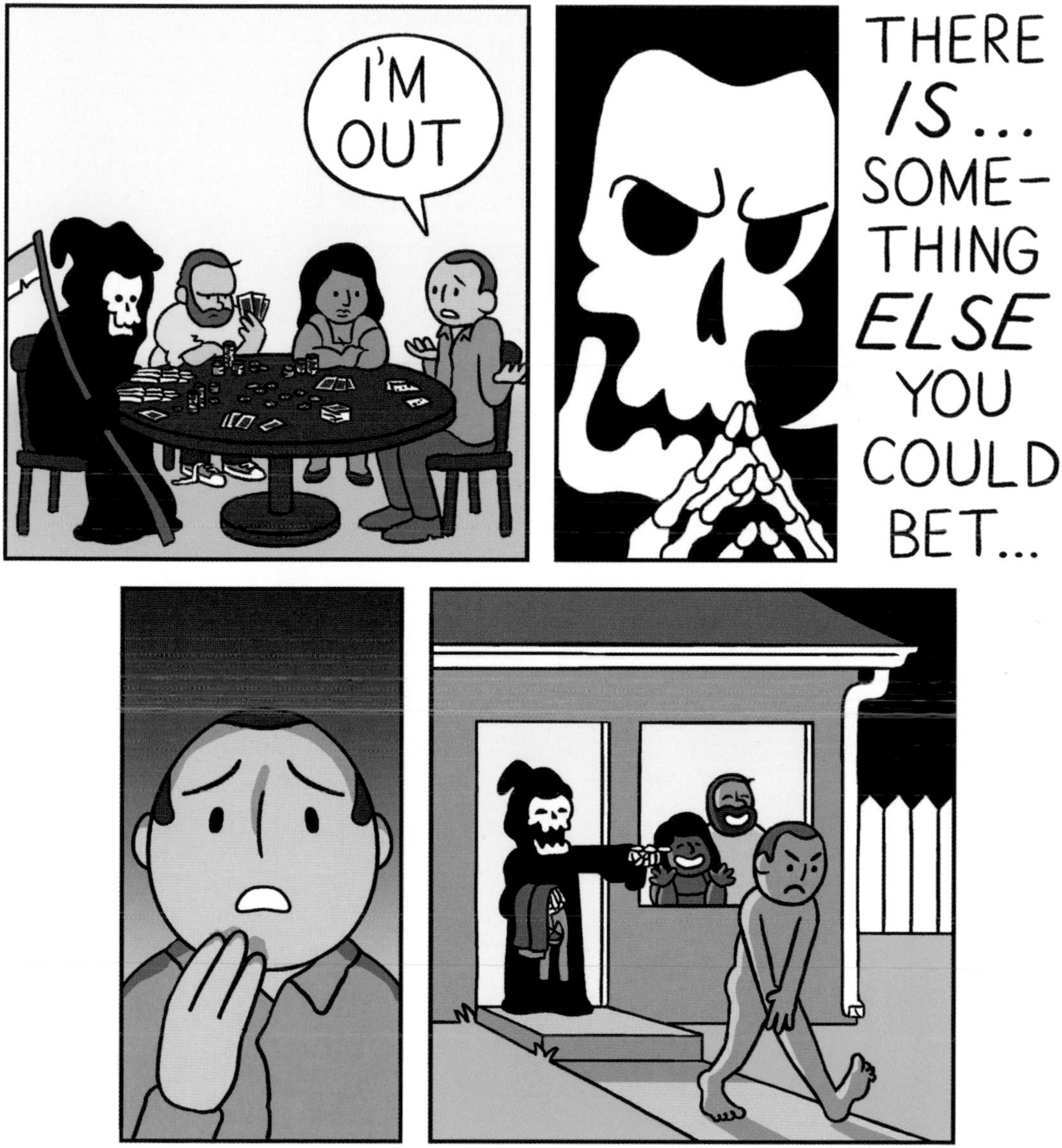
I'M OUT
THERE *IS* ... SOME-THING *ELSE* YOU COULD BET...

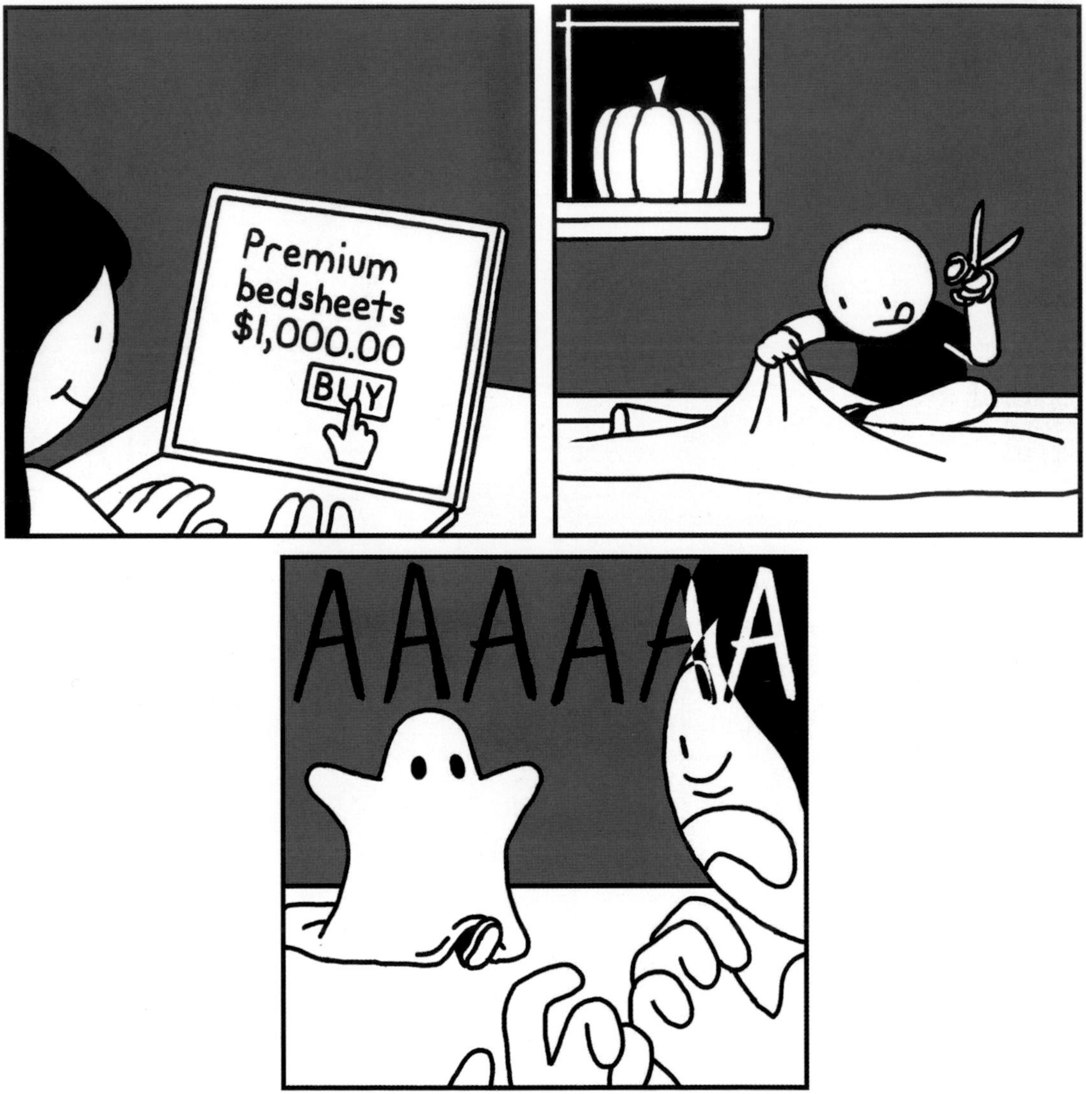
Premium
bedsheets
$1,000.00
BUY
AAAAAA

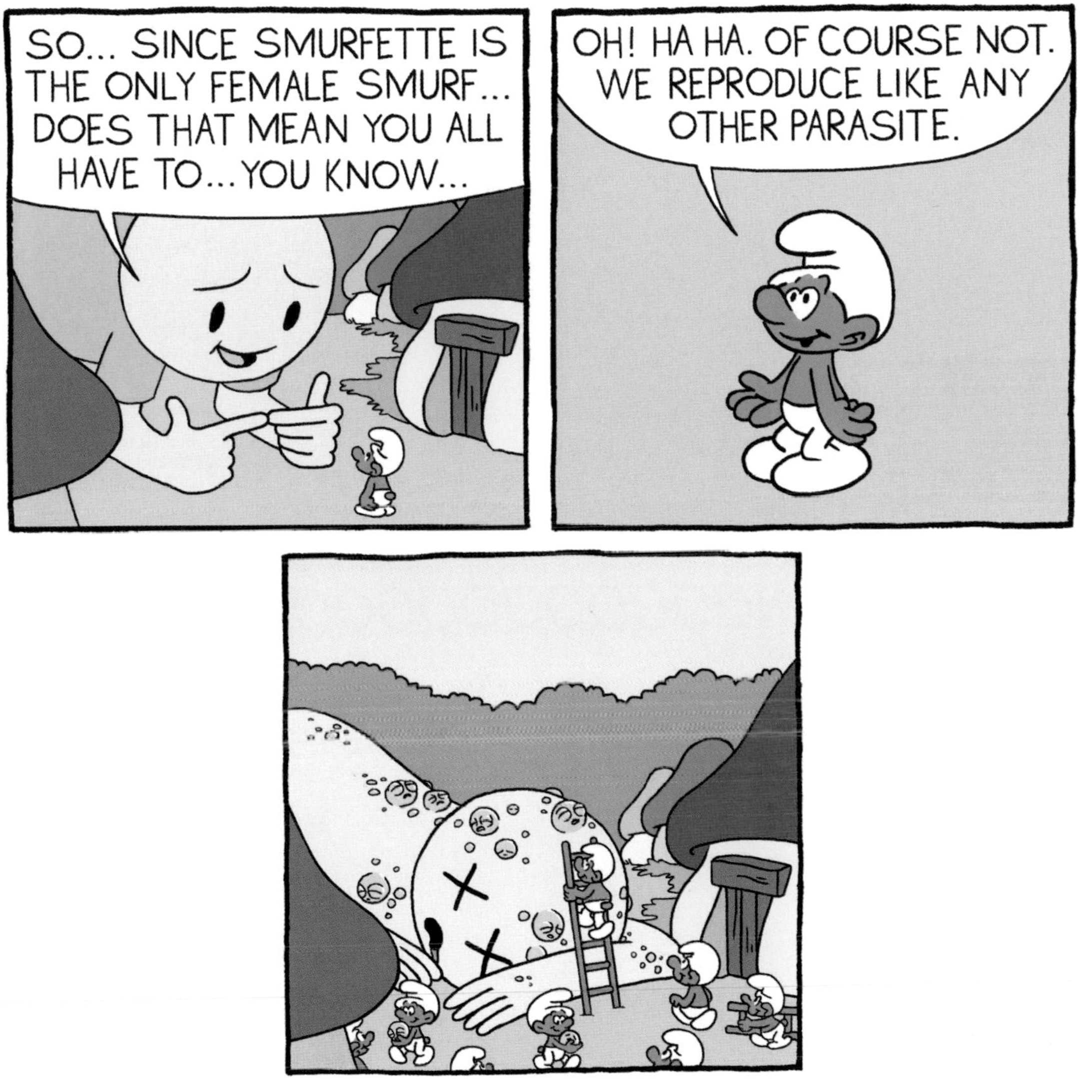
SO... SINCE SMURFETTE IS THE ONLY FEMALE SMURF... DOES THAT MEAN YOU ALL HAVE TO... YOU KNOW...
OH! HA HA. OF COURSE NOT. WE REPRODUCE LIKE ANY OTHER PARASITE.

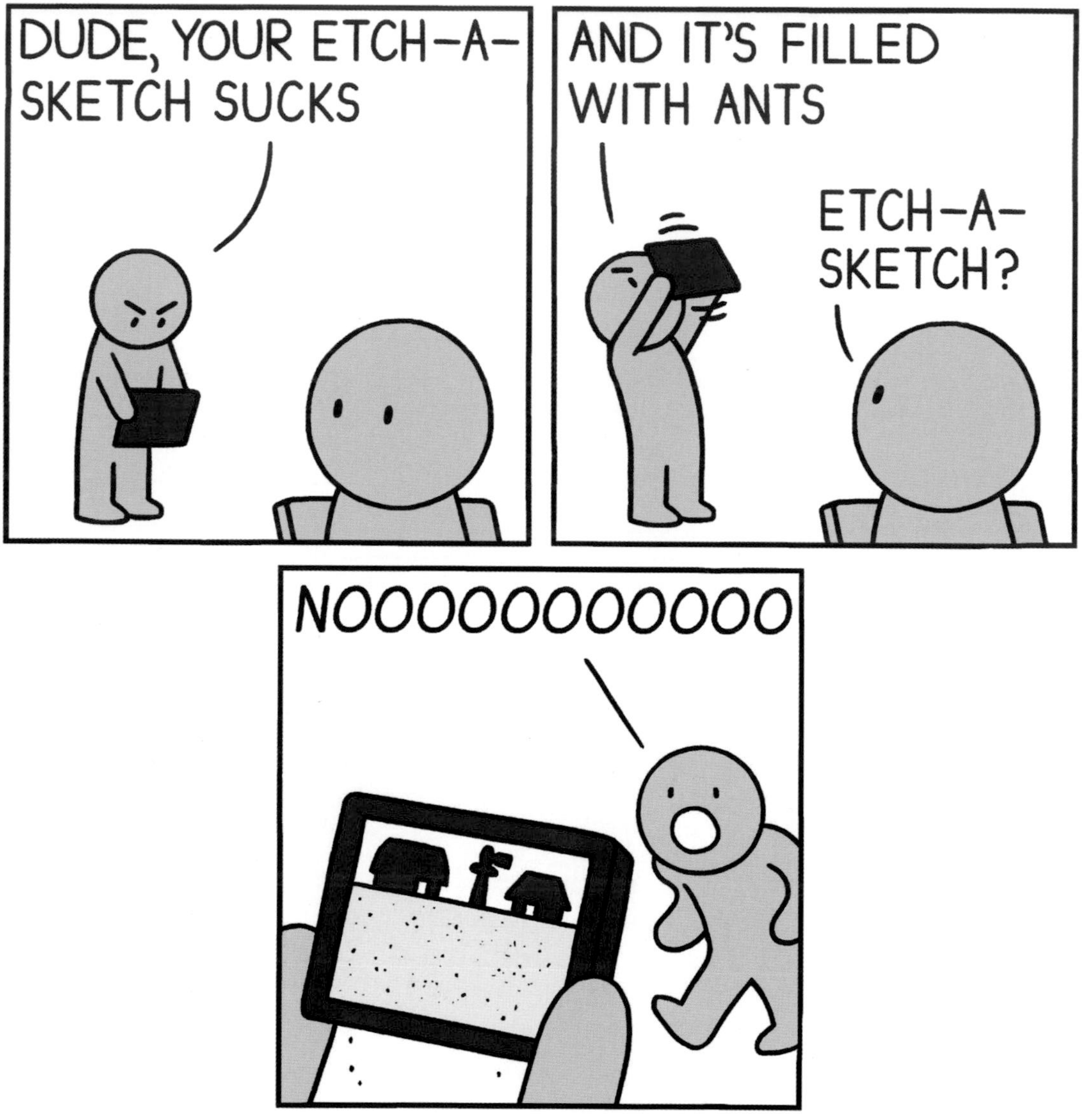
DUDE, YOUR ETCH-A-SKETCH SUCKS
AND IT'S FILLED WITH ANTS
ETCH-A-SKETCH?
NOOOOOOOOOOOO

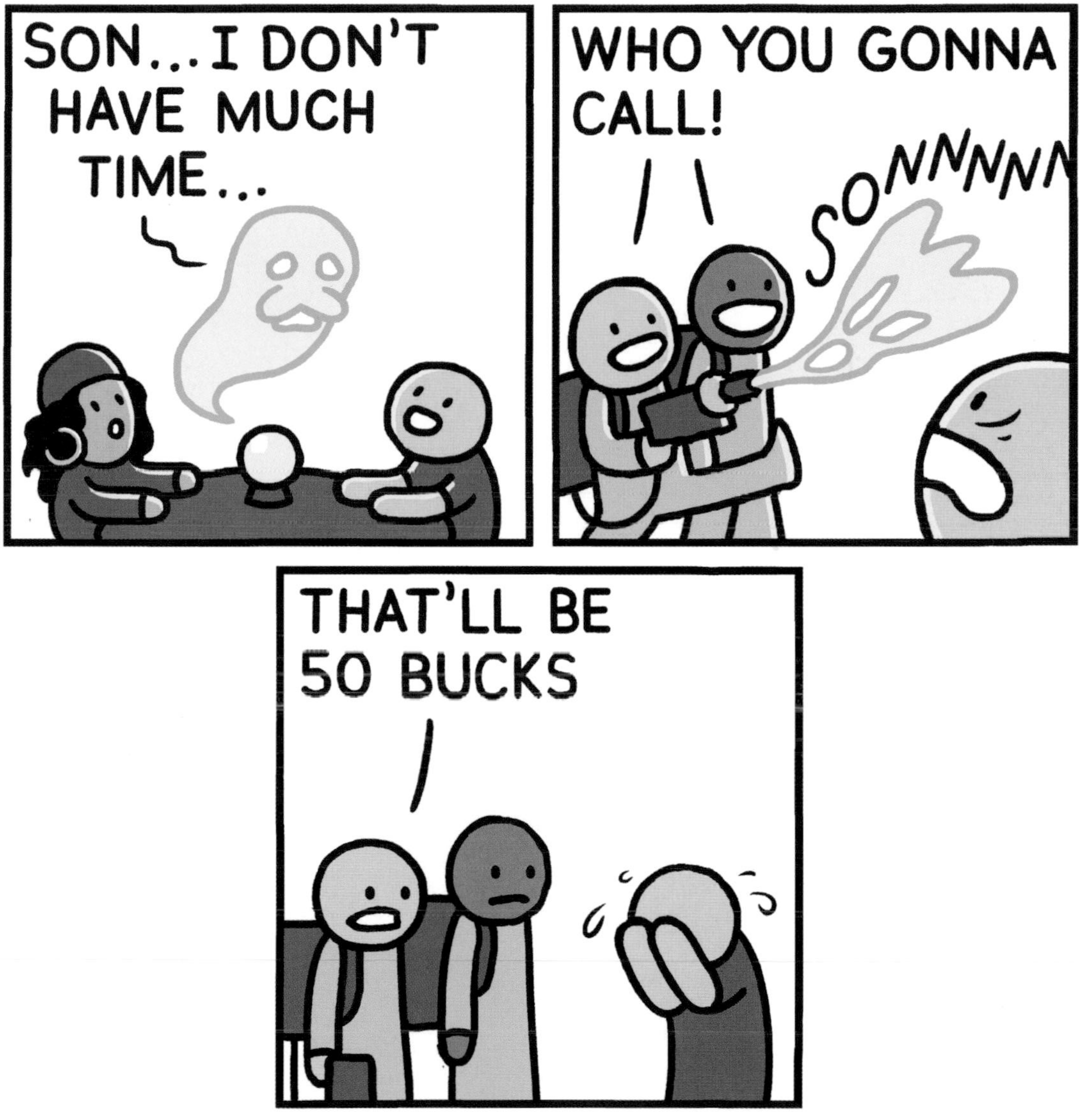
SON... I DON'T HAVE MUCH TIME...
WHO YOU GONNA CALL!
SONNNNNN
THAT'LL BE 50 BUCKS

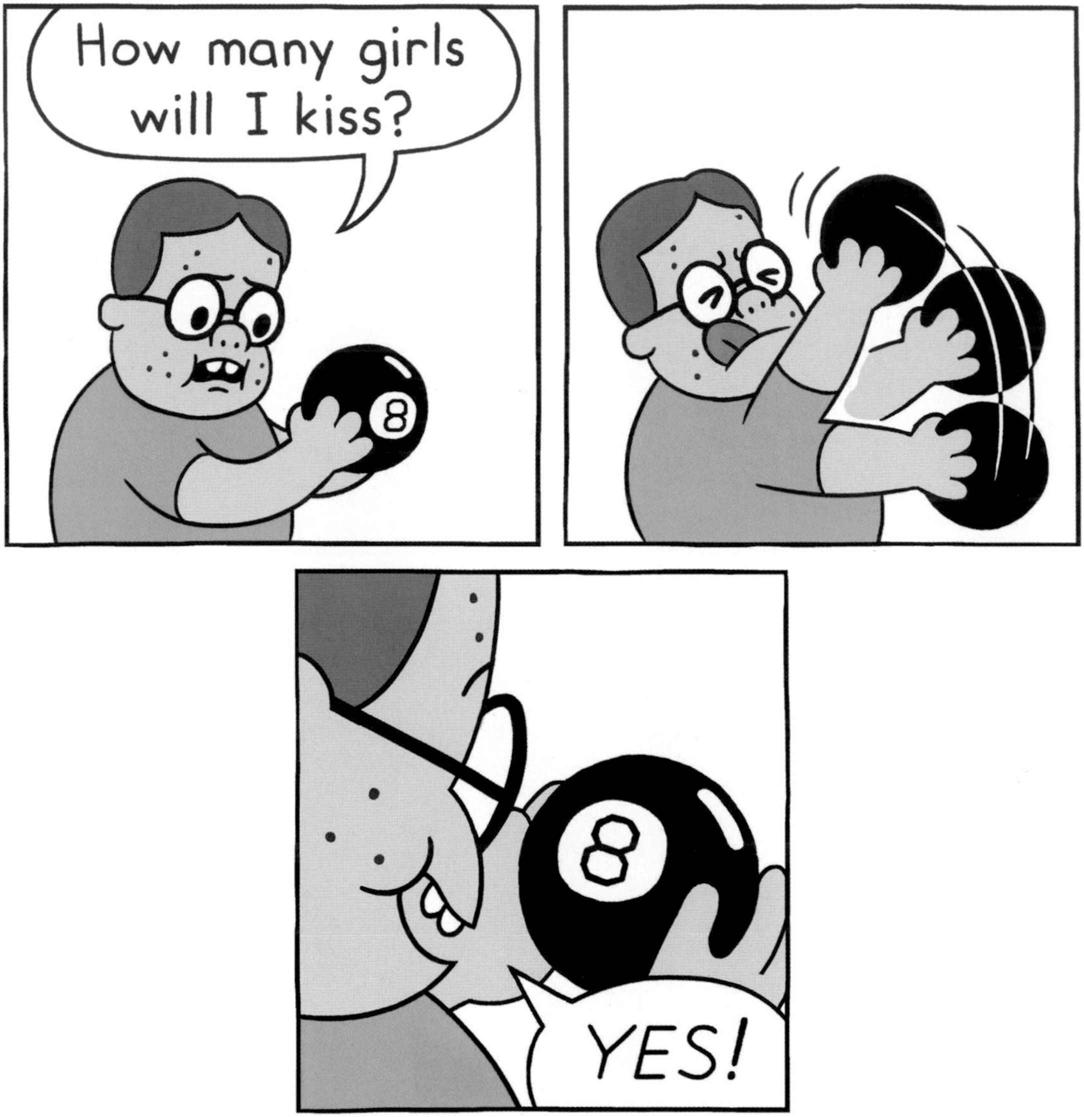
How many girls will I kiss?
8
8
YES!

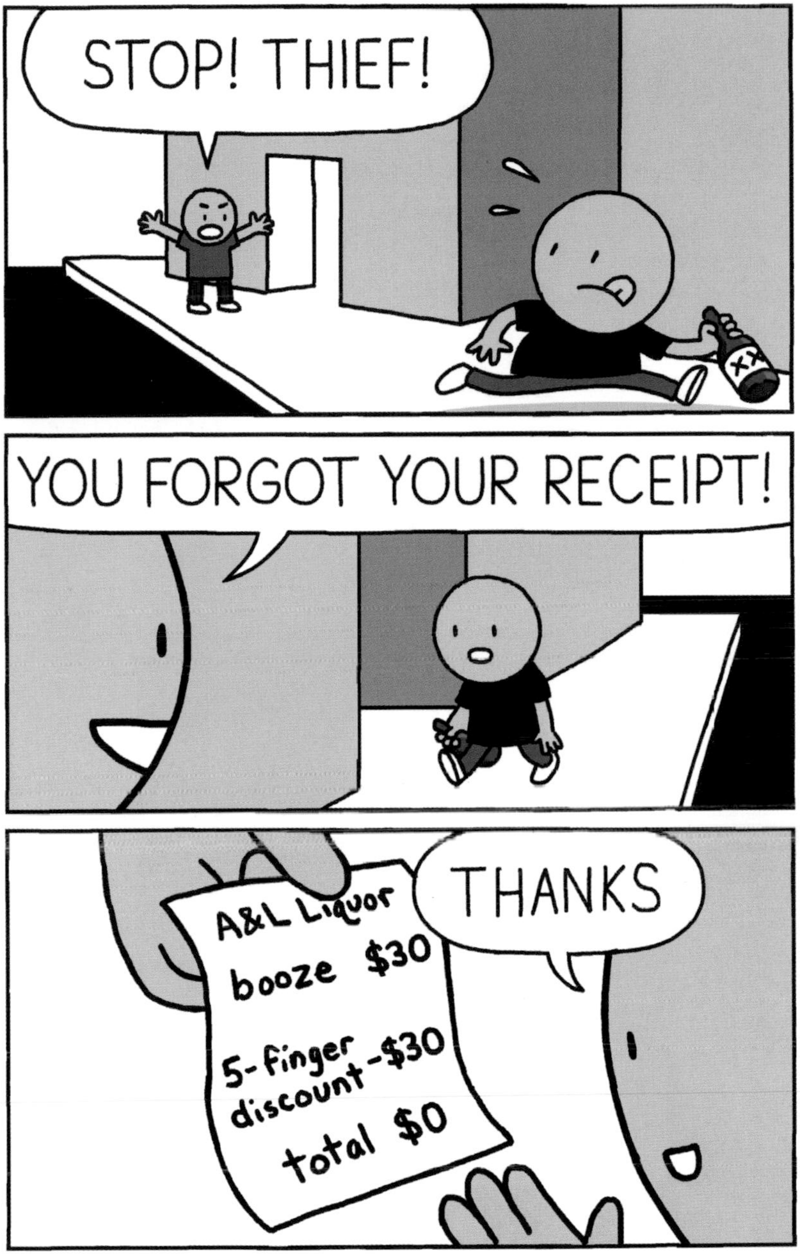
STOP! THIEF!
YOU FORGOT YOUR RECEIPT!
A&L Liquor
booze $30
5-finger discount -$30
total $0
THANKS

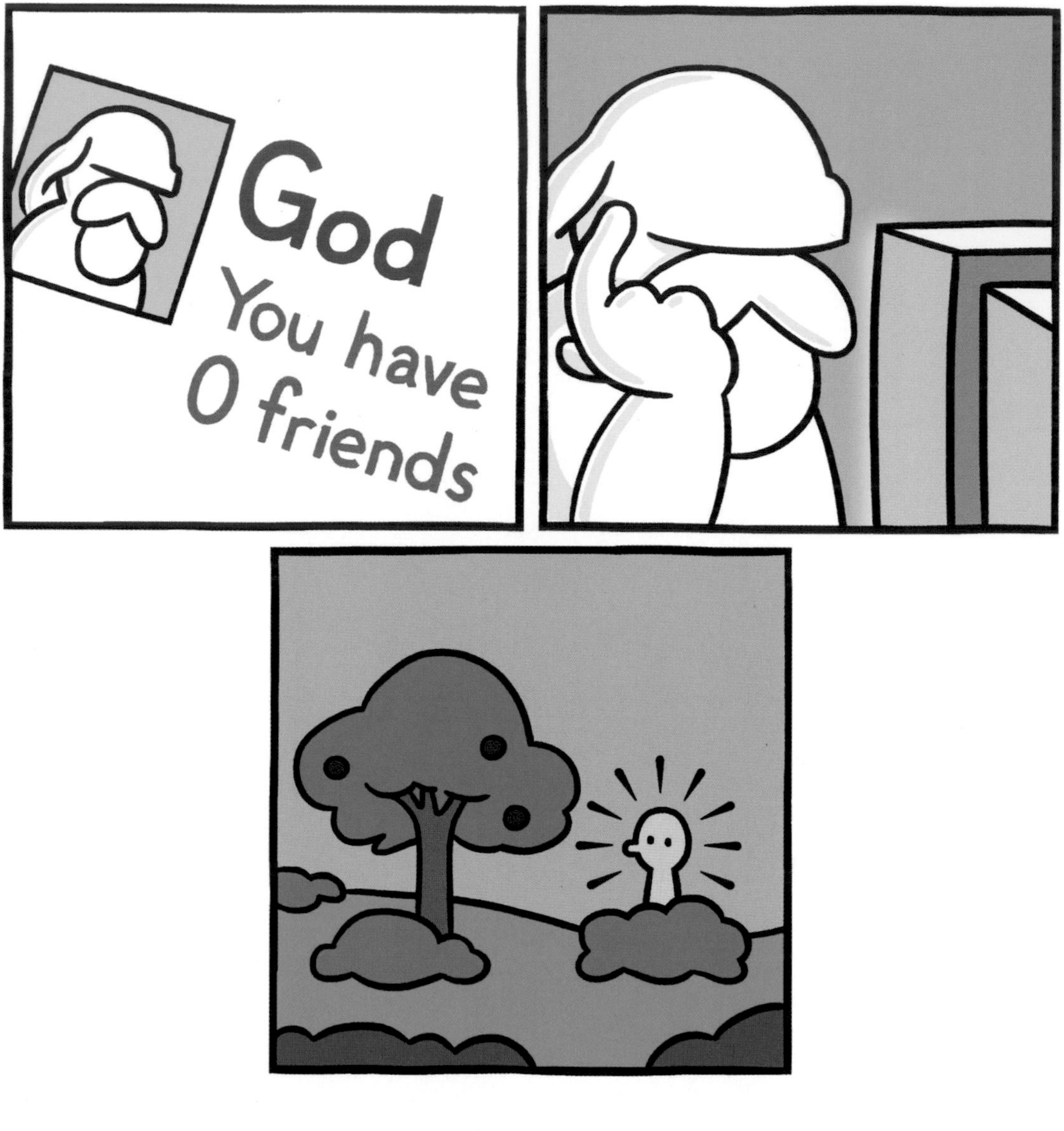
God
You have
0 friends

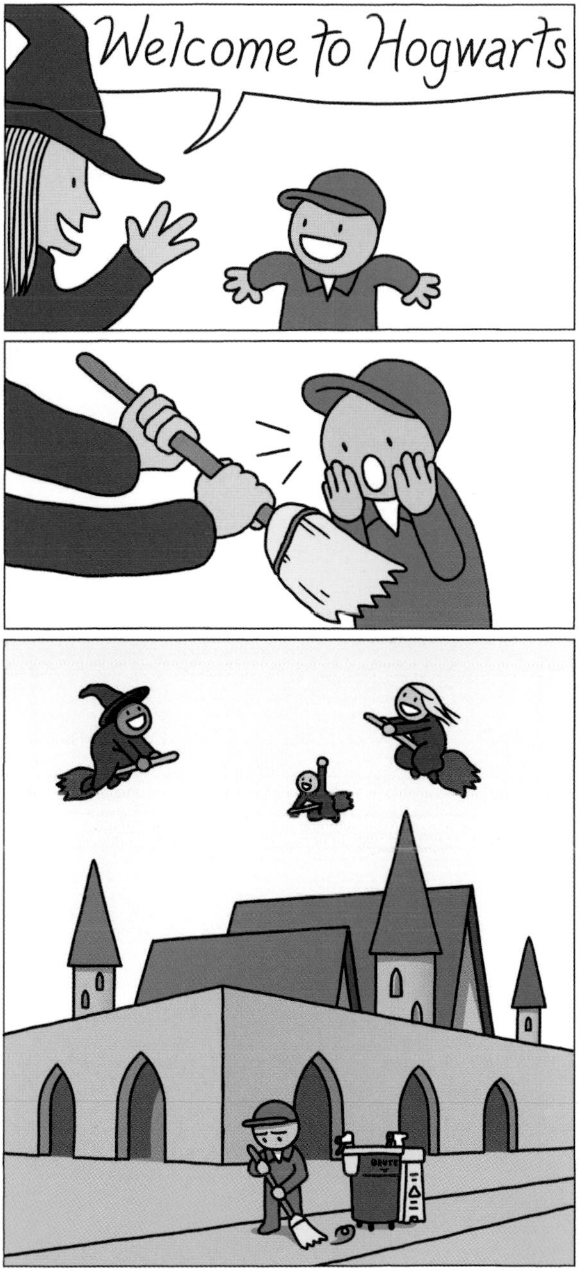
Welcome to Hogwarts

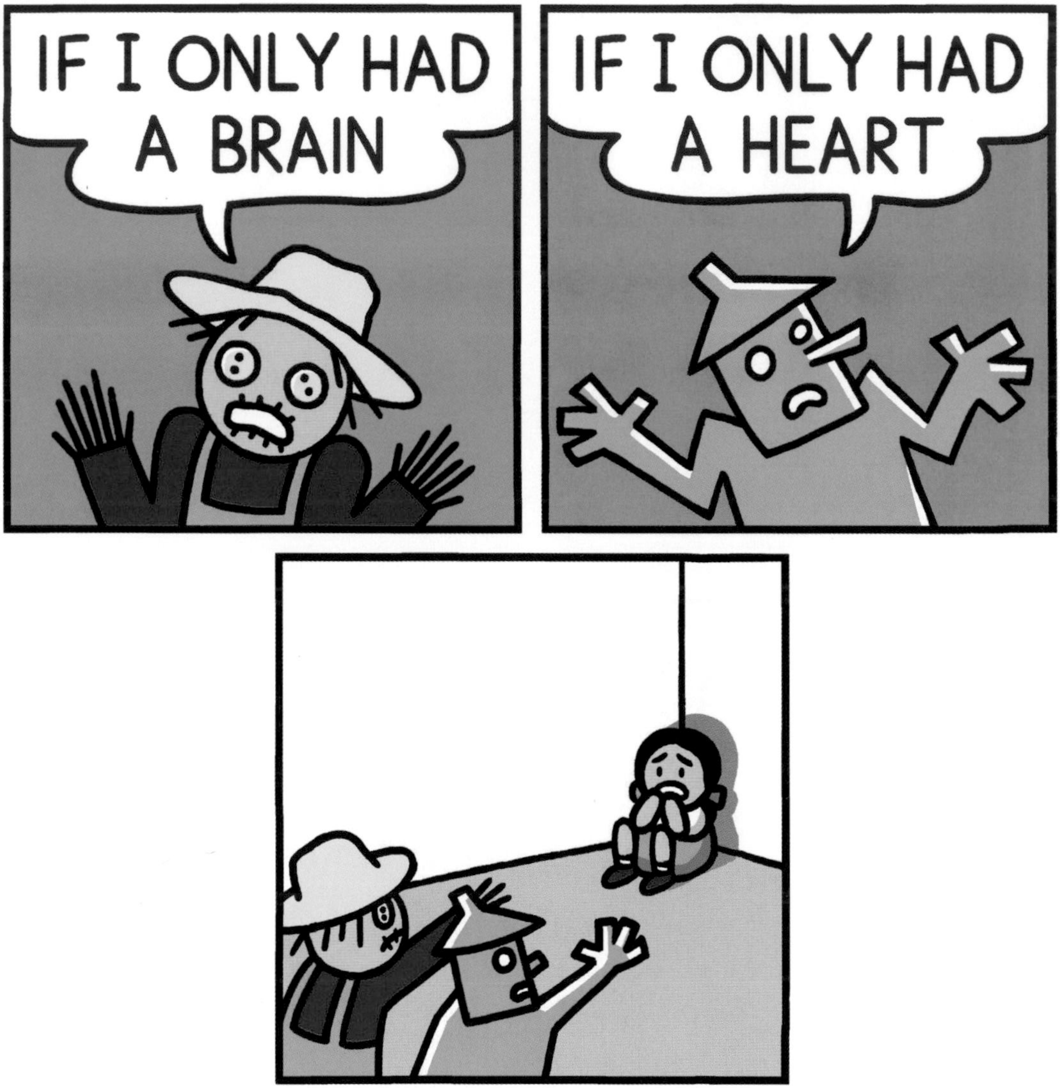
IF I ONLY HAD A BRAIN
IF I ONLY HAD A HEART

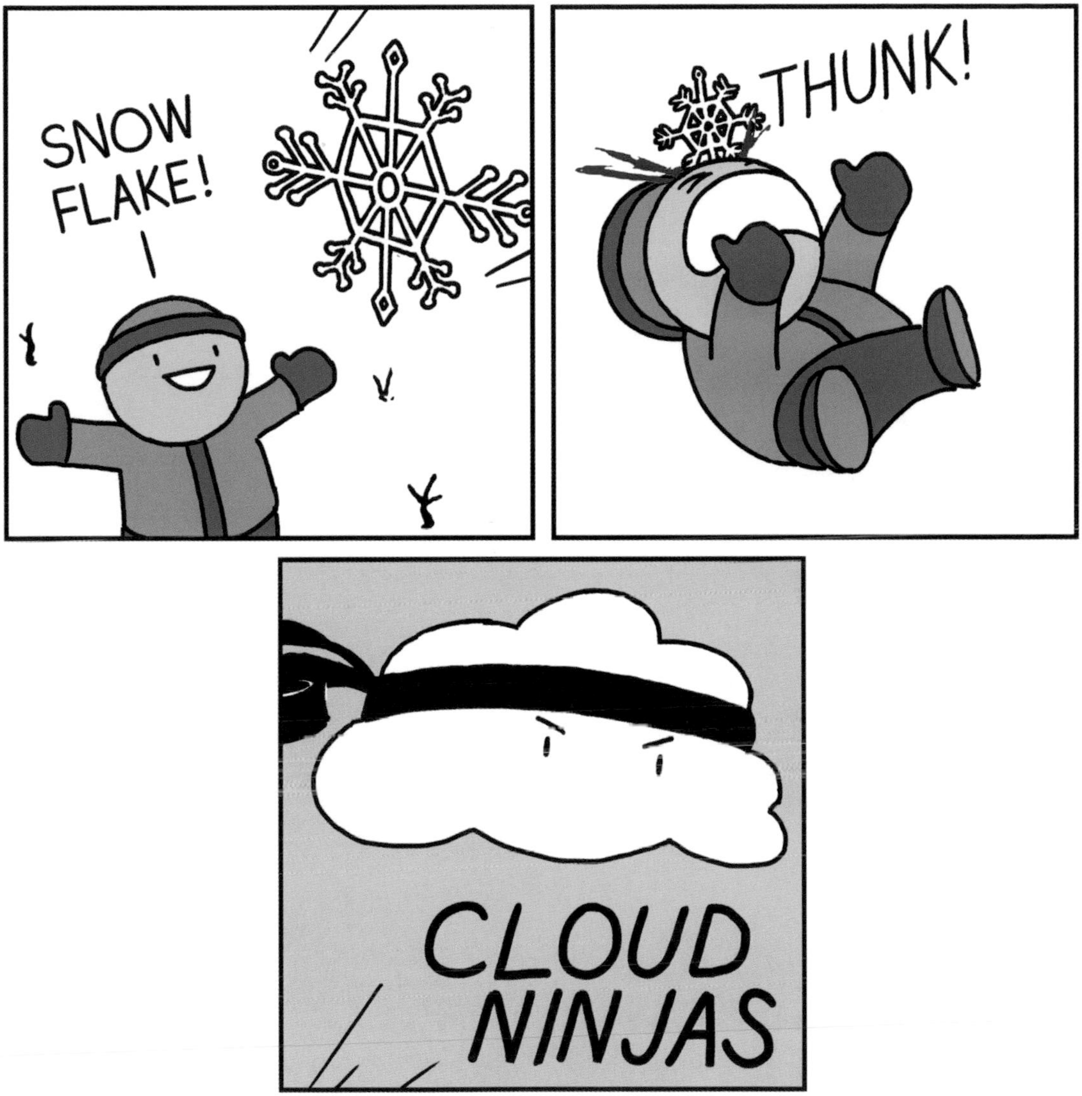
SNOW FLAKE!
THUNK!
CLOUD NINJAS

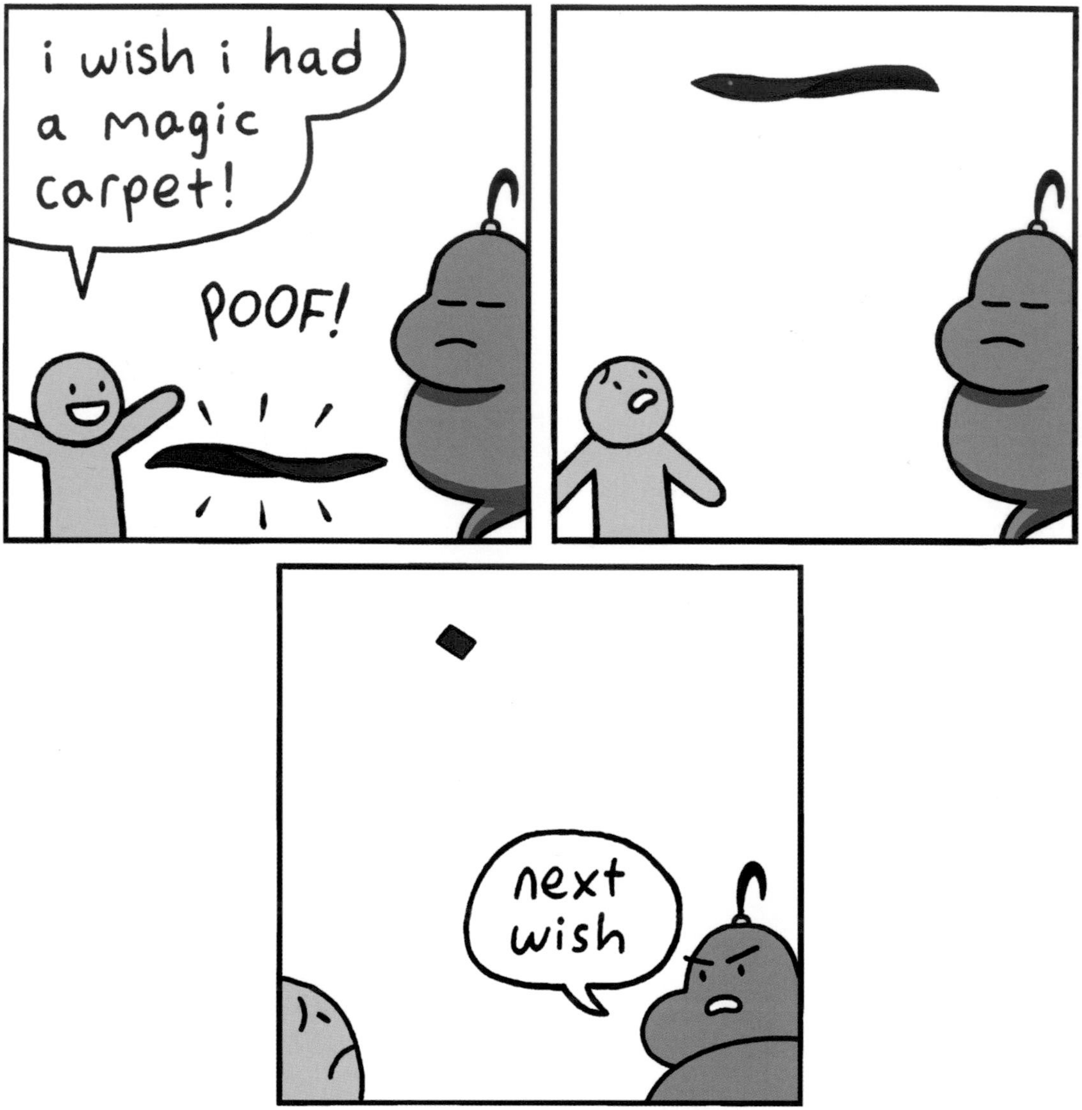
i wish i had a magic carpet!
POOF!
next wish

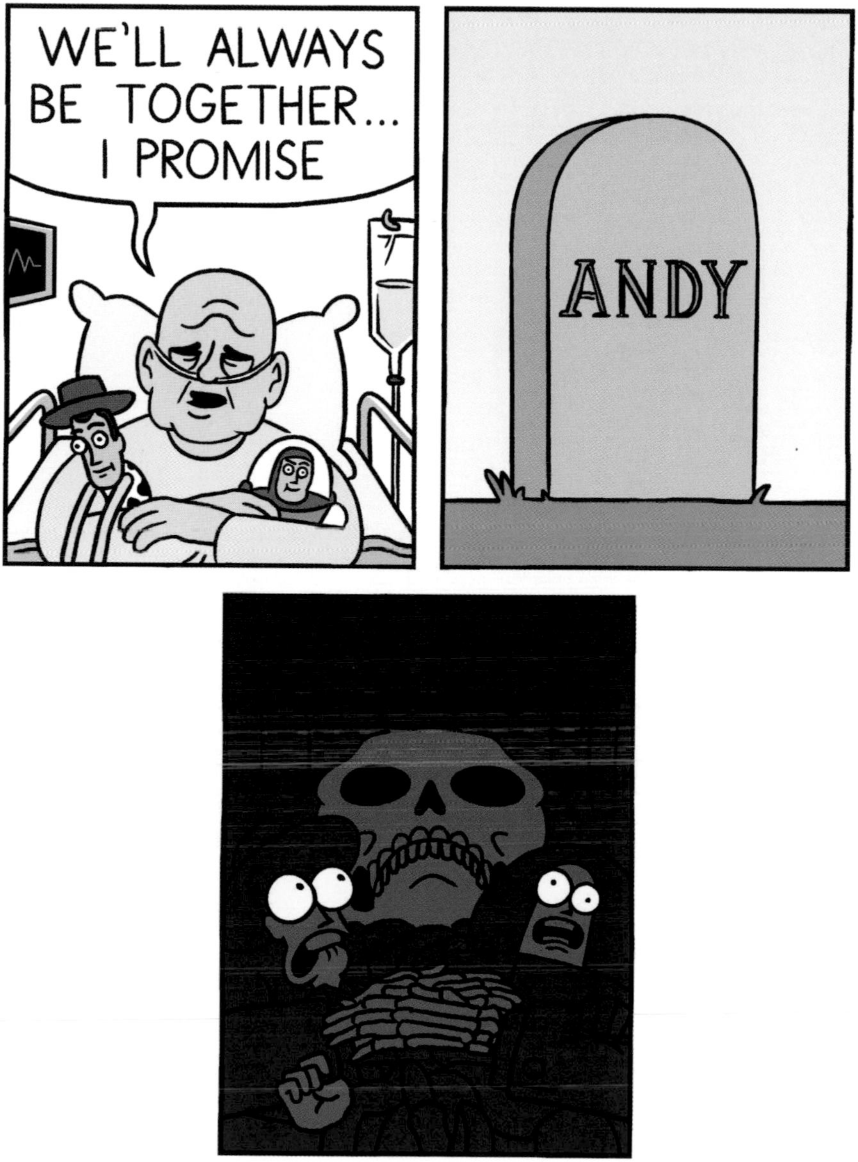
WE'LL ALWAYS BE TOGETHER... I PROMISE
ANDY

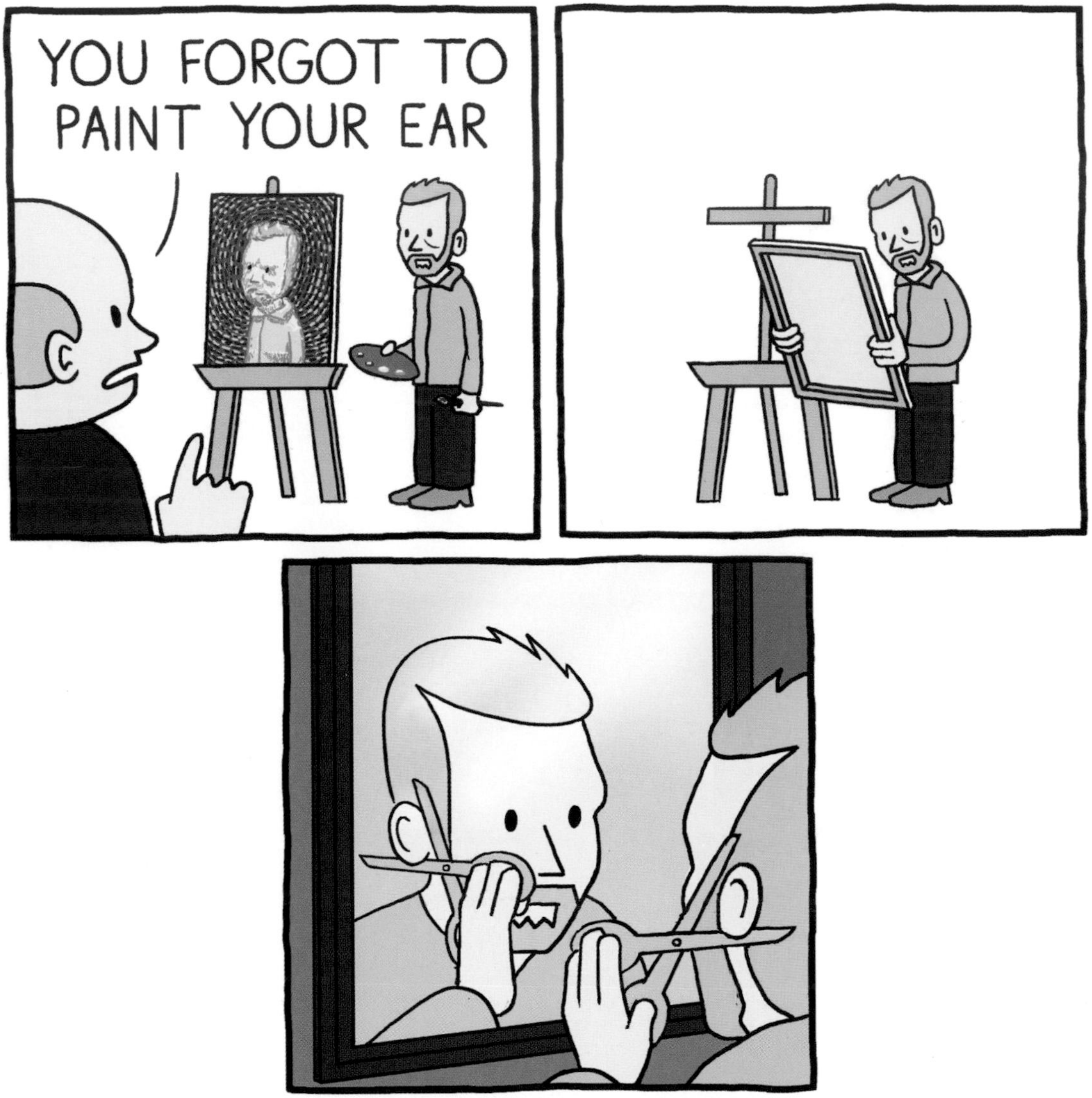
YOU FORGOT TO PAINT YOUR EAR

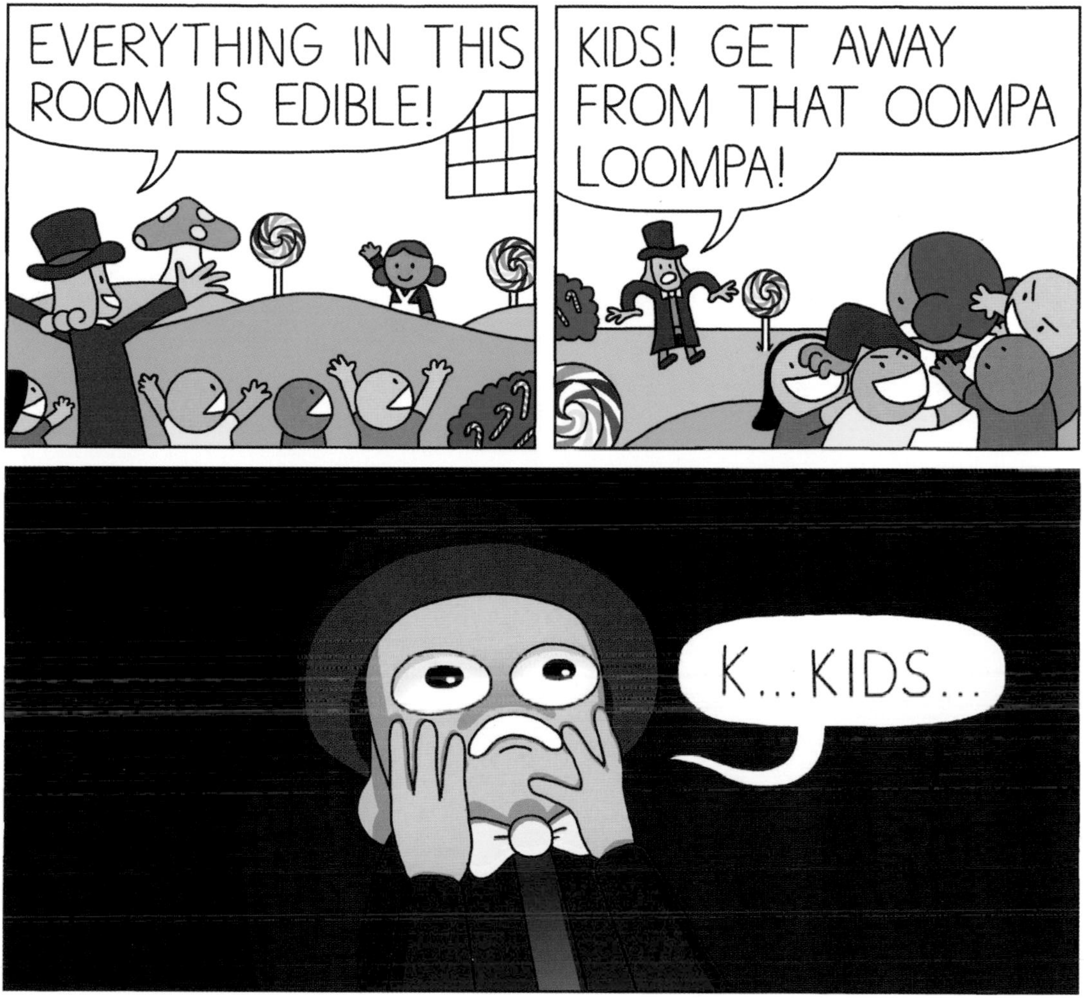
EVERYTHING IN THIS ROOM IS EDIBLE!
KIDS! GET AWAY FROM THAT OOMPA LOOMPA!
K...KIDS...

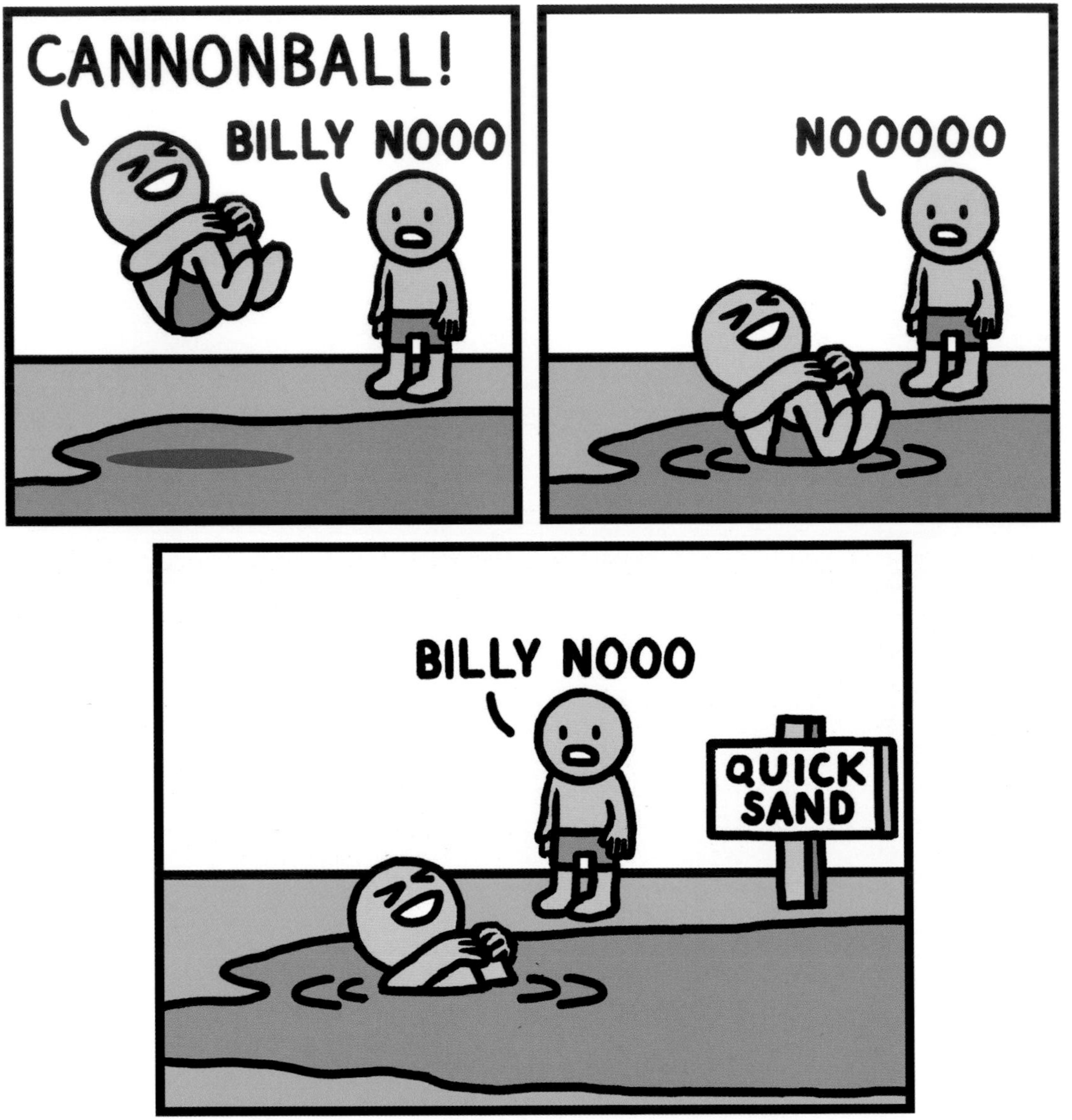
CANNONBALL!
BILLY NOOO
NOOOOO
BILLY NOOO
QUICK SAND

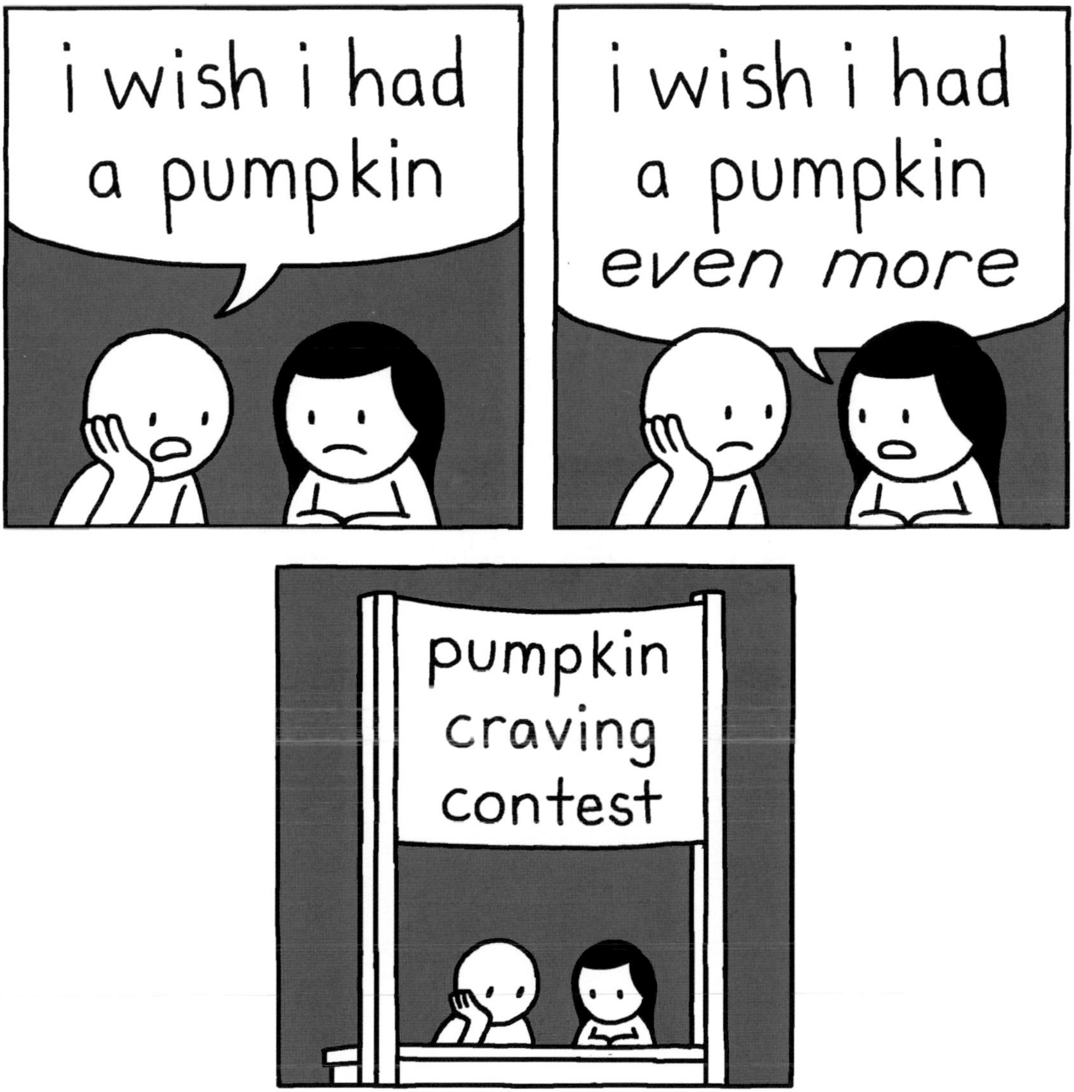

i wish i had a pumpkin
i wish i had a pumpkin *even more*
pumpkin craving contest

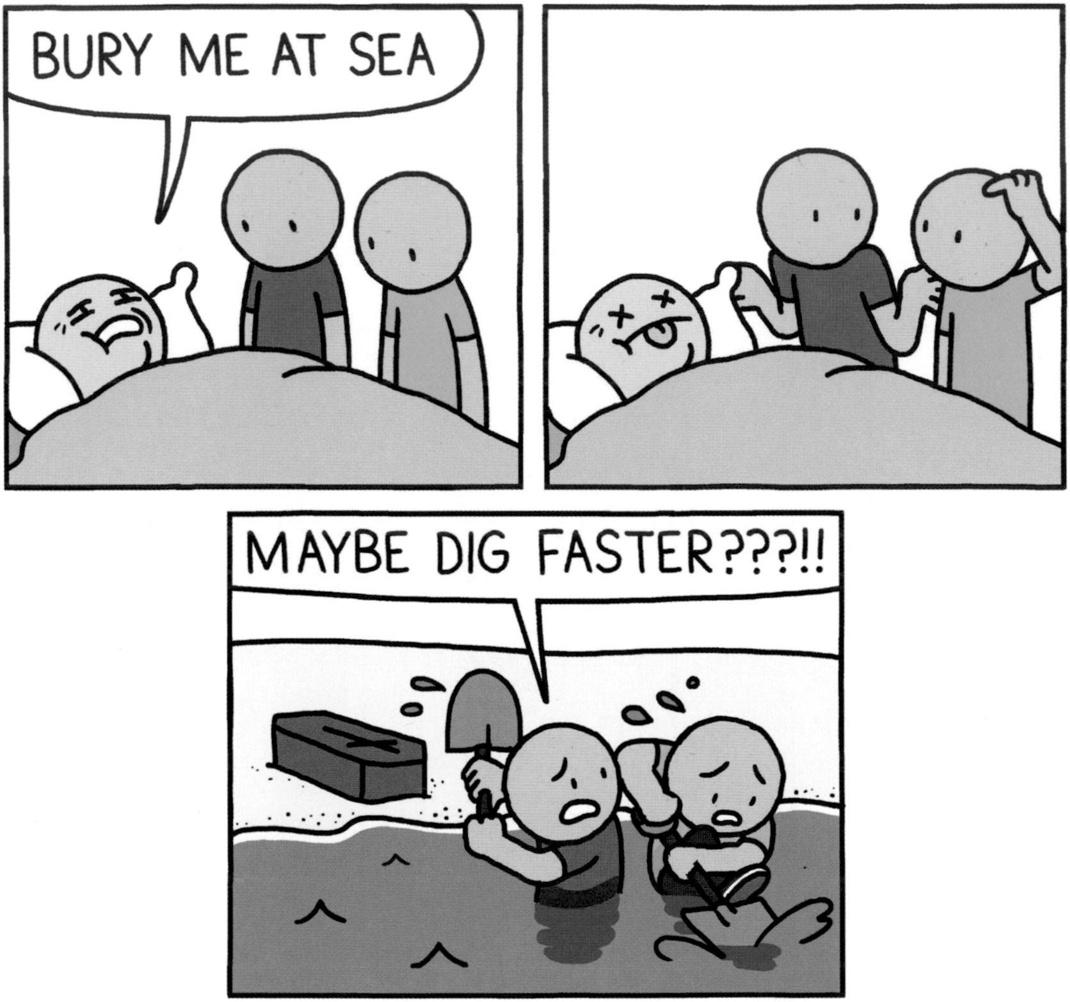
BURY ME AT SEA
MAYBE DIG FASTER???!!

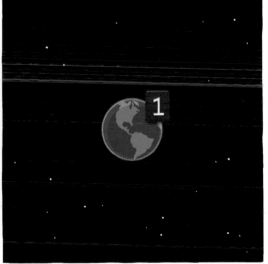

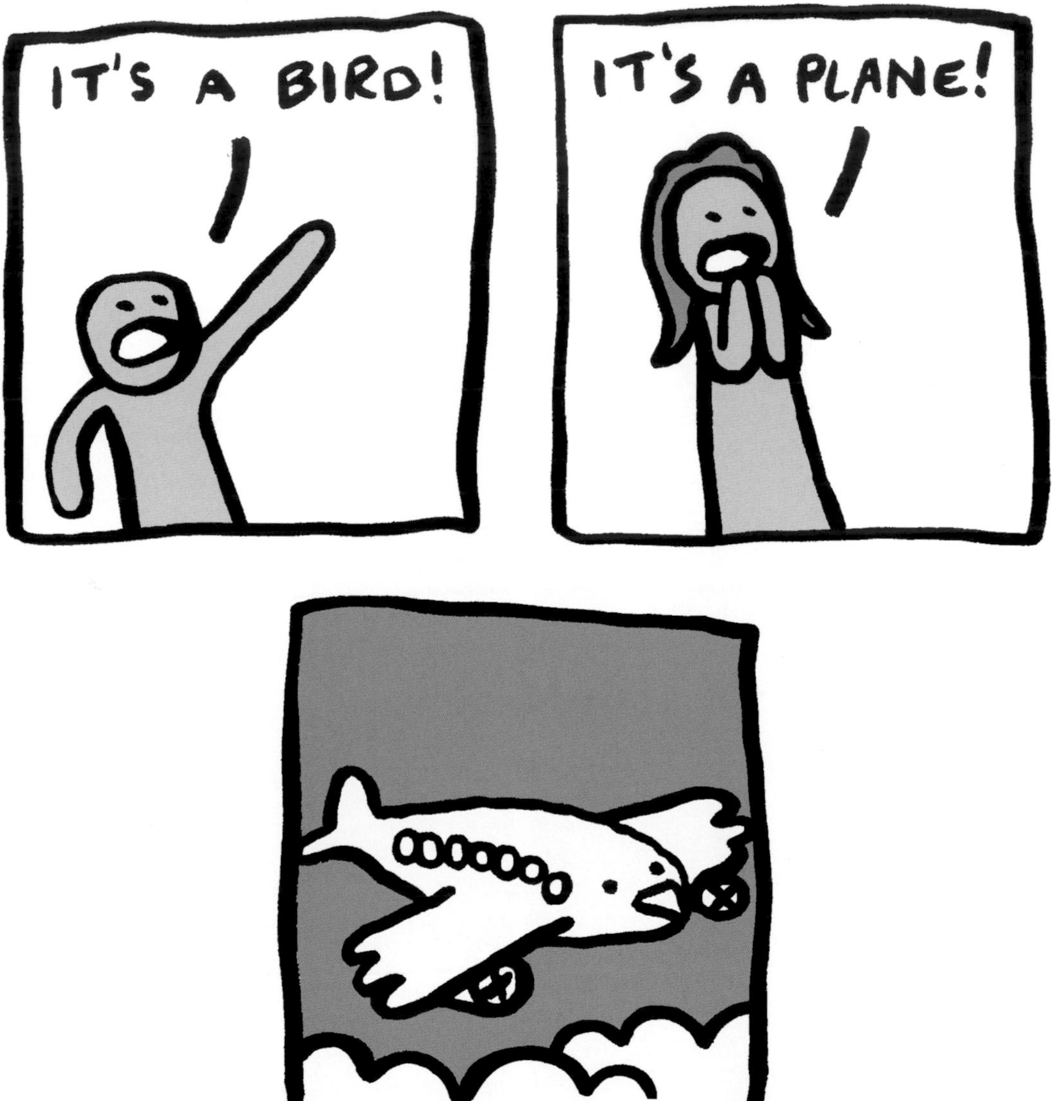
IT'S A BIRD!
IT'S A PLANE!

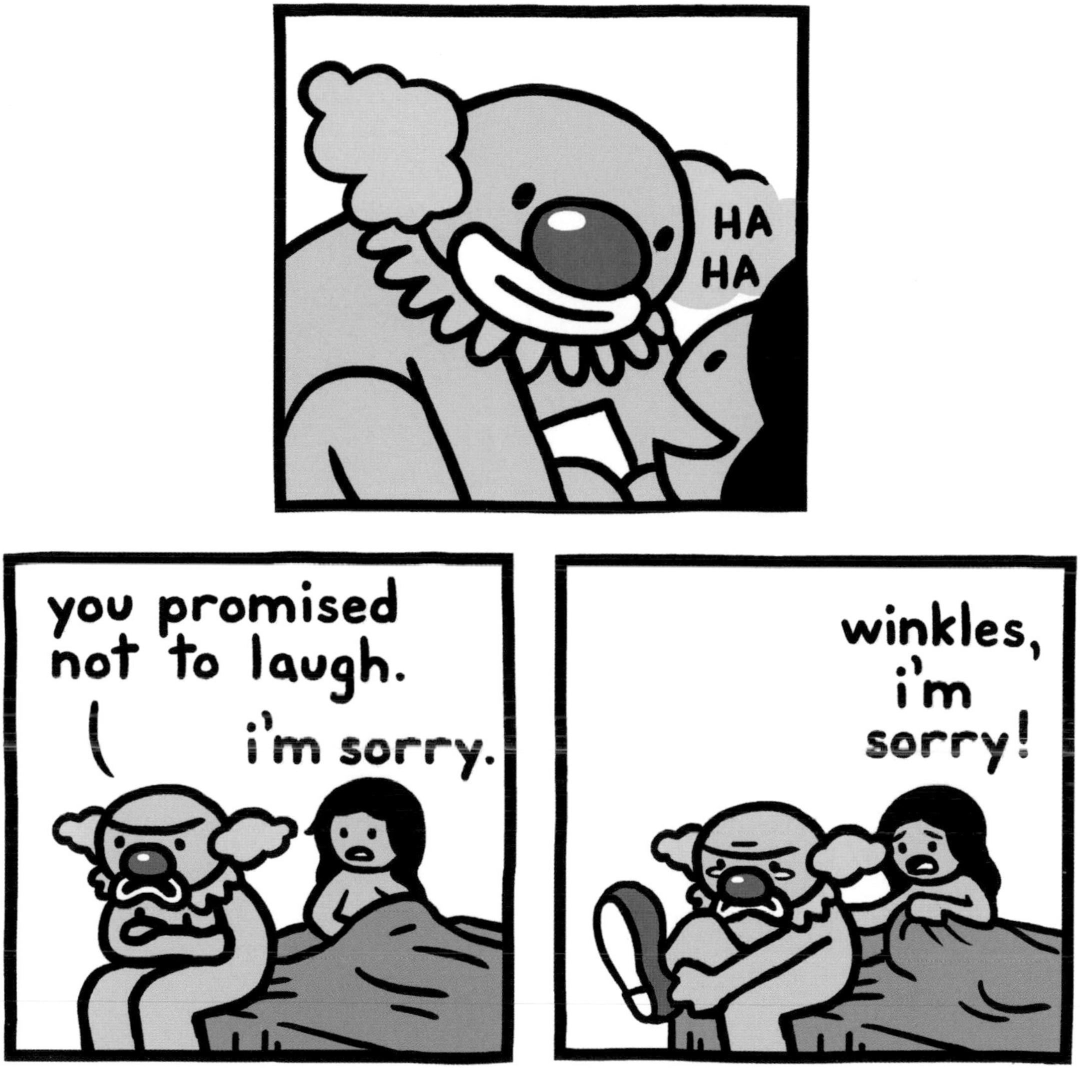
HA
HA
you promised not to laugh.
i'm sorry.
winkles, i'm sorry!

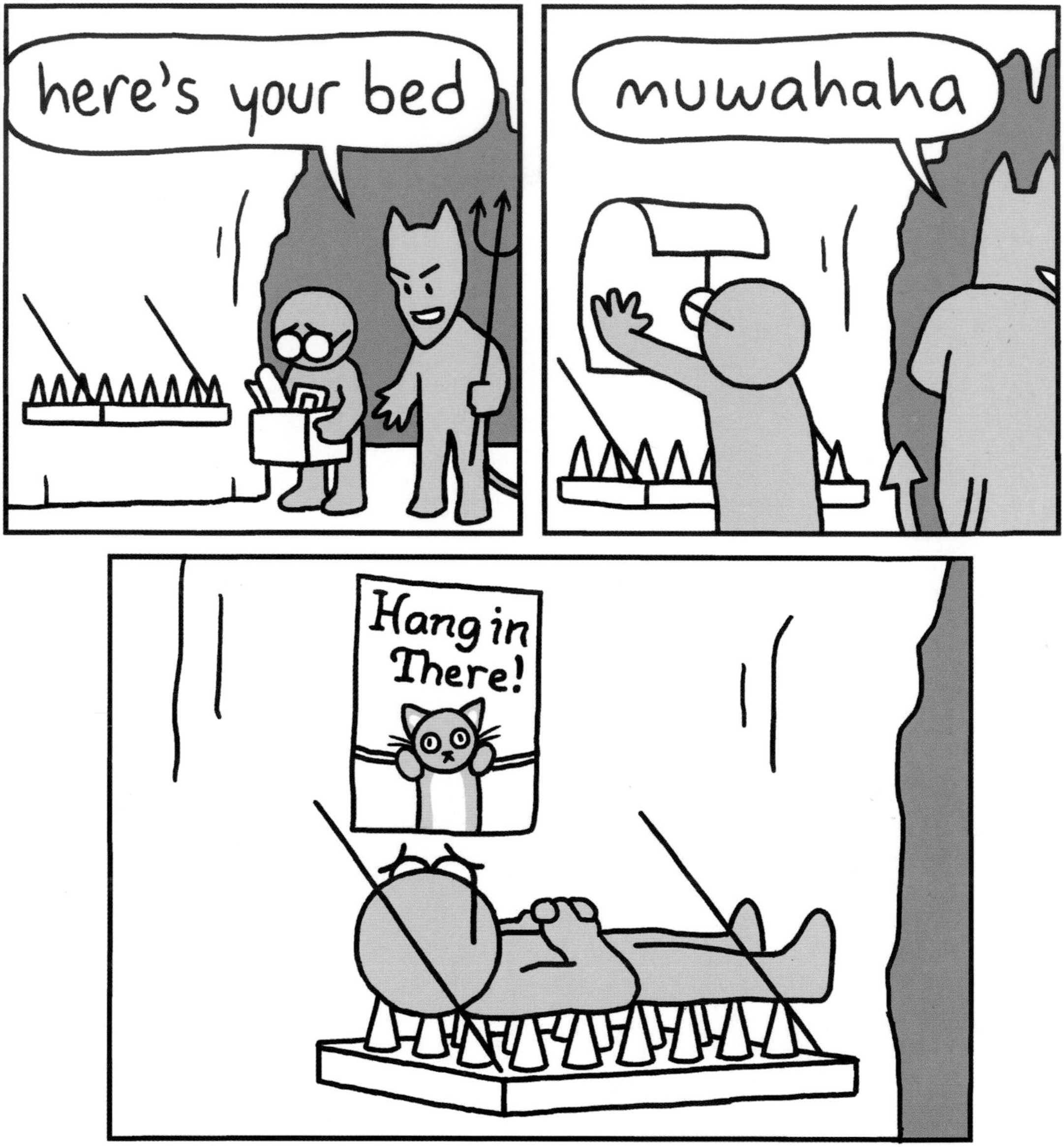
here's your bed
muwahaha
Hang in There!

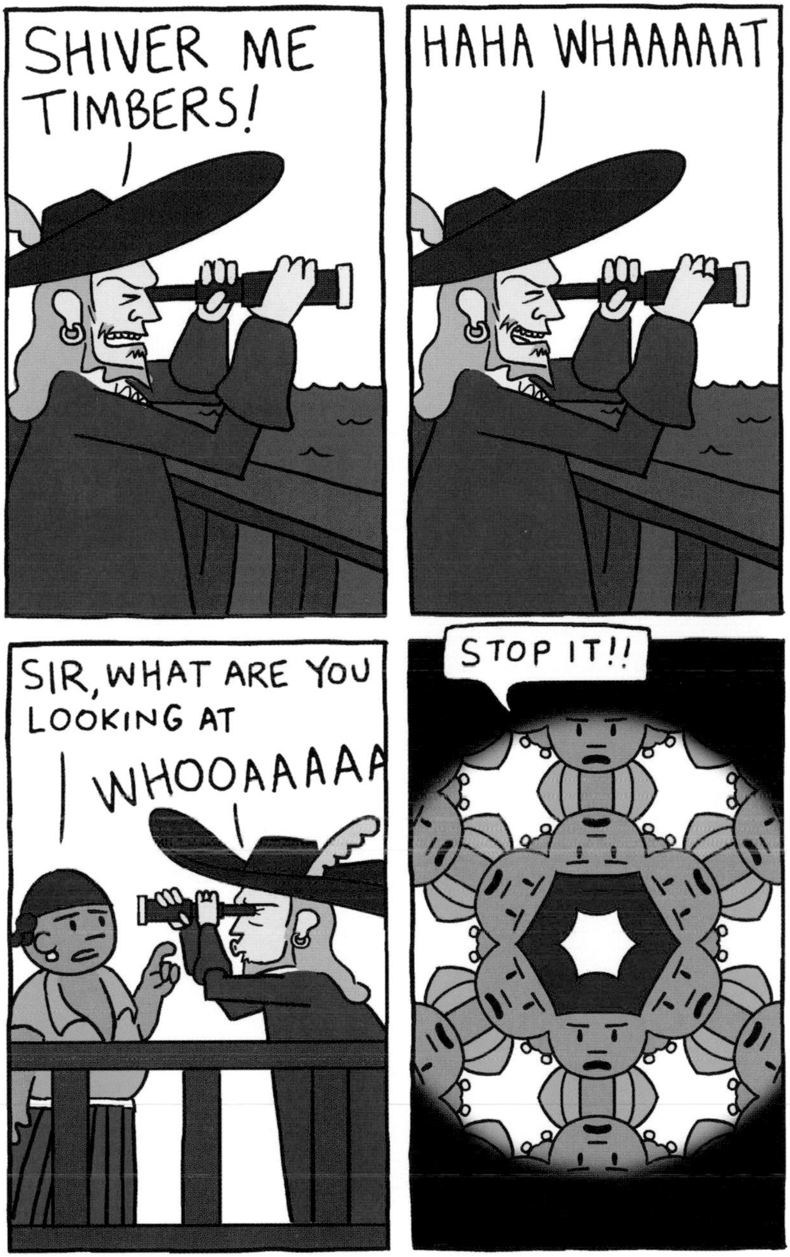
SHIVER ME TIMBERS!
HAHA WHAAAAAT
SIR, WHAT ARE YOU LOOKING AT
WHOOAAAAA
STOP IT!!

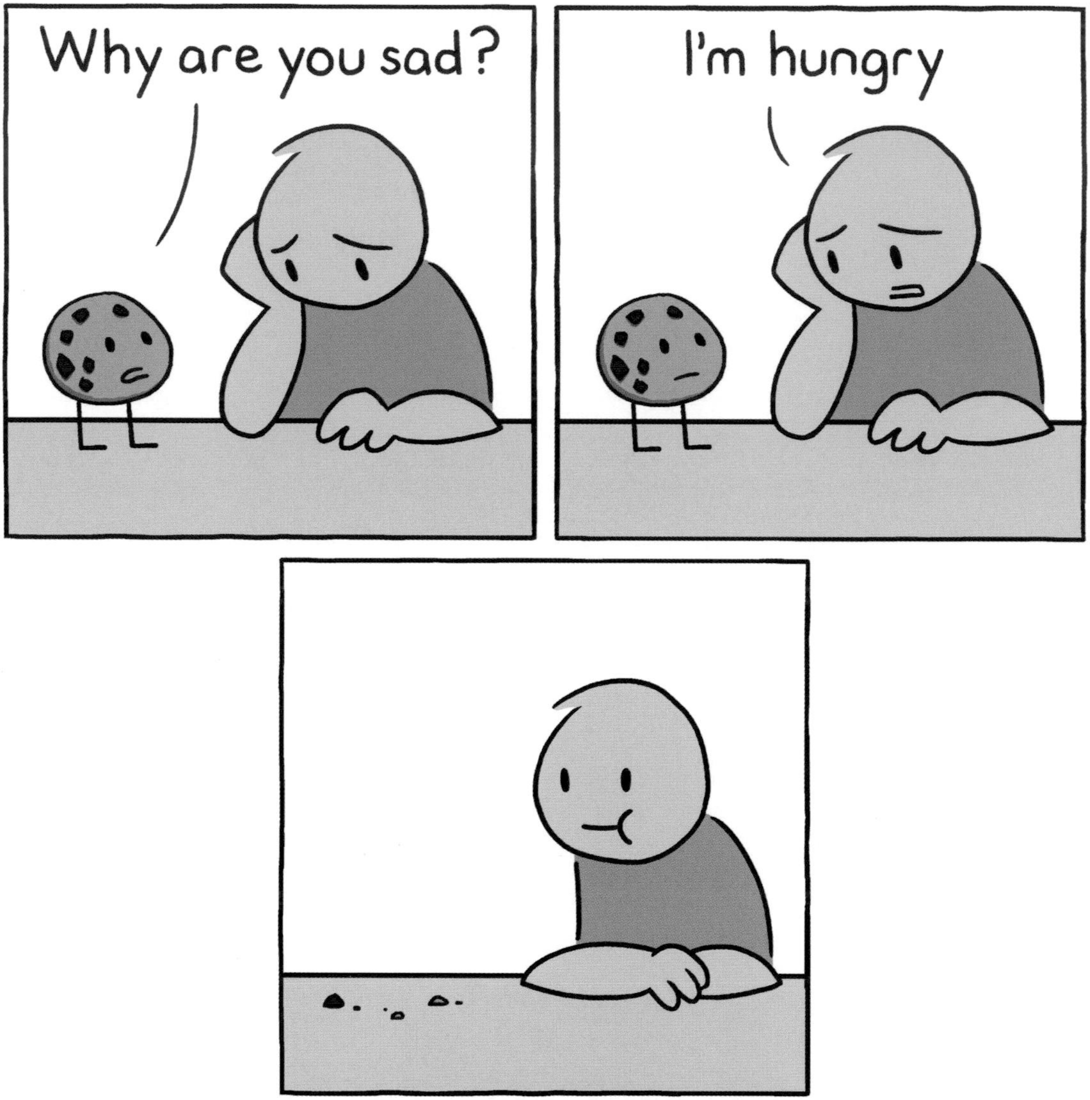
Why are you sad?
I'm hungry

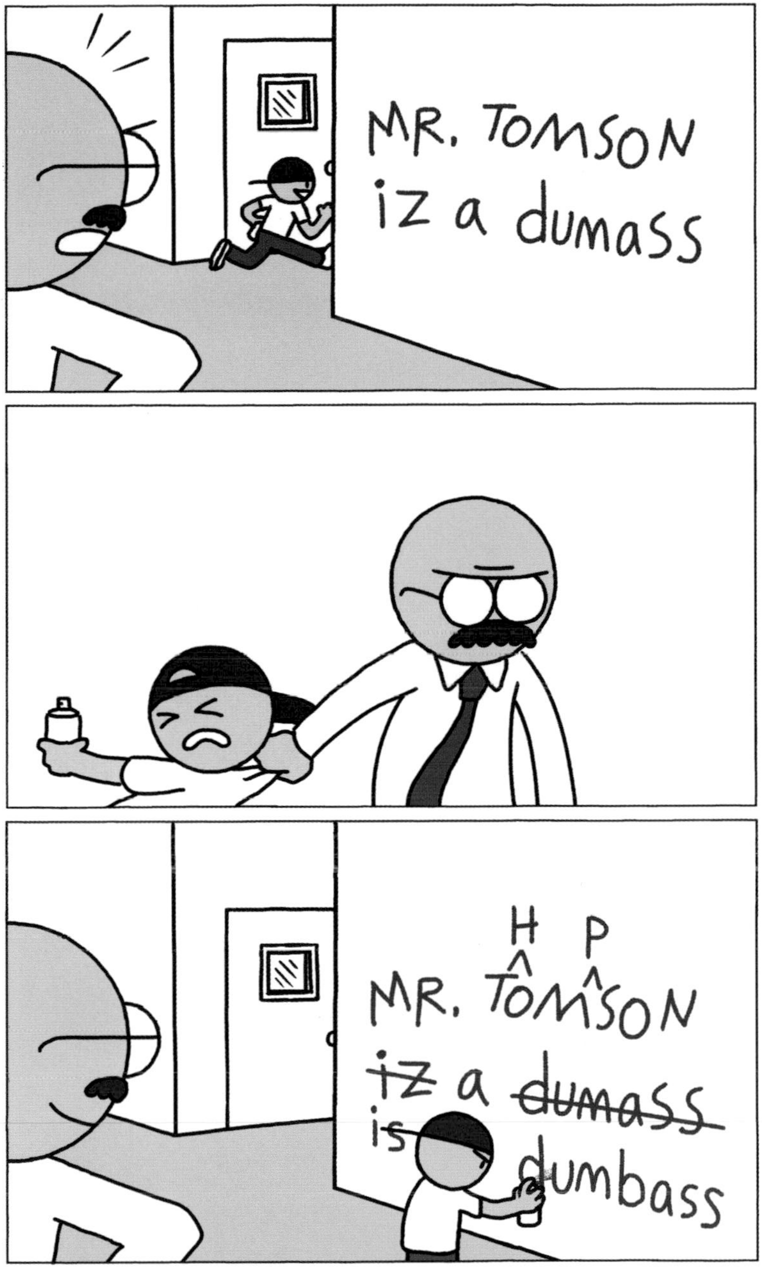
MR. TOMSON
iz a dumass
H P
MR. TOMSON
iz a dumass
is dumbass

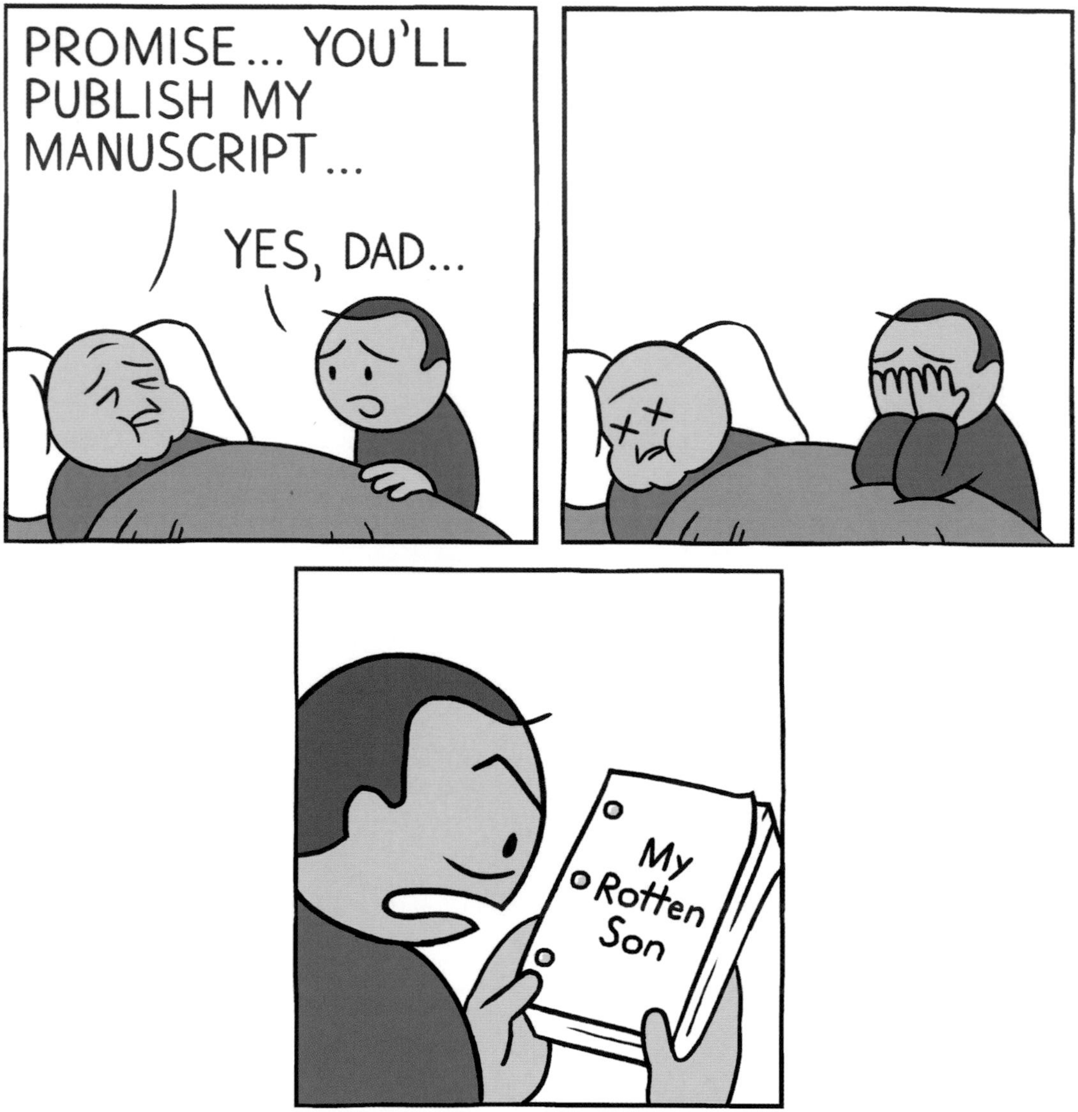
PROMISE... YOU'LL PUBLISH MY MANUSCRIPT...
YES, DAD...
My Rotten Son

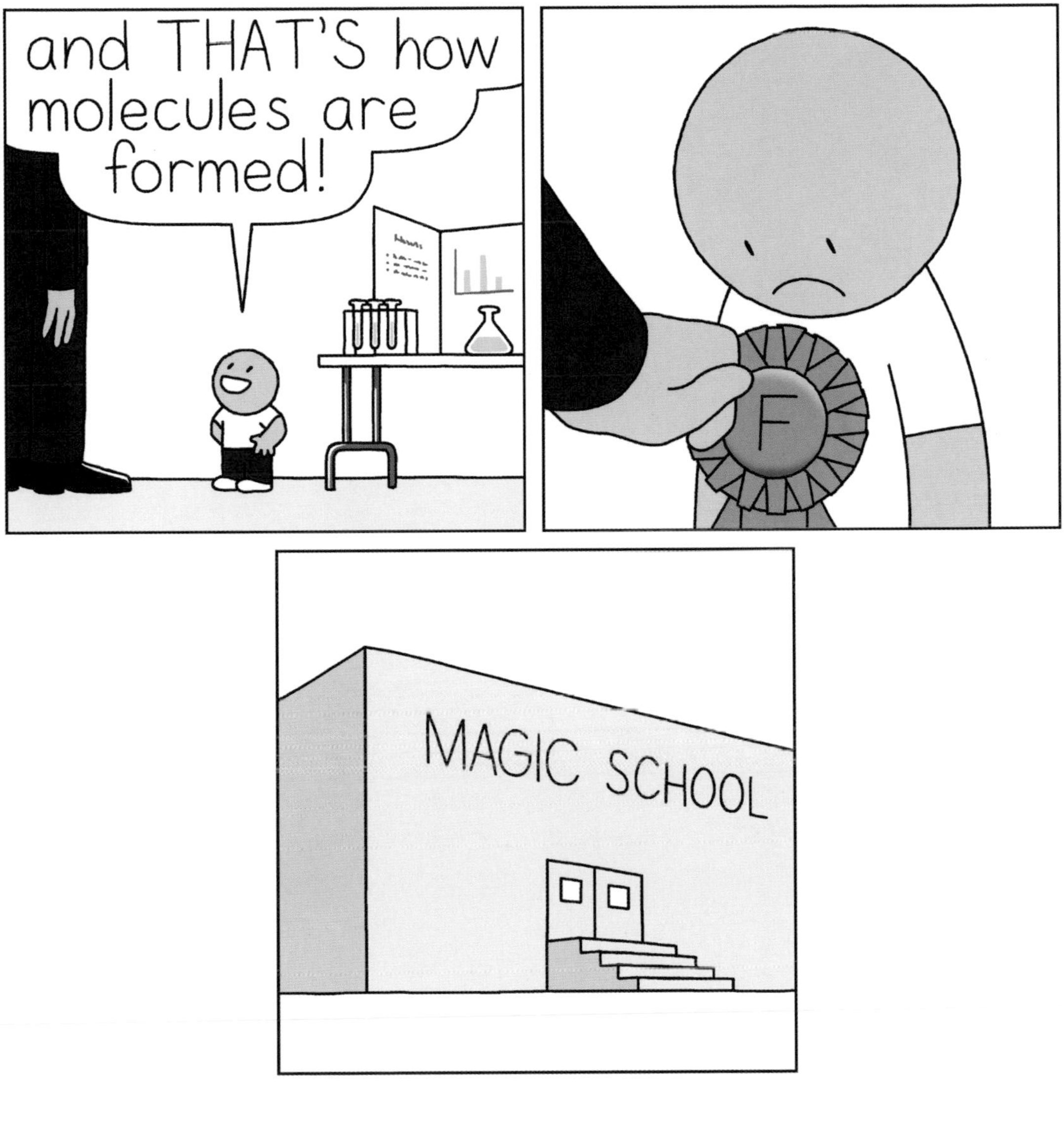
and THAT'S how molecules are formed!
F
MAGIC SCHOOL

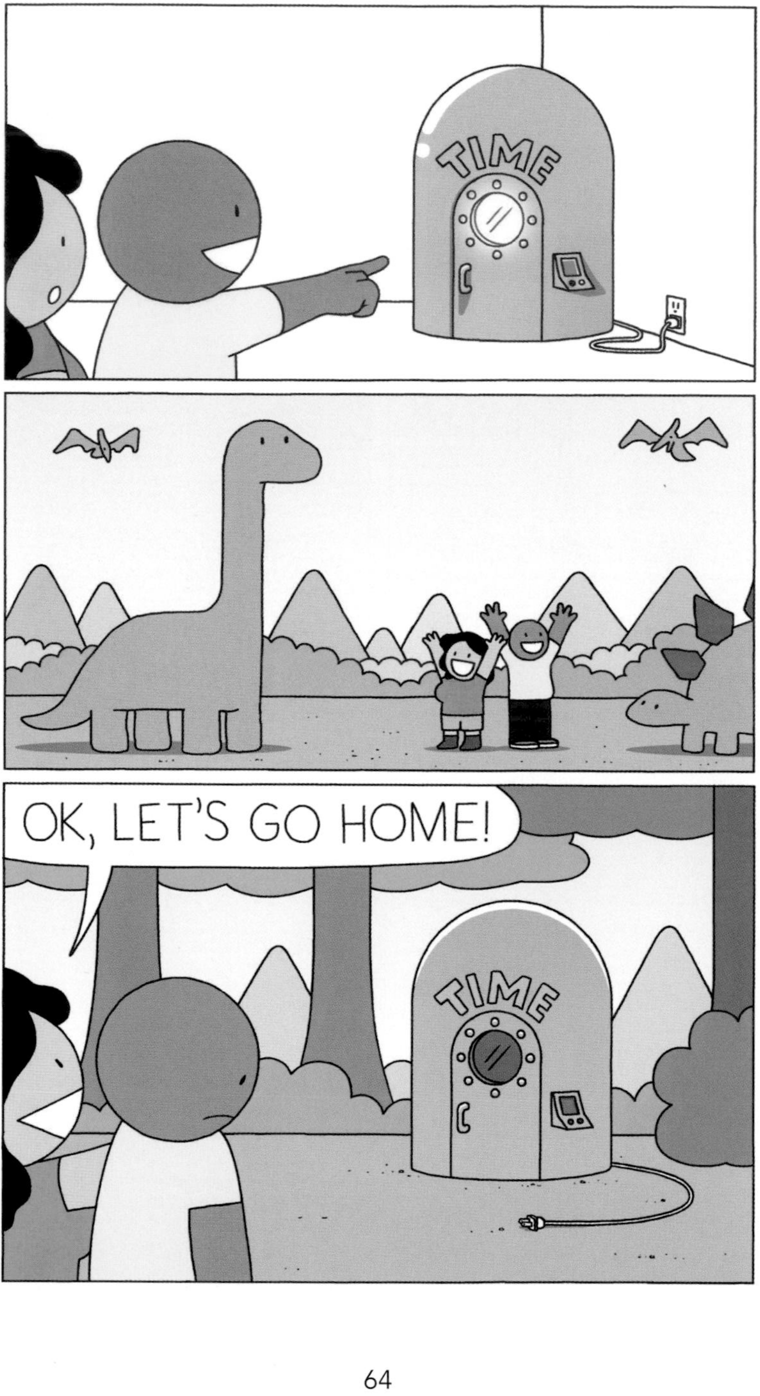
TIME
OK, LET'S GO HOME!
TIME

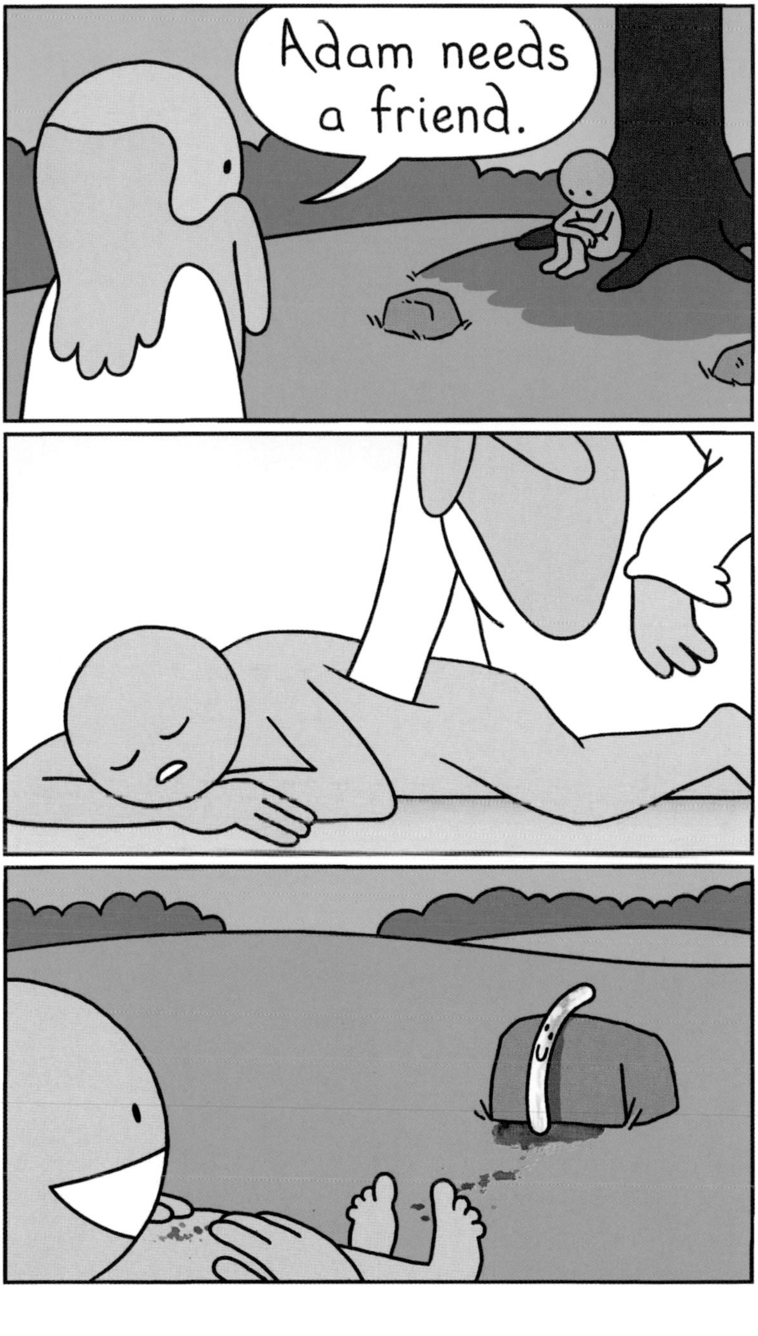
Adam needs a friend.

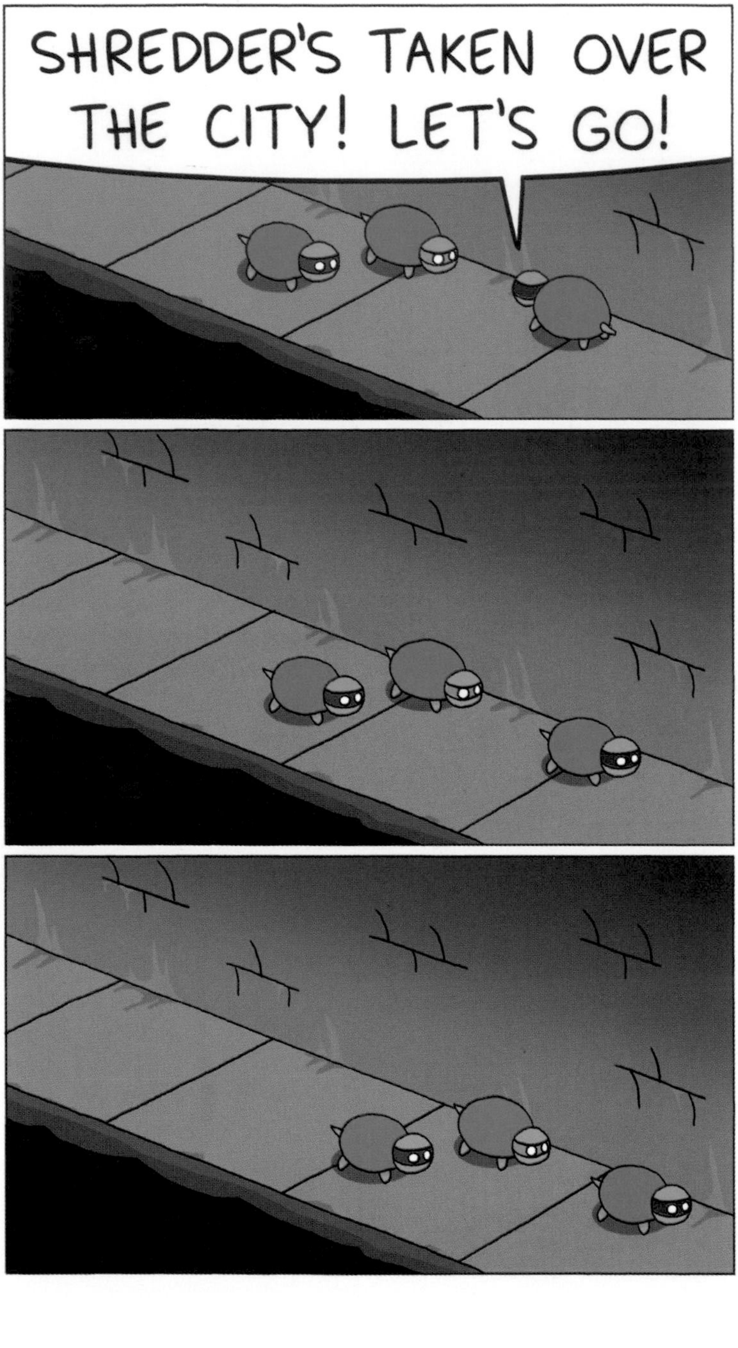
SHREDDER'S TAKEN OVER THE CITY! LET'S GO!

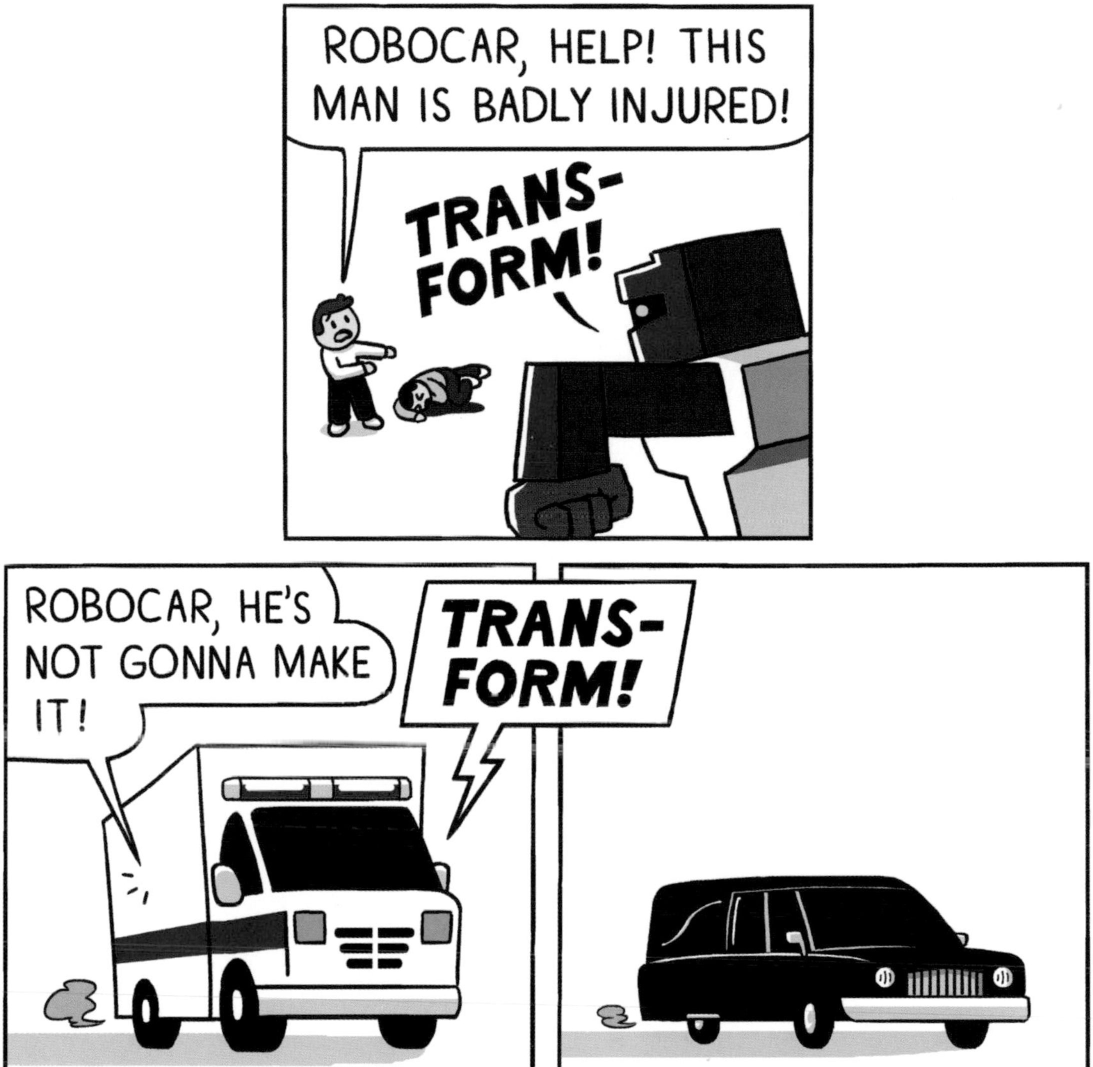
ROBOCAR, HELP! THIS MAN IS BADLY INJURED!
TRANS-FORM!
ROBOCAR, HE'S NOT GONNA MAKE IT!
TRANS-FORM!

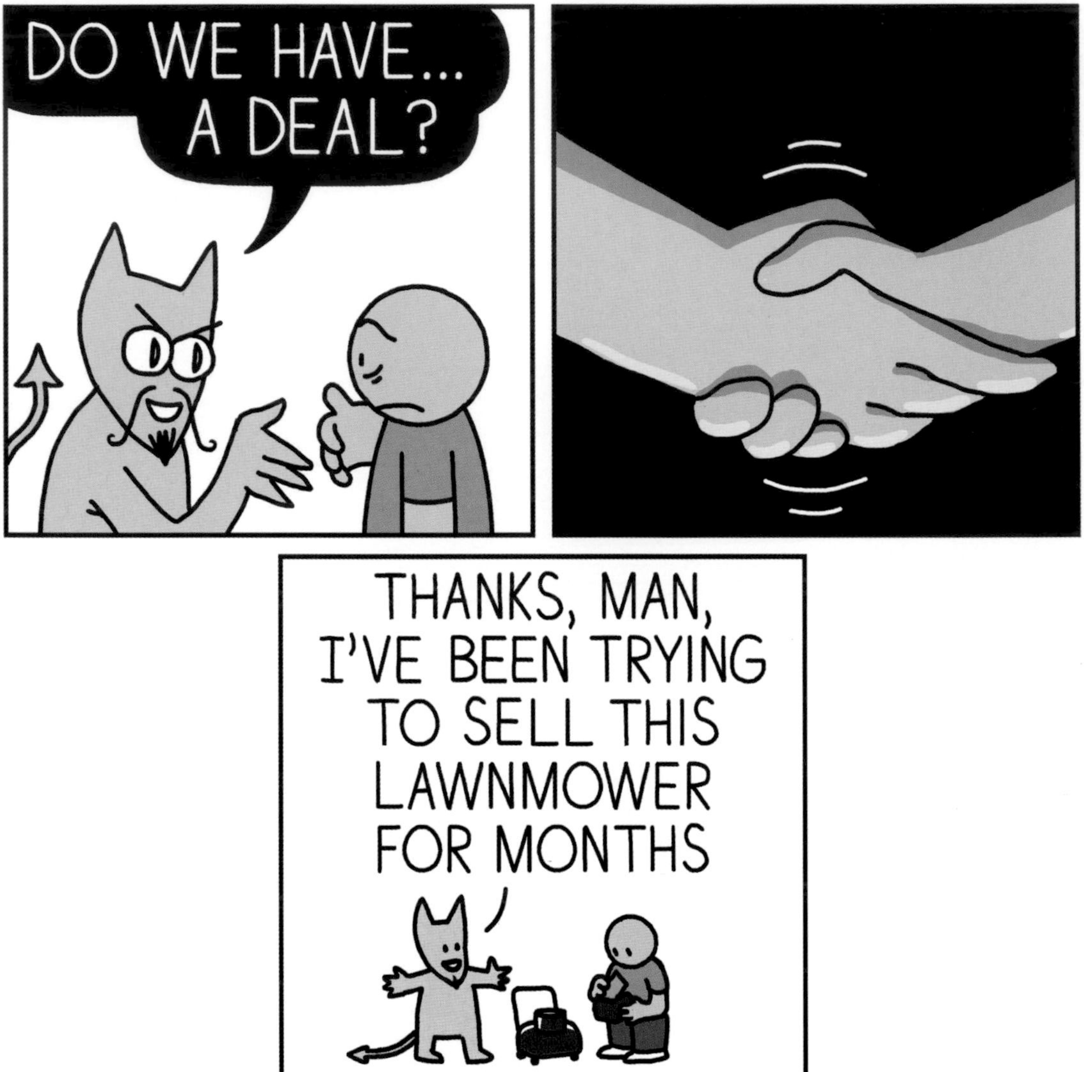
DO WE HAVE... A DEAL?
THANKS, MAN, I'VE BEEN TRYING TO SELL THIS LAWNMOWER FOR MONTHS

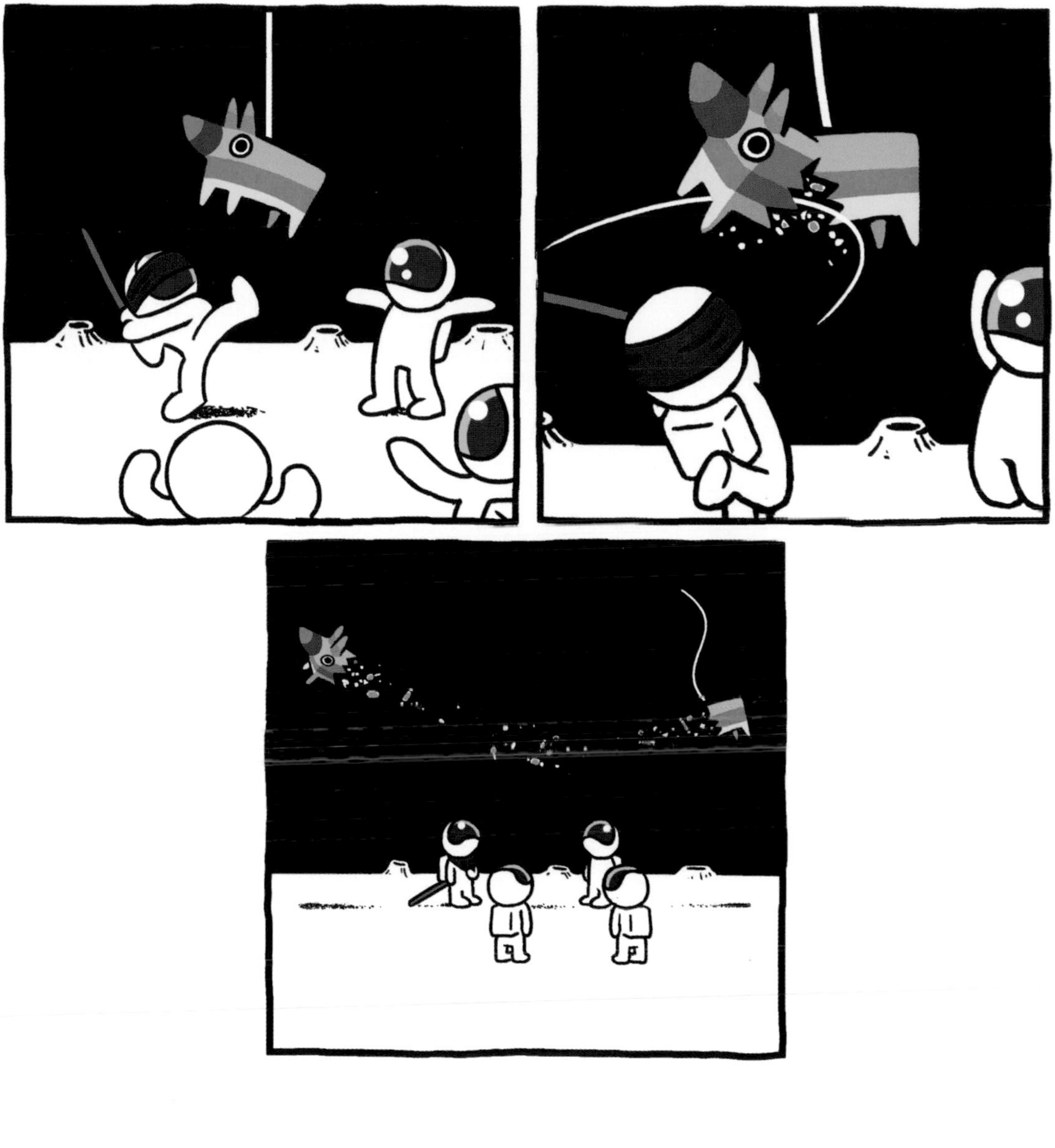

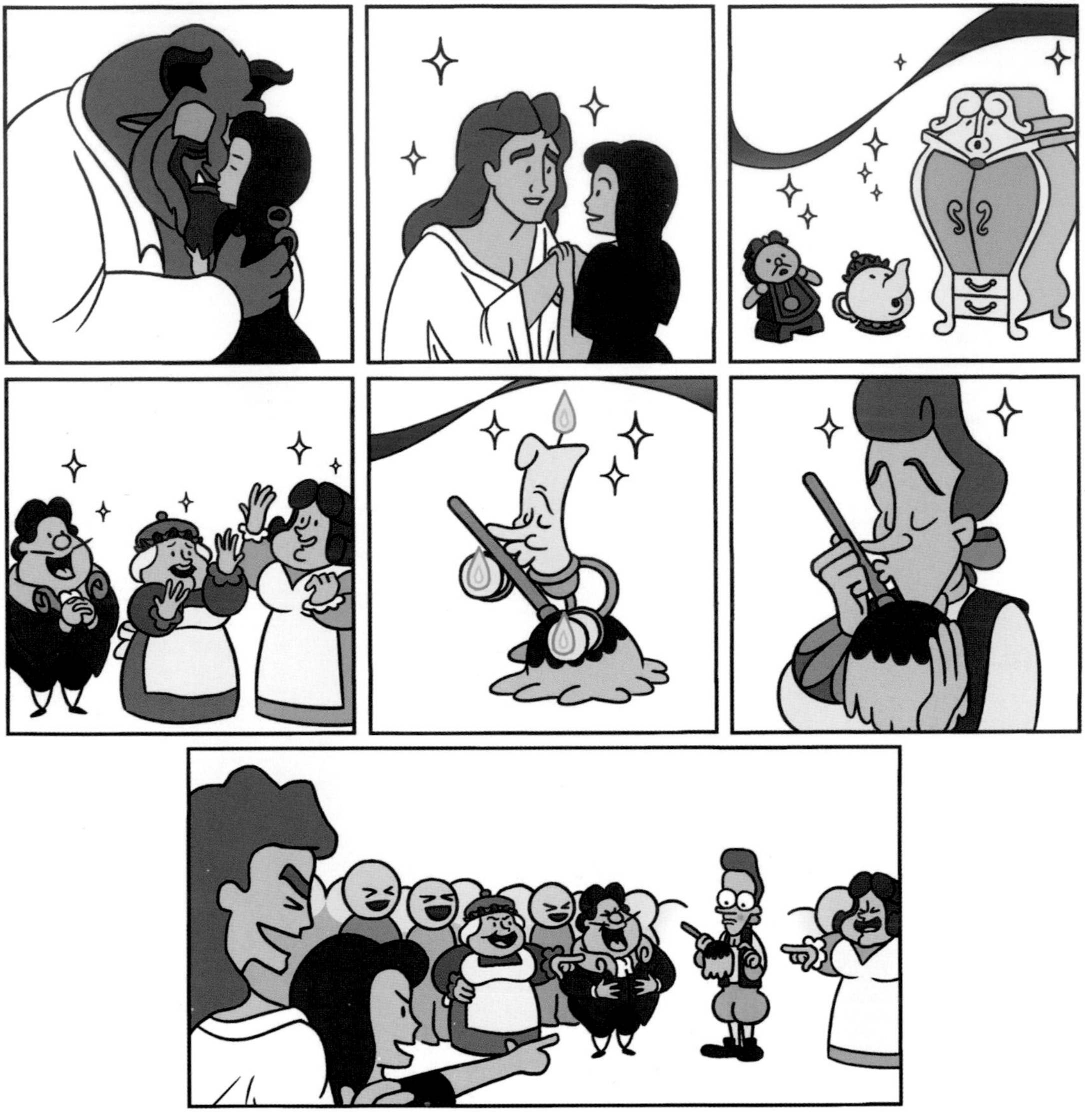

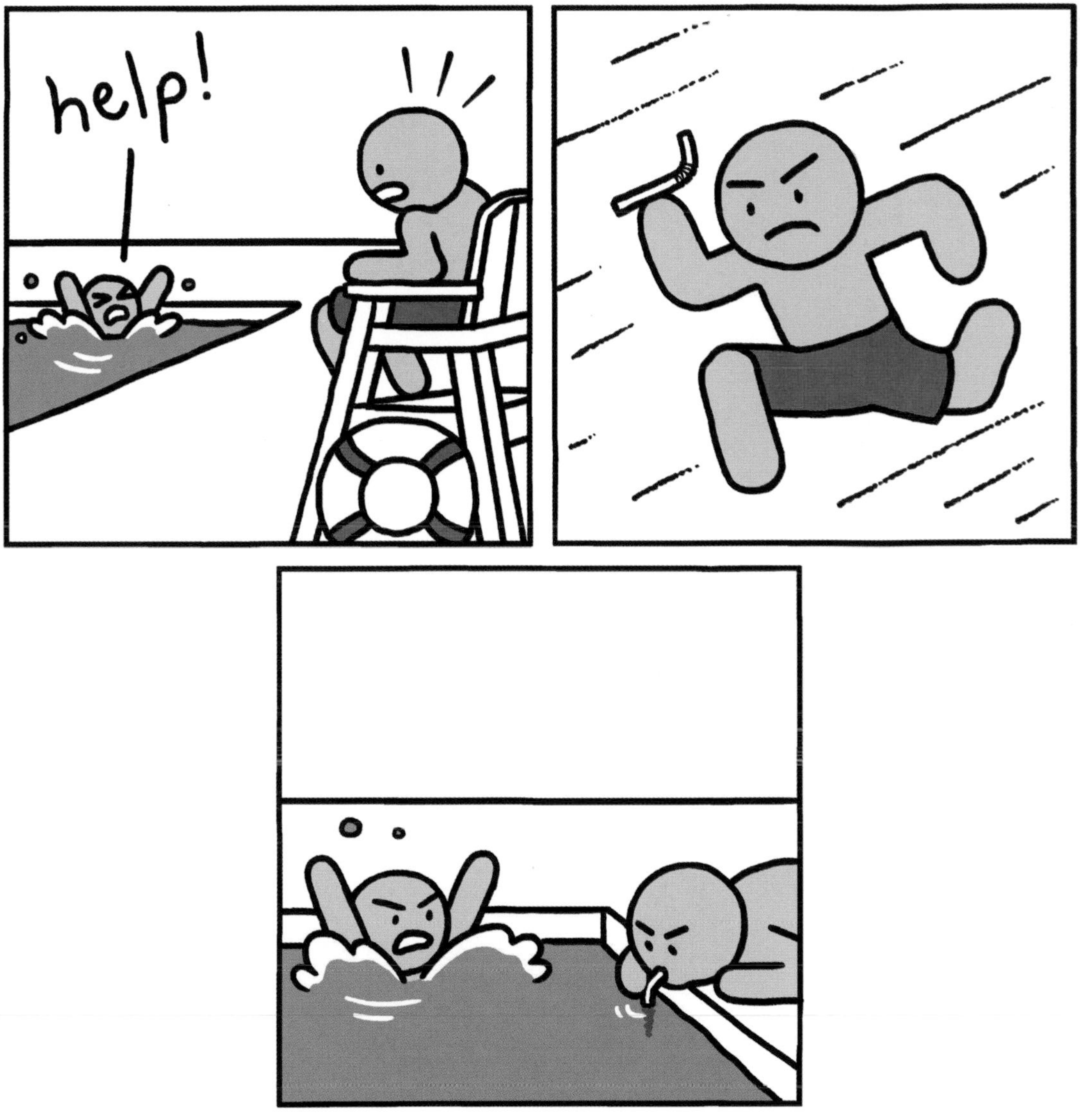
help!

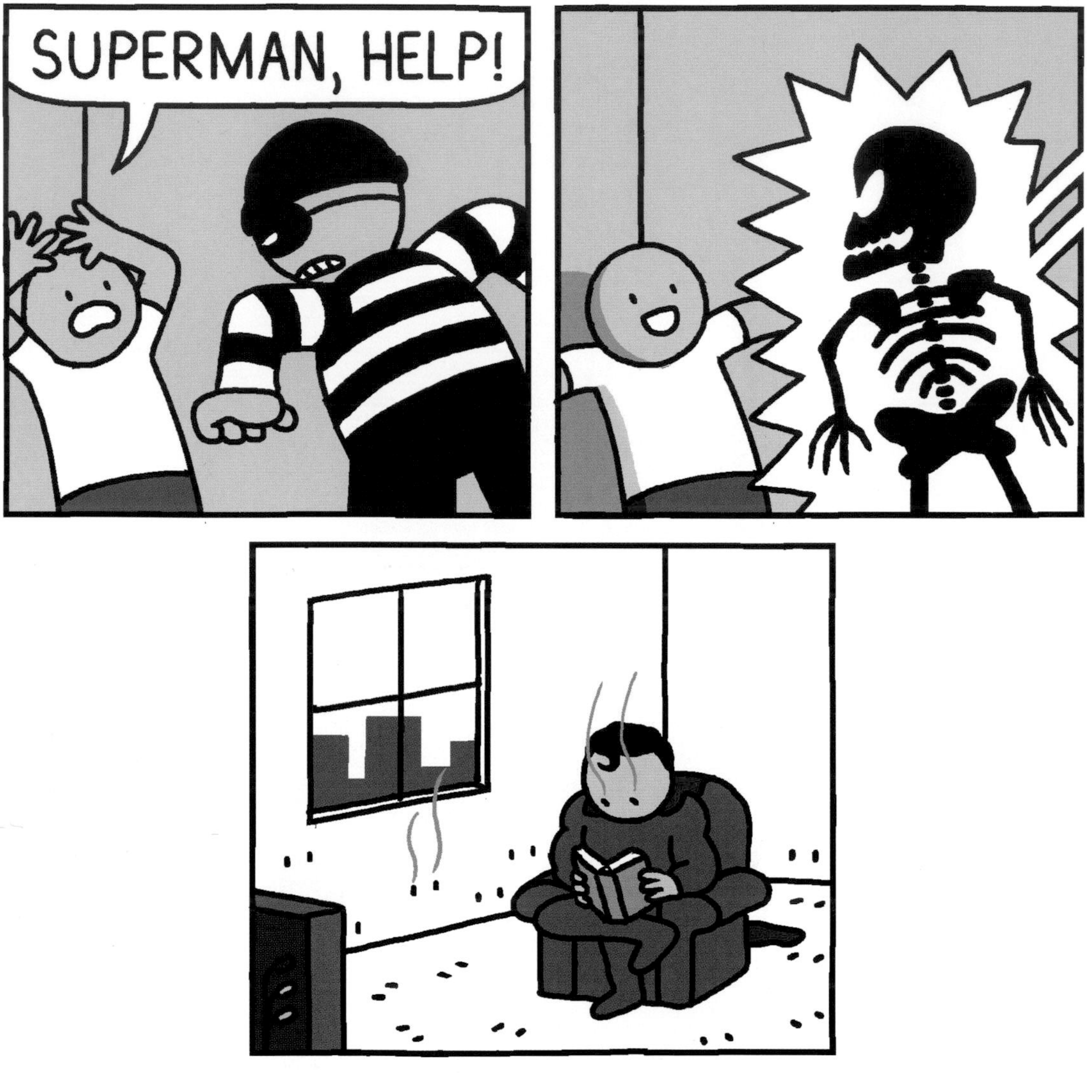
SUPERMAN, HELP!

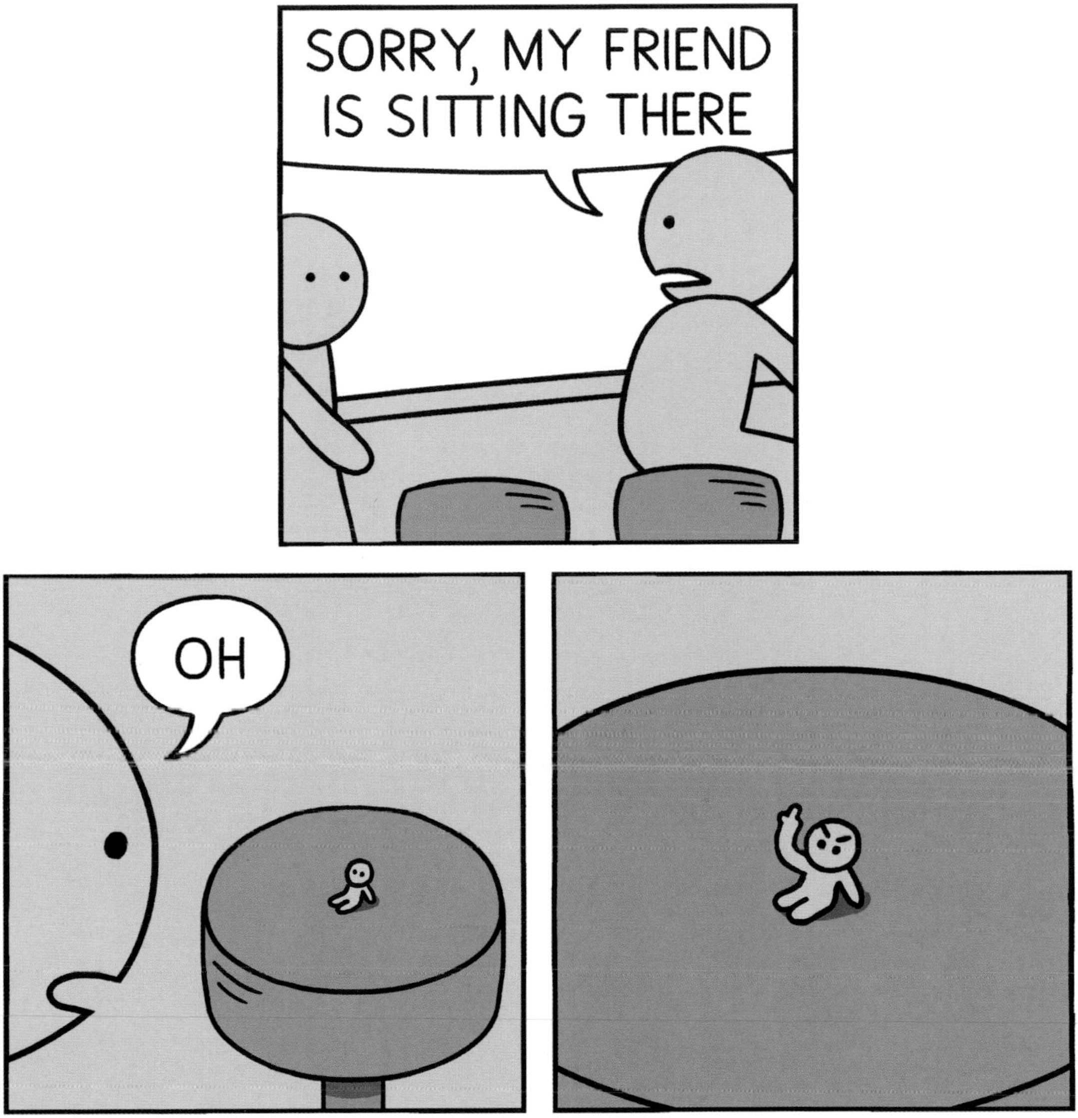
SORRY, MY FRIEND IS SITTING THERE
OH

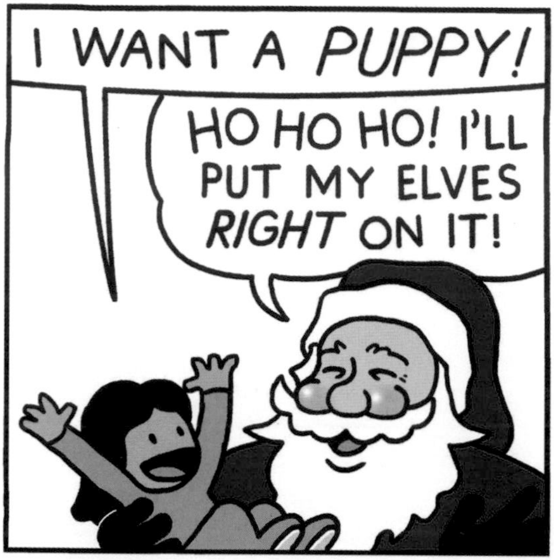
I WANT A PUPPY!
HO HO HO! I'LL PUT MY ELVES RIGHT ON IT!

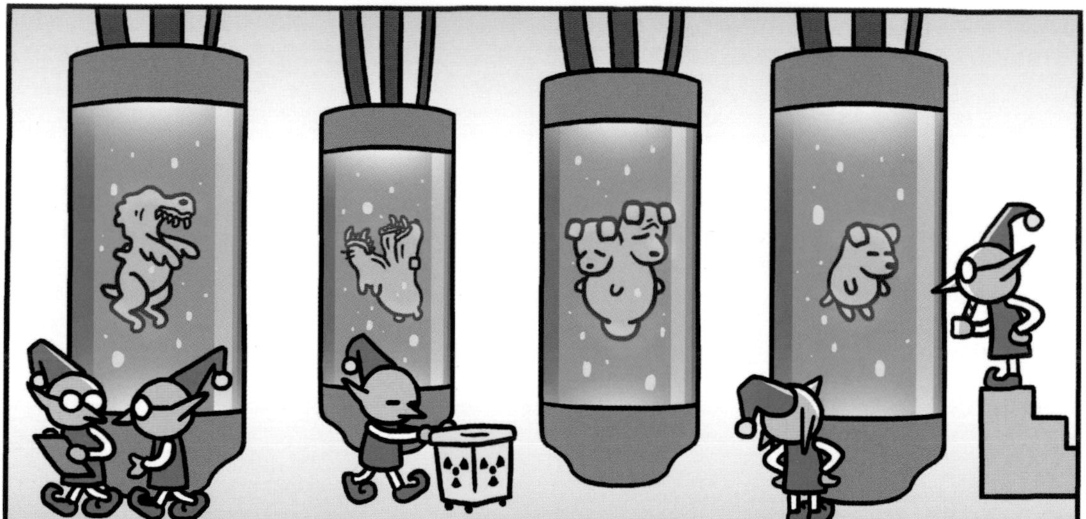

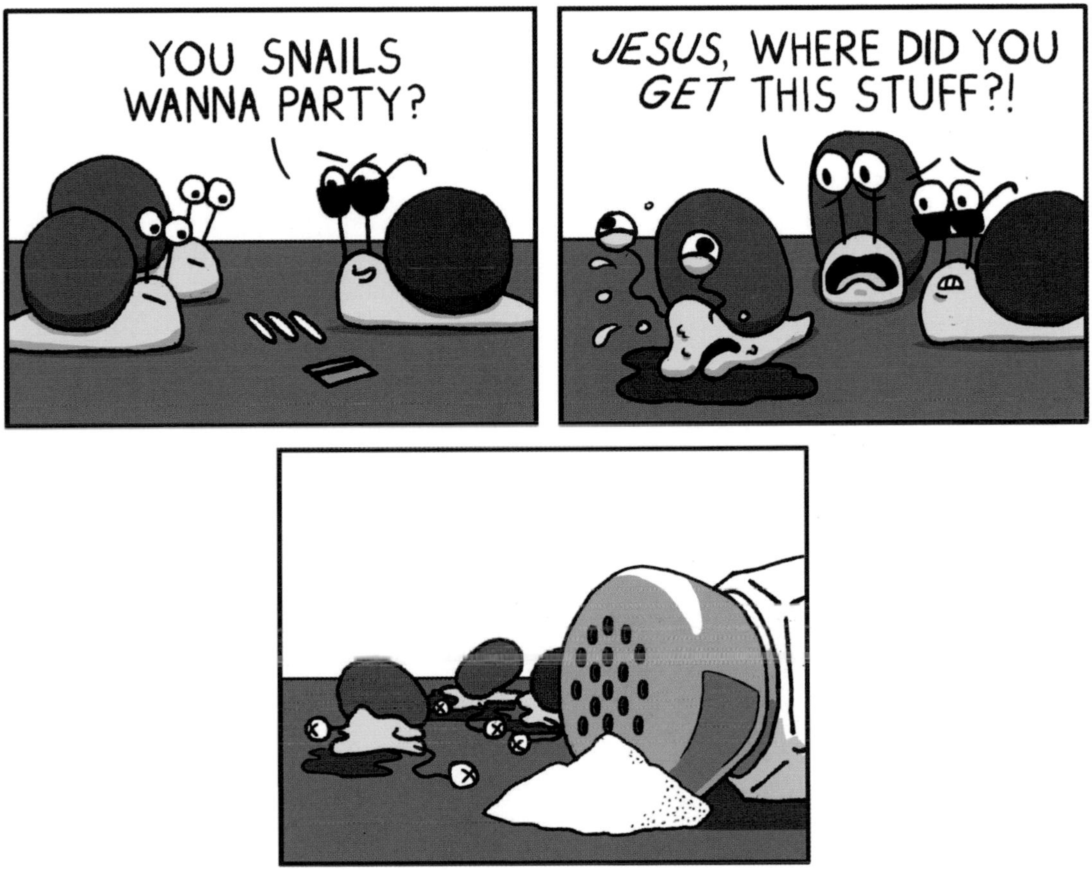
YOU SNAILS WANNA PARTY?
JESUS, WHERE DID YOU *GET* THIS STUFF?!

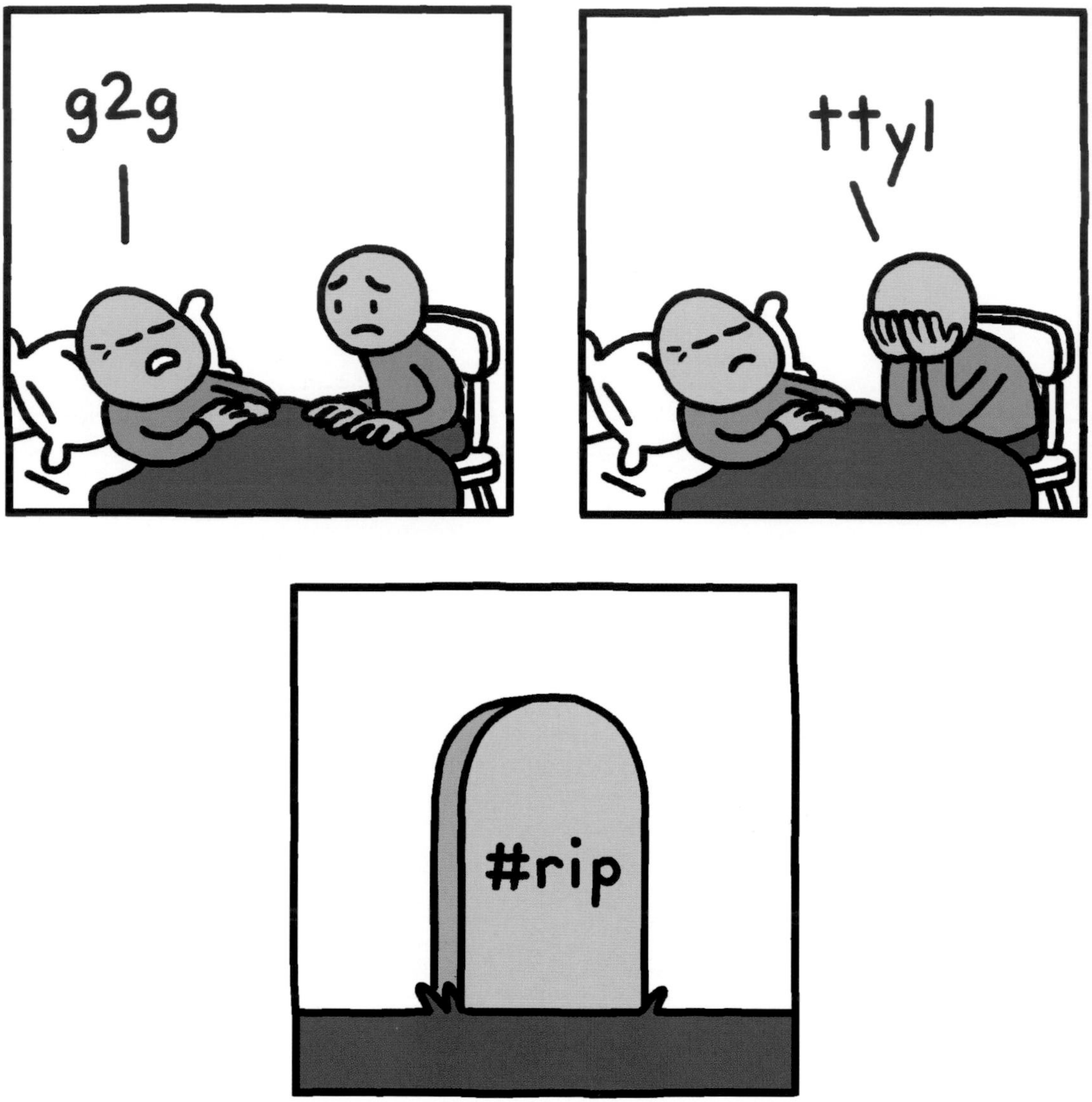
g2g
ttyl
#rip

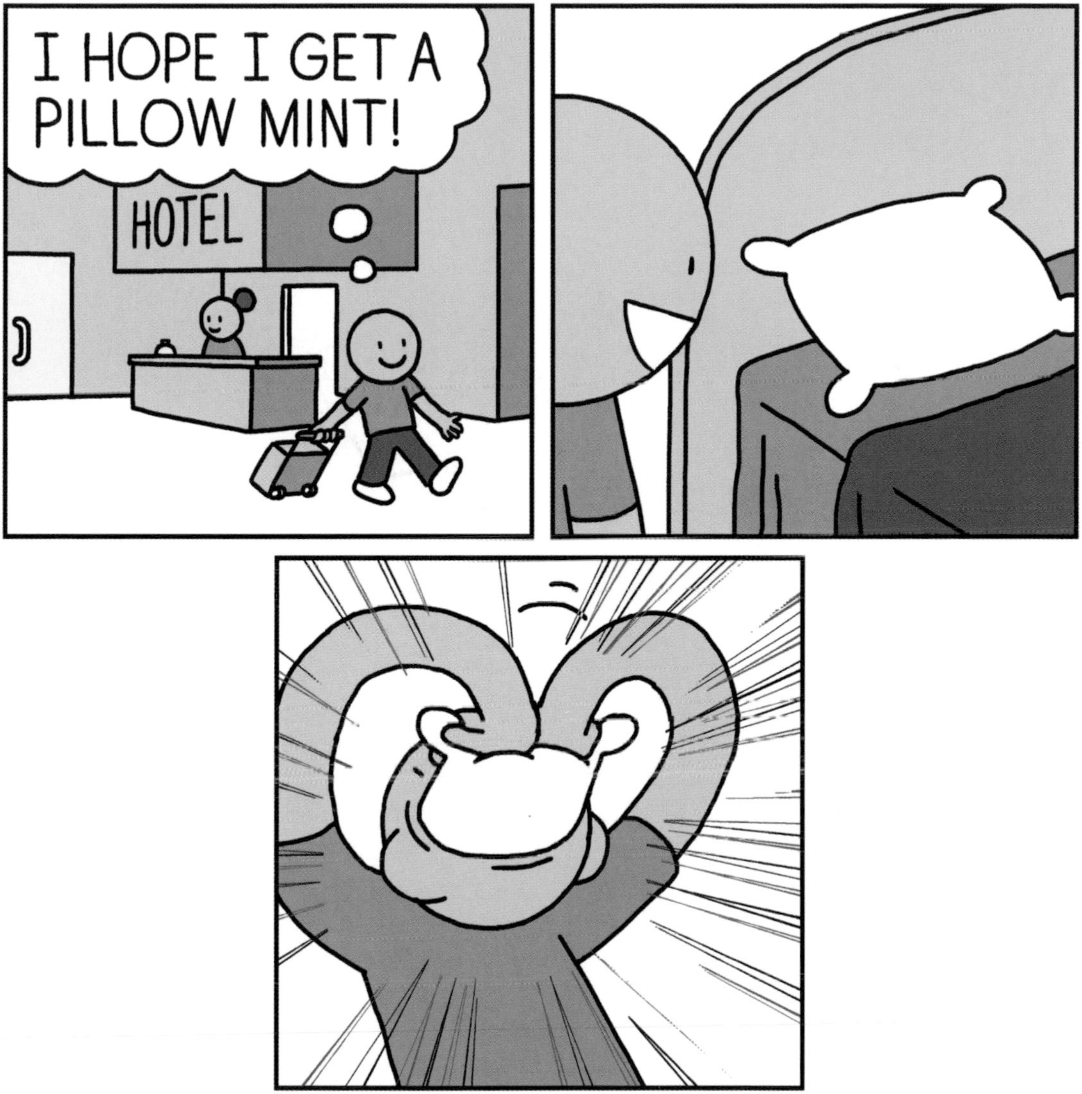
I HOPE I GET A PILLOW MINT!
HOTEL

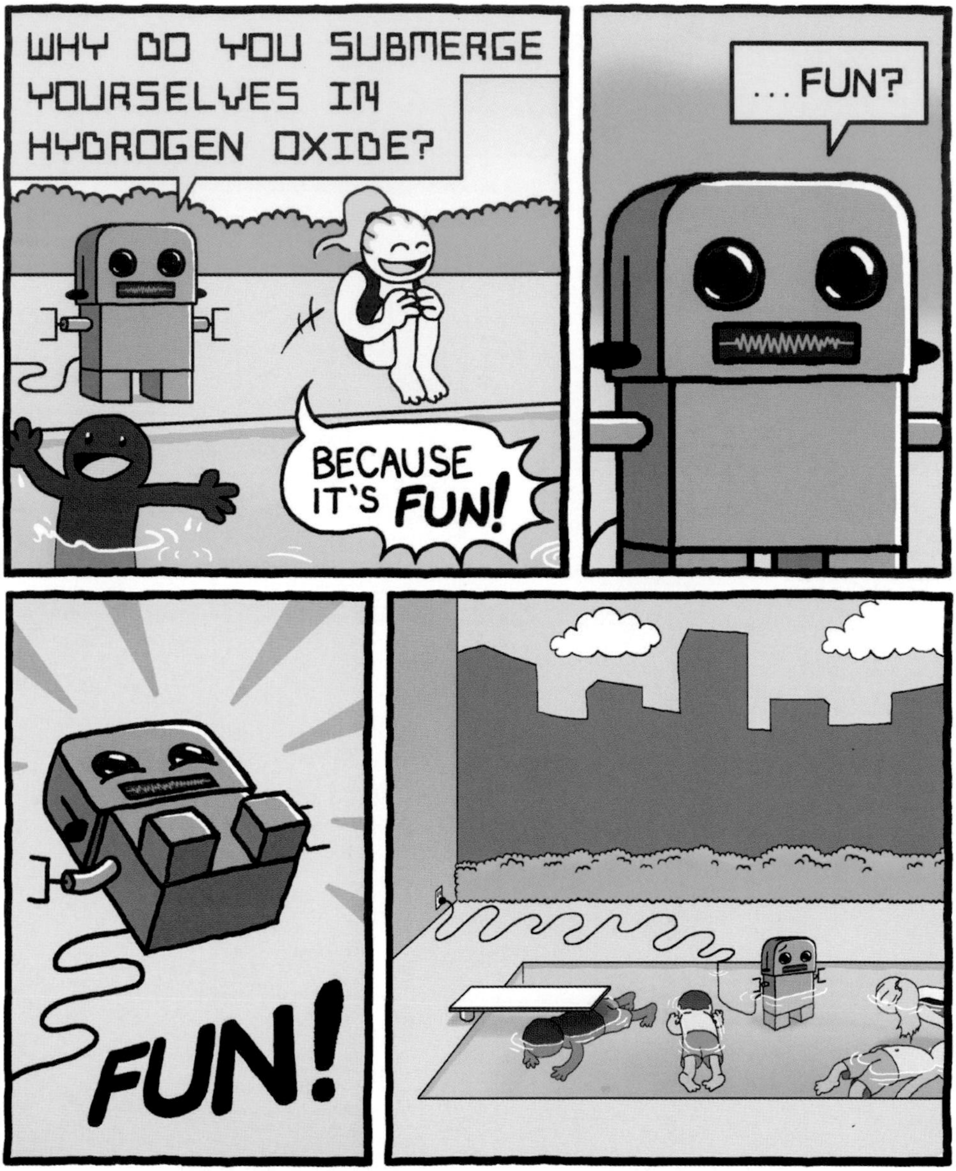
WHY DO YOU SUBMERGE YOURSELVES IN HYDROGEN OXIDE?
BECAUSE IT'S FUN!
...FUN?
FUN!

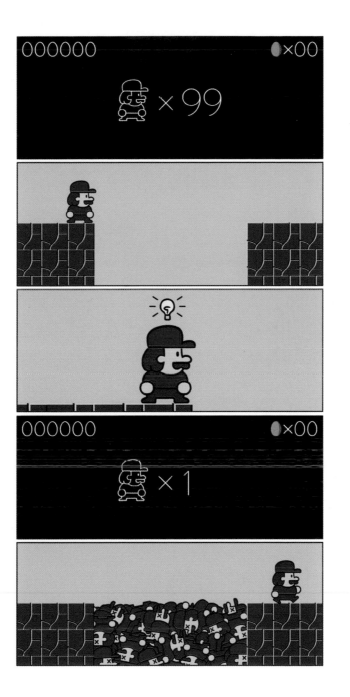

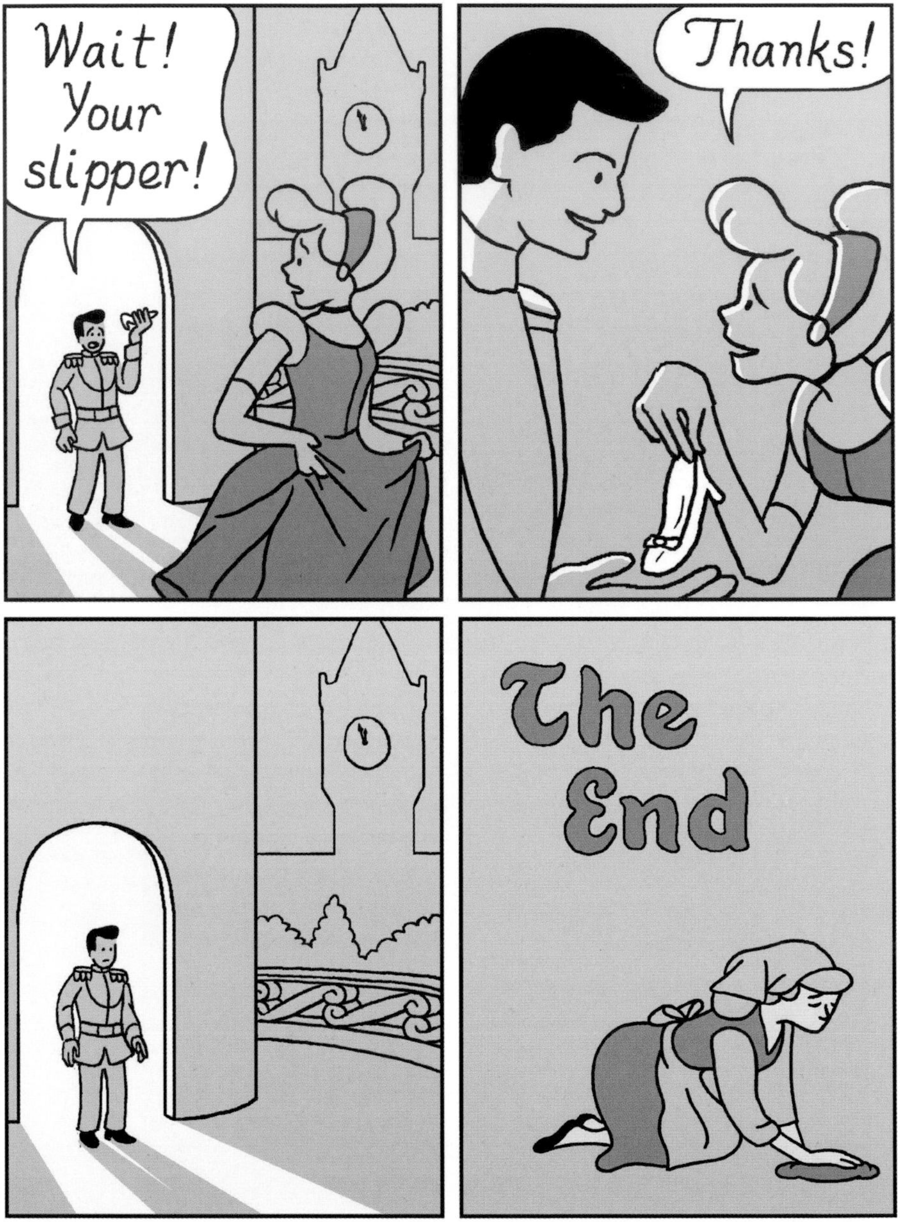

Wait! Your slipper!
Thanks!
The End

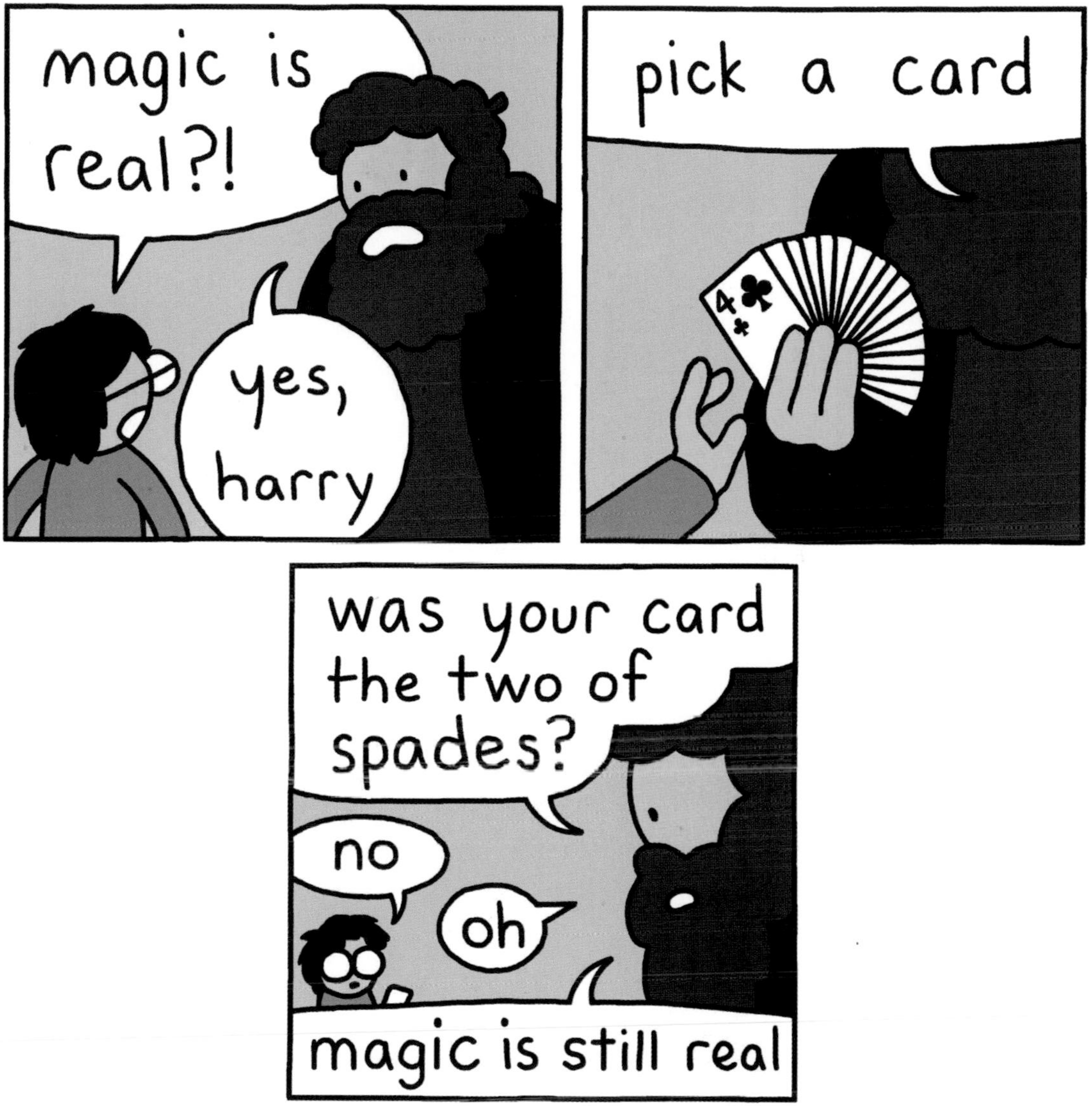
magic is real?!
yes, harry
pick a card
was your card the two of spades?
no
oh
magic is still real

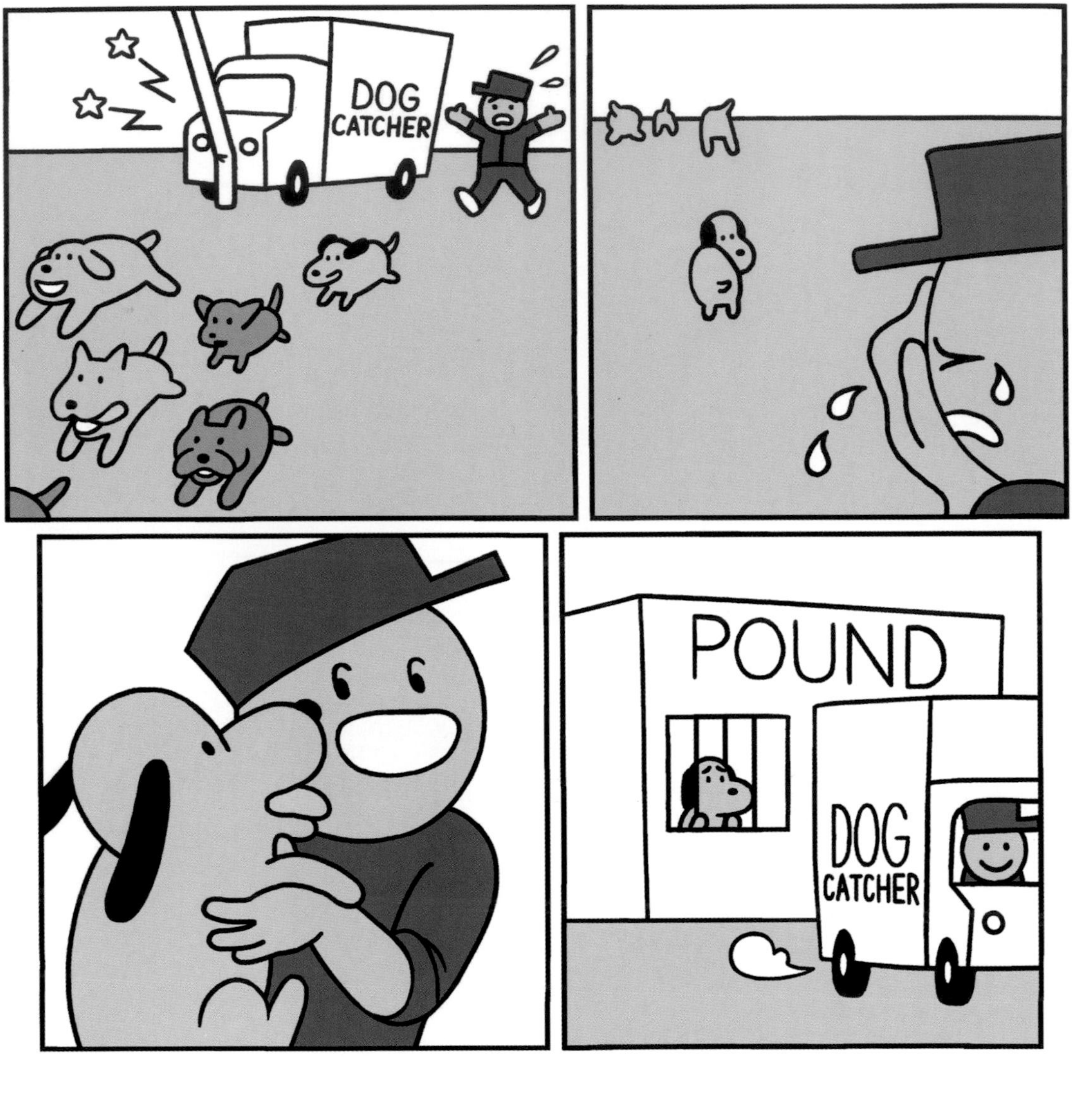
DOG
CATCHER
POUND
DOG
CATCHER

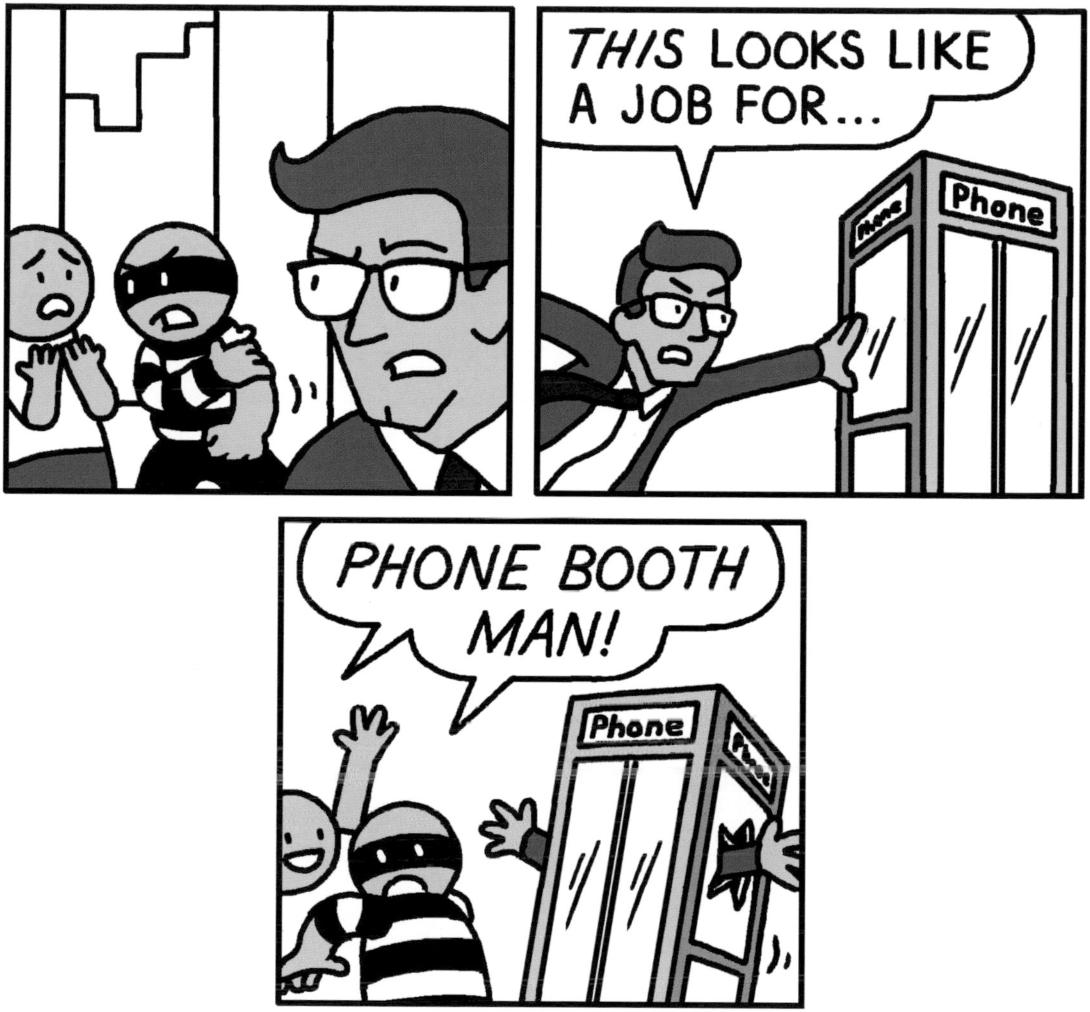
THIS LOOKS LIKE A JOB FOR...
Phone
PHONE BOOTH MAN!
Phone

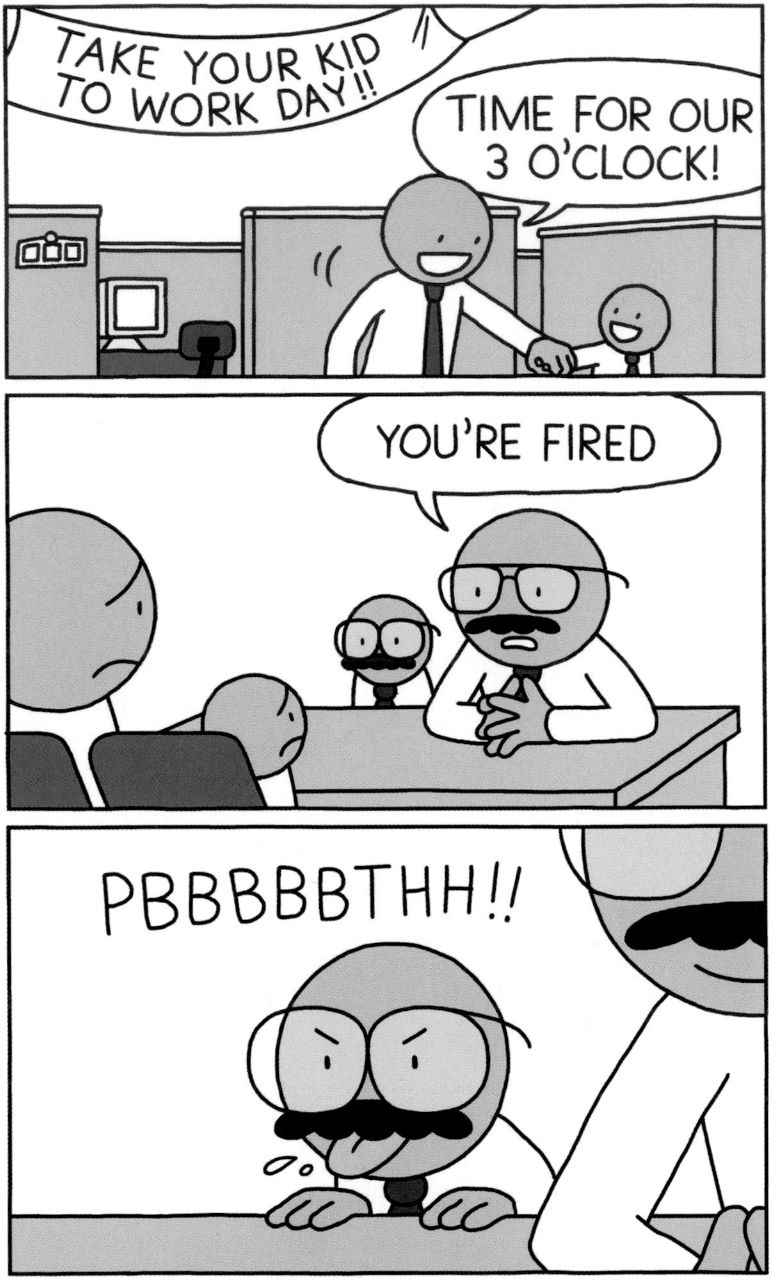
TAKE YOUR KID TO WORK DAY!!
TIME FOR OUR 3 O'CLOCK!
YOU'RE FIRED
PBBBBBTHH!!

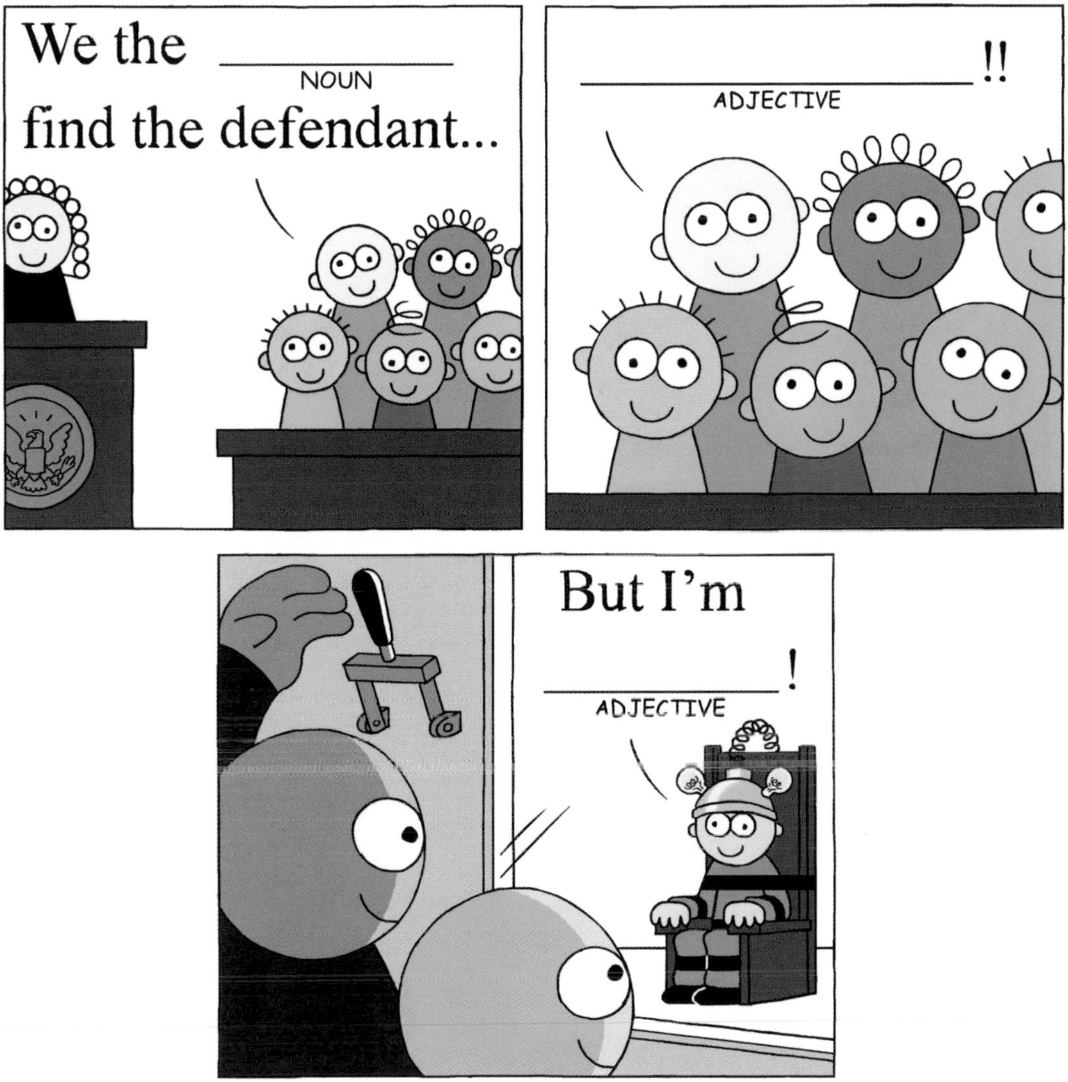
We the ____________ find the defendant...
NOUN
____________!!
ADJECTIVE
But I'm ____________!
ADJECTIVE

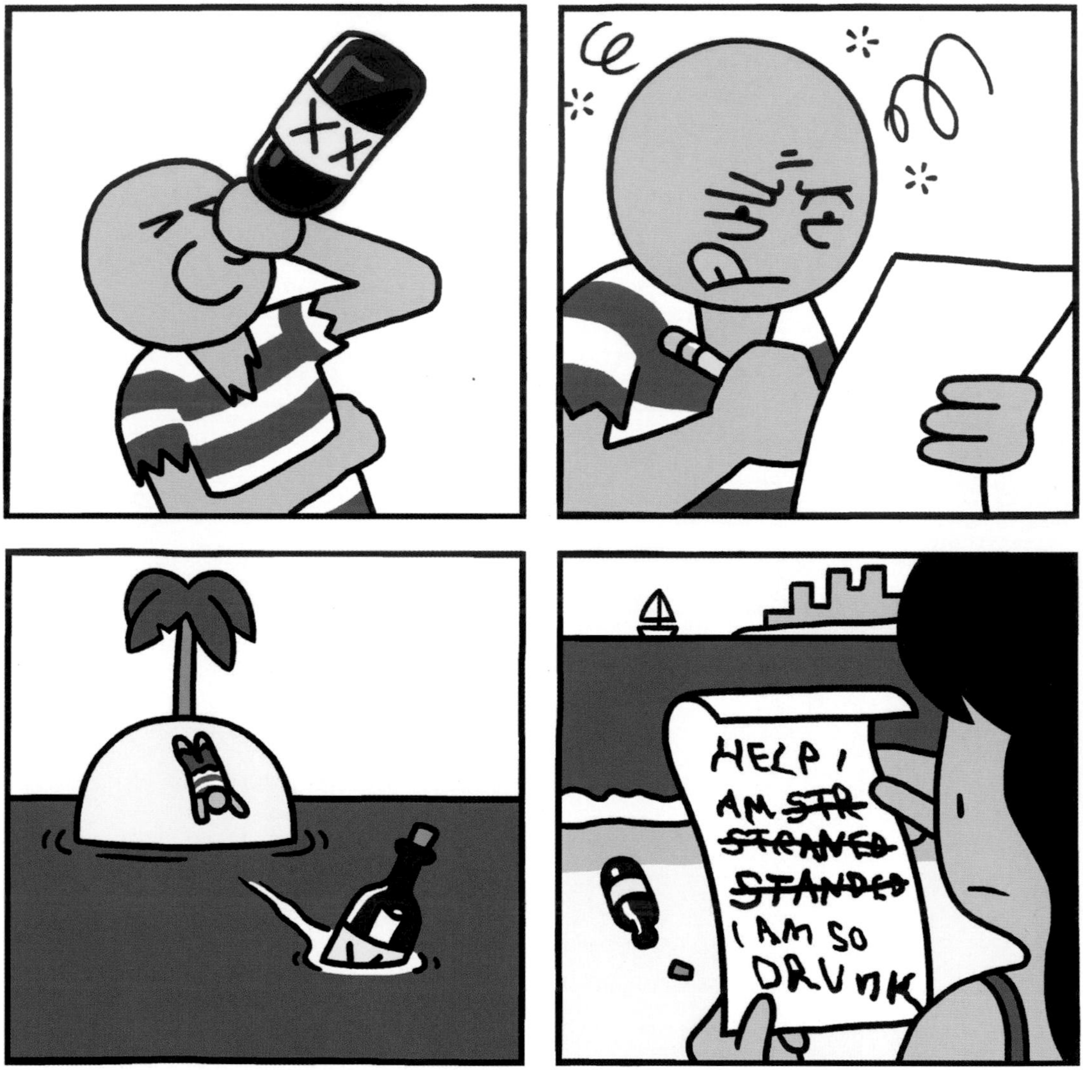
HELP I
AM ~~STR~~
~~STRANED~~
~~STANDED~~
I AM SO
DRUNK

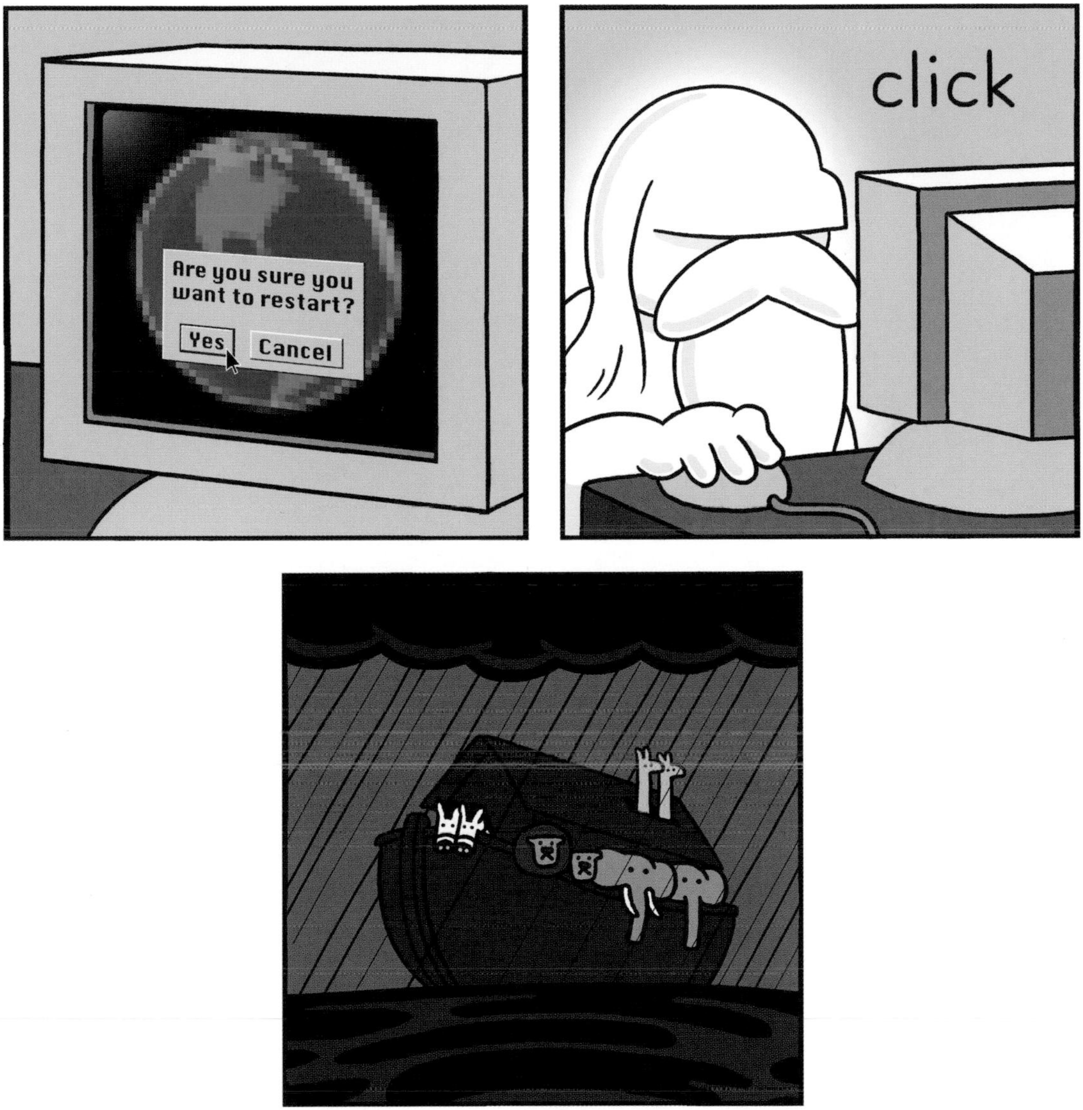
Are you sure you want to restart?
Yes
Cancel
click

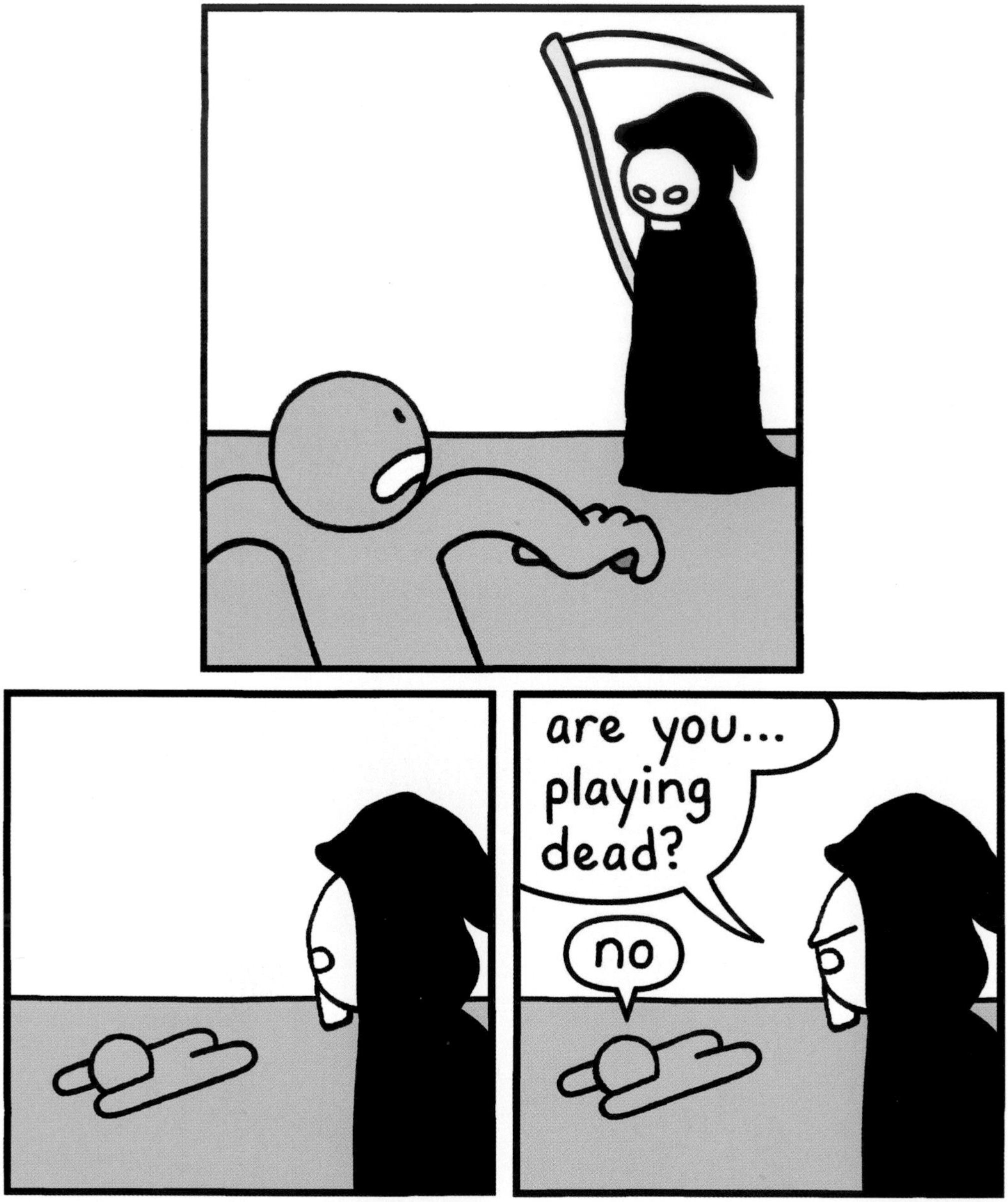
are you...
playing
dead?
no

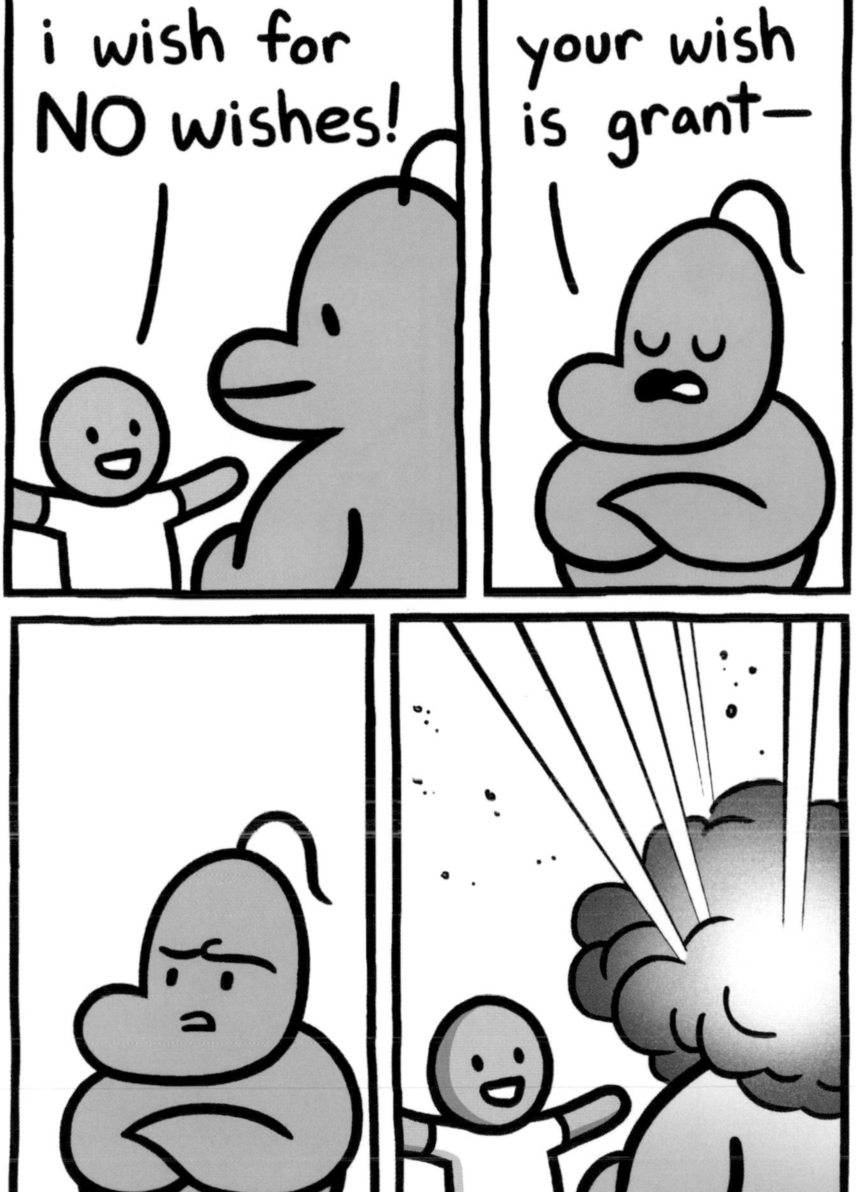
i wish for NO wishes!
your wish is grant—

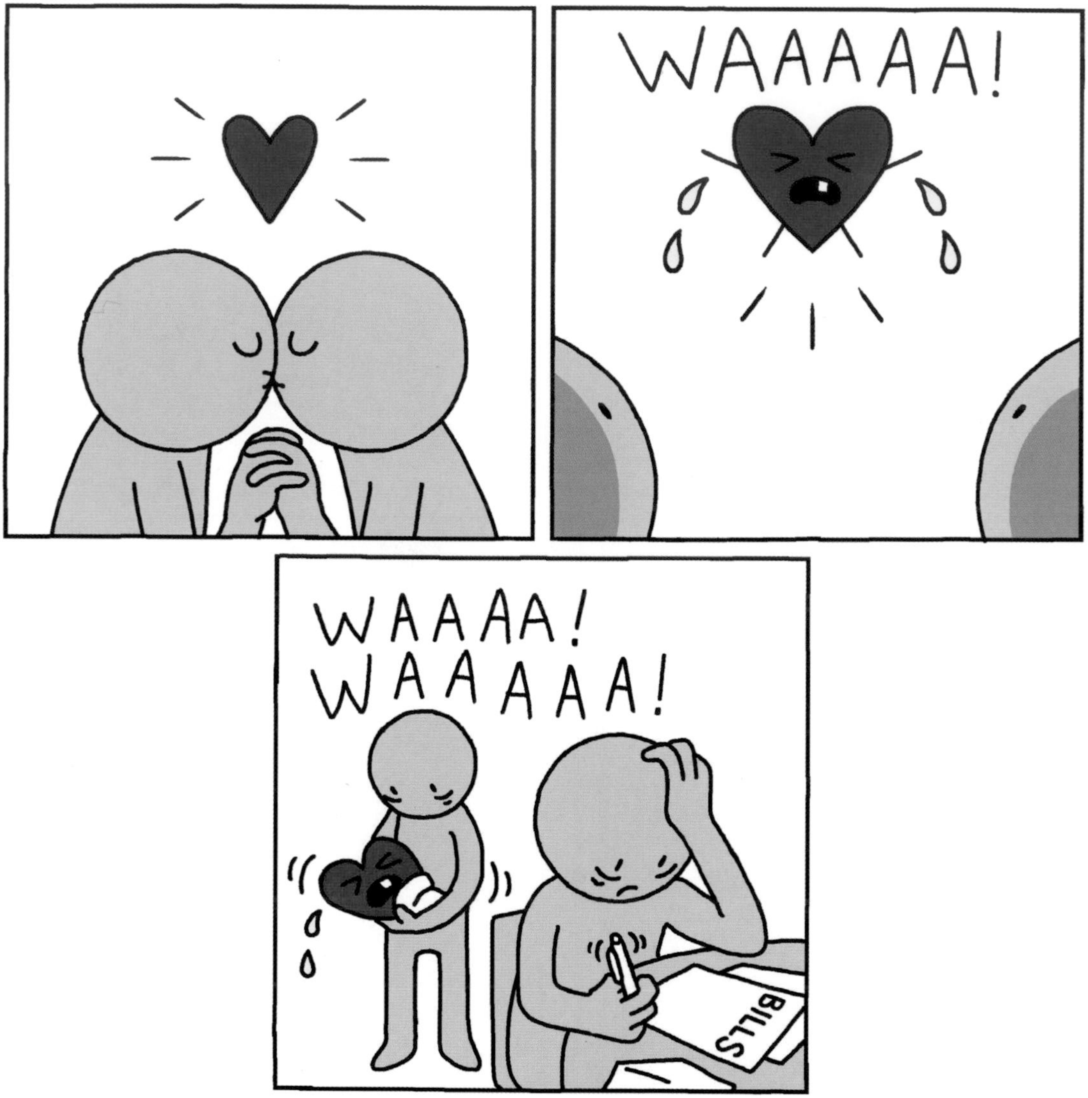
WAAAAA!
WAAAA!
WAAAAA!
BILLS

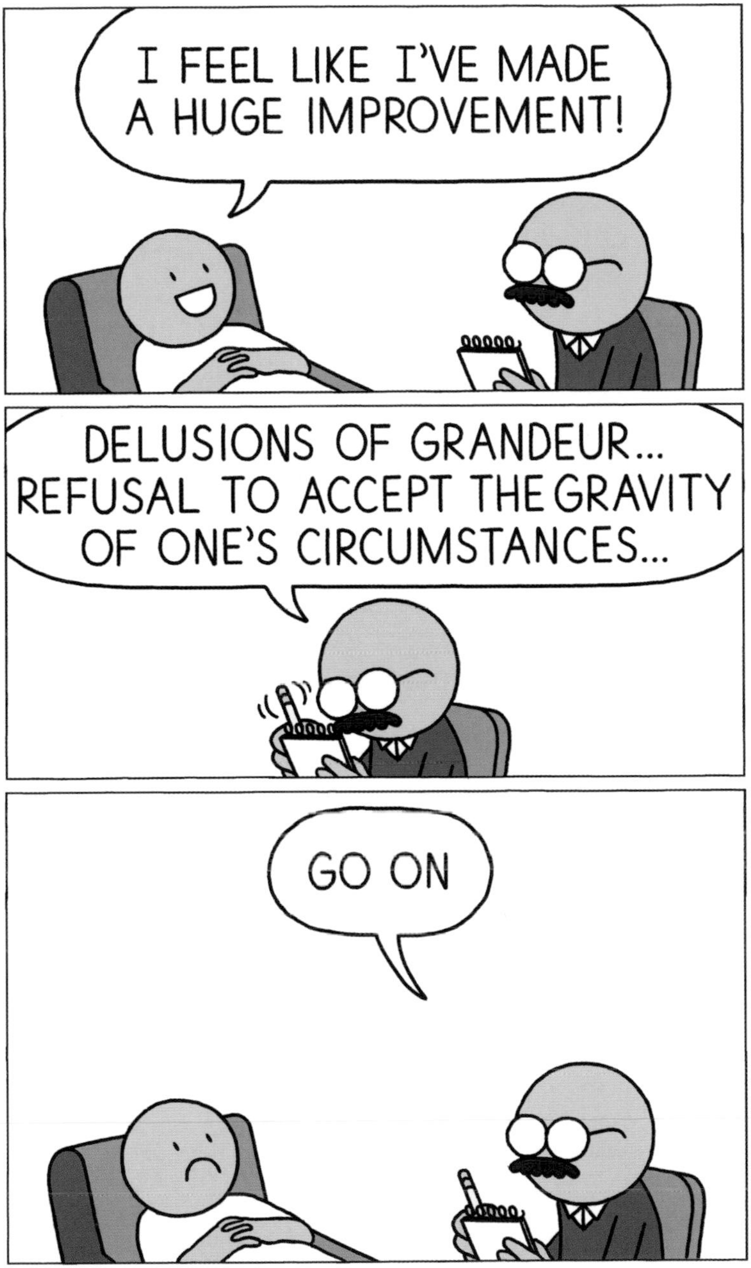
I FEEL LIKE I'VE MADE A HUGE IMPROVEMENT!
DELUSIONS OF GRANDEUR... REFUSAL TO ACCEPT THE GRAVITY OF ONE'S CIRCUMSTANCES...
GO ON

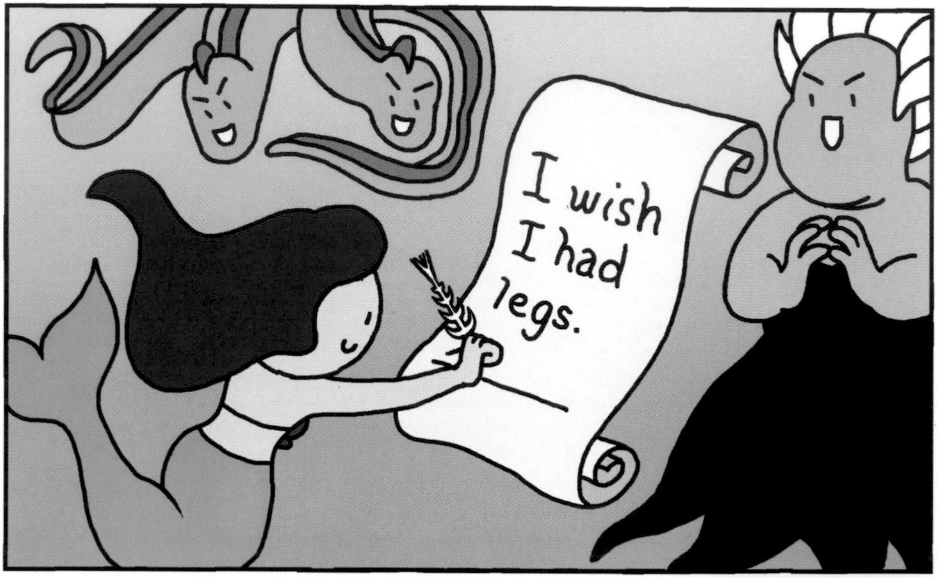
I wish
I had
legs.

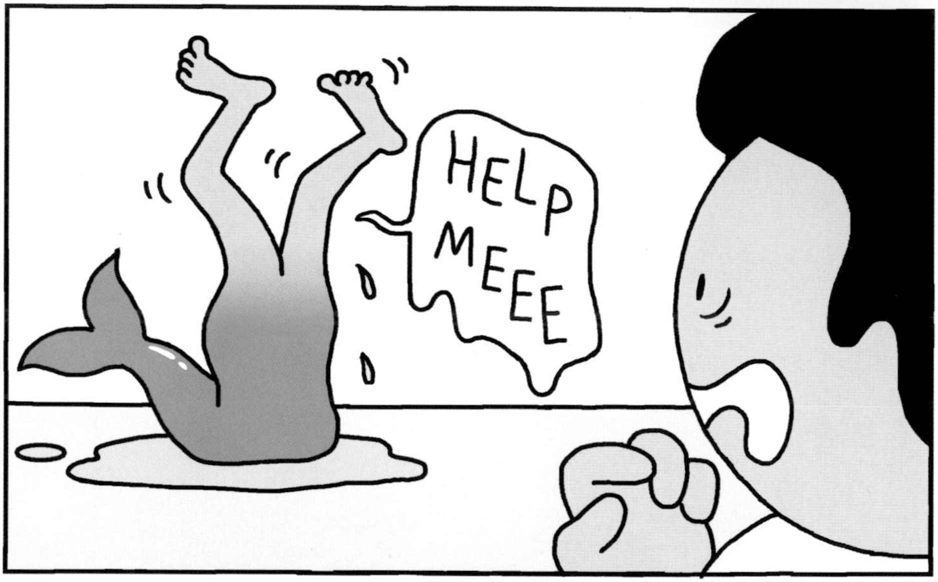
HELP
MEEE

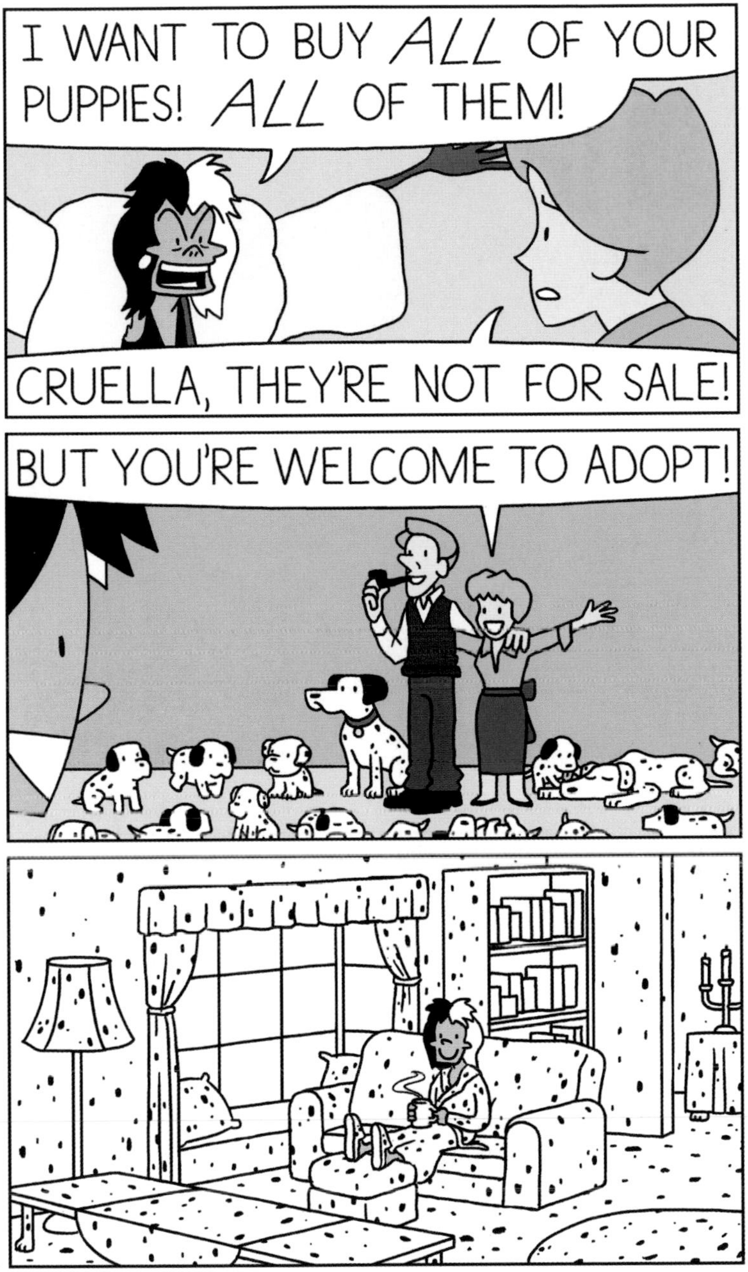
I WANT TO BUY ALL OF YOUR PUPPIES! ALL OF THEM!
CRUELLA, THEY'RE NOT FOR SALE!
BUT YOU'RE WELCOME TO ADOPT!

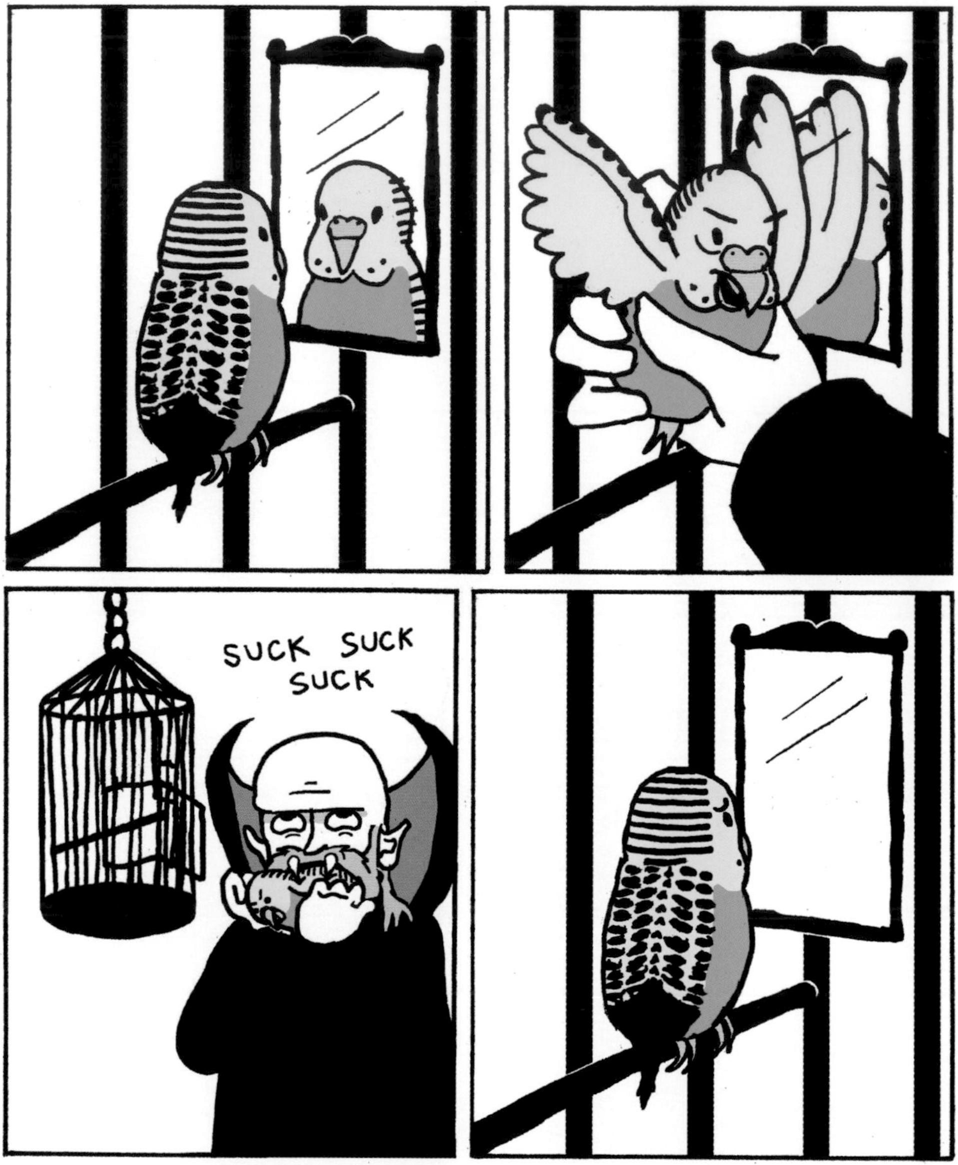
SUCK SUCK
SUCK

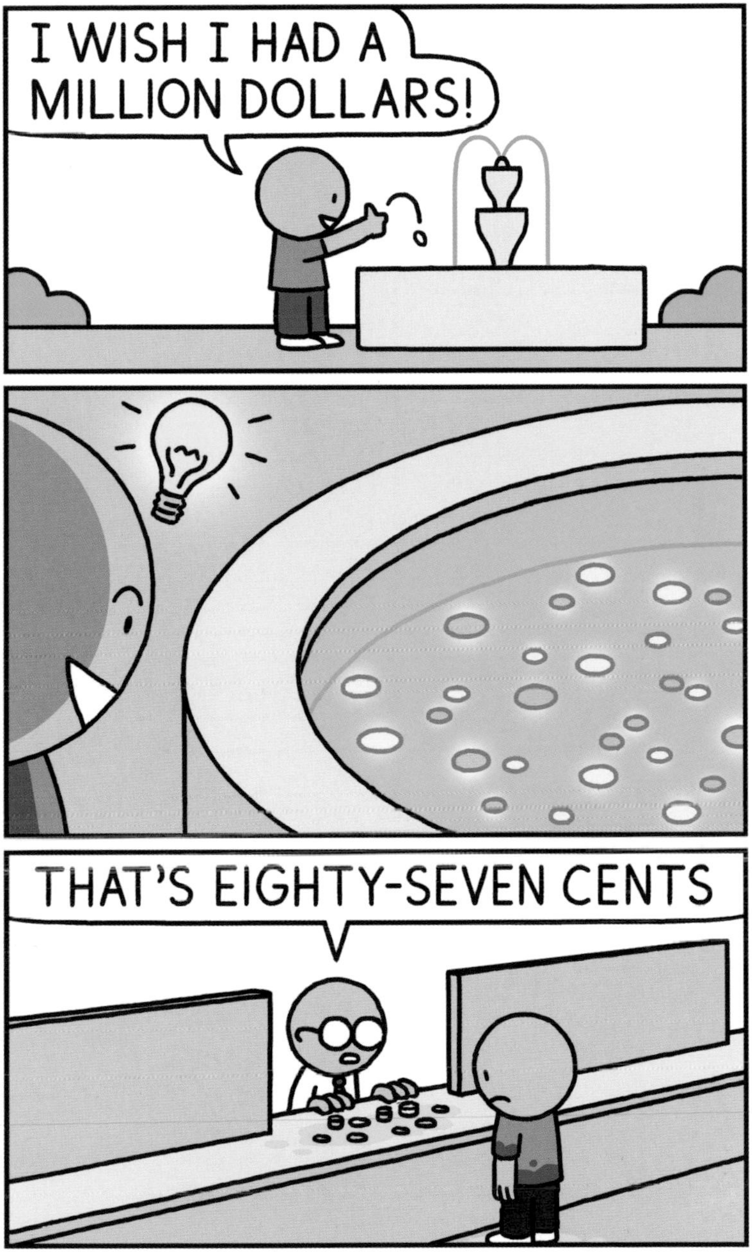
I WISH I HAD A MILLION DOLLARS!
THAT'S EIGHTY-SEVEN CENTS

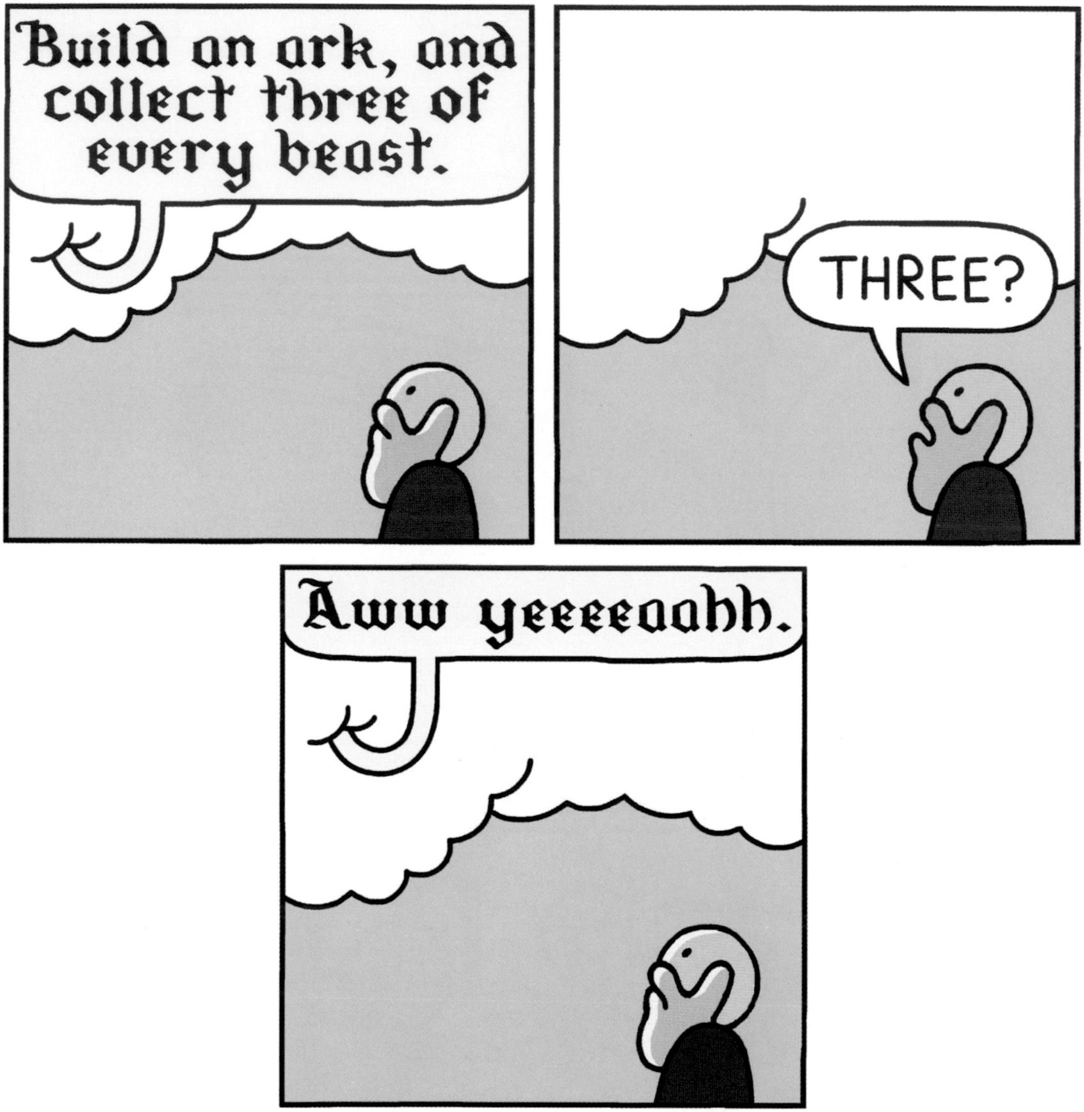
Build an ark, and collect three of every beast.
THREE?
Aww yeeeeaahh.

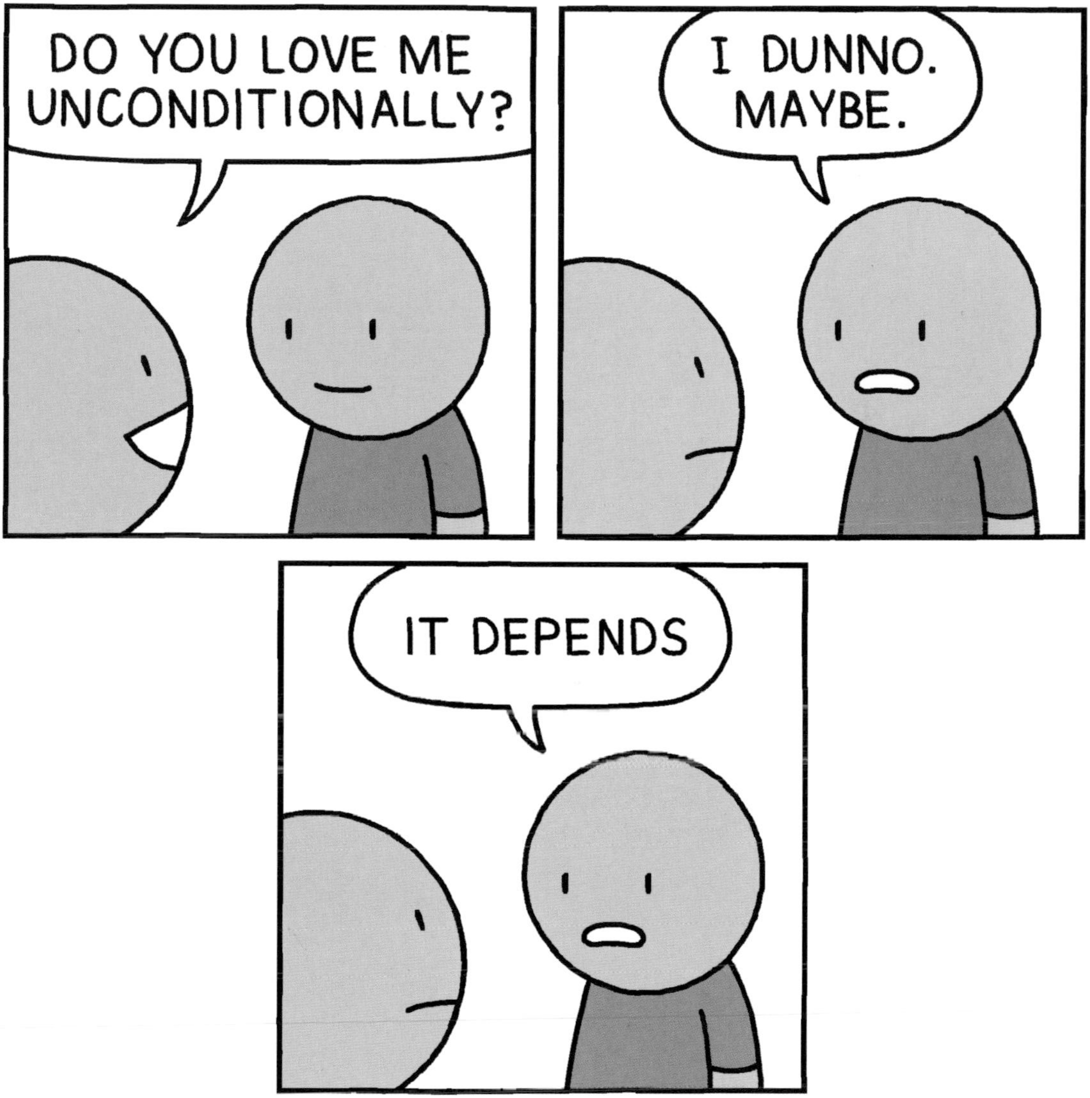
DO YOU LOVE ME UNCONDITIONALLY?
I DUNNO. MAYBE.
IT DEPENDS

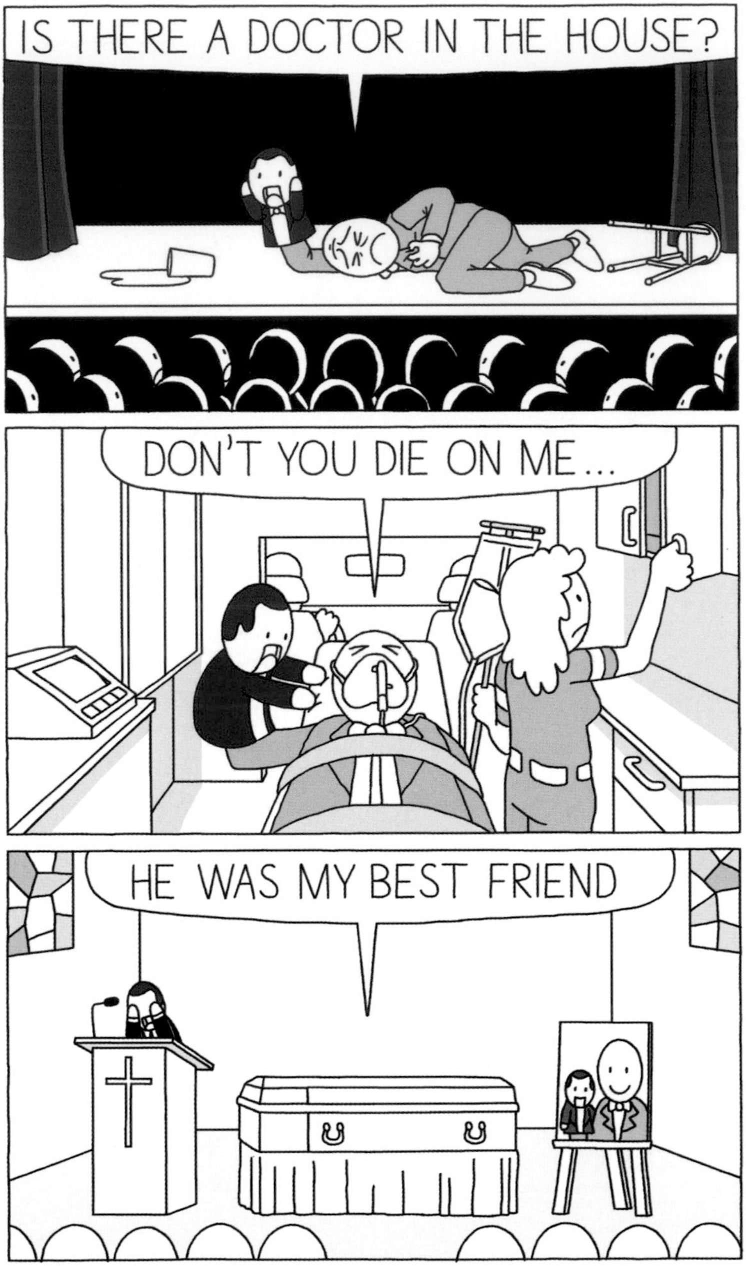
IS THERE A DOCTOR IN THE HOUSE?
DON'T YOU DIE ON ME...
HE WAS MY BEST FRIEND

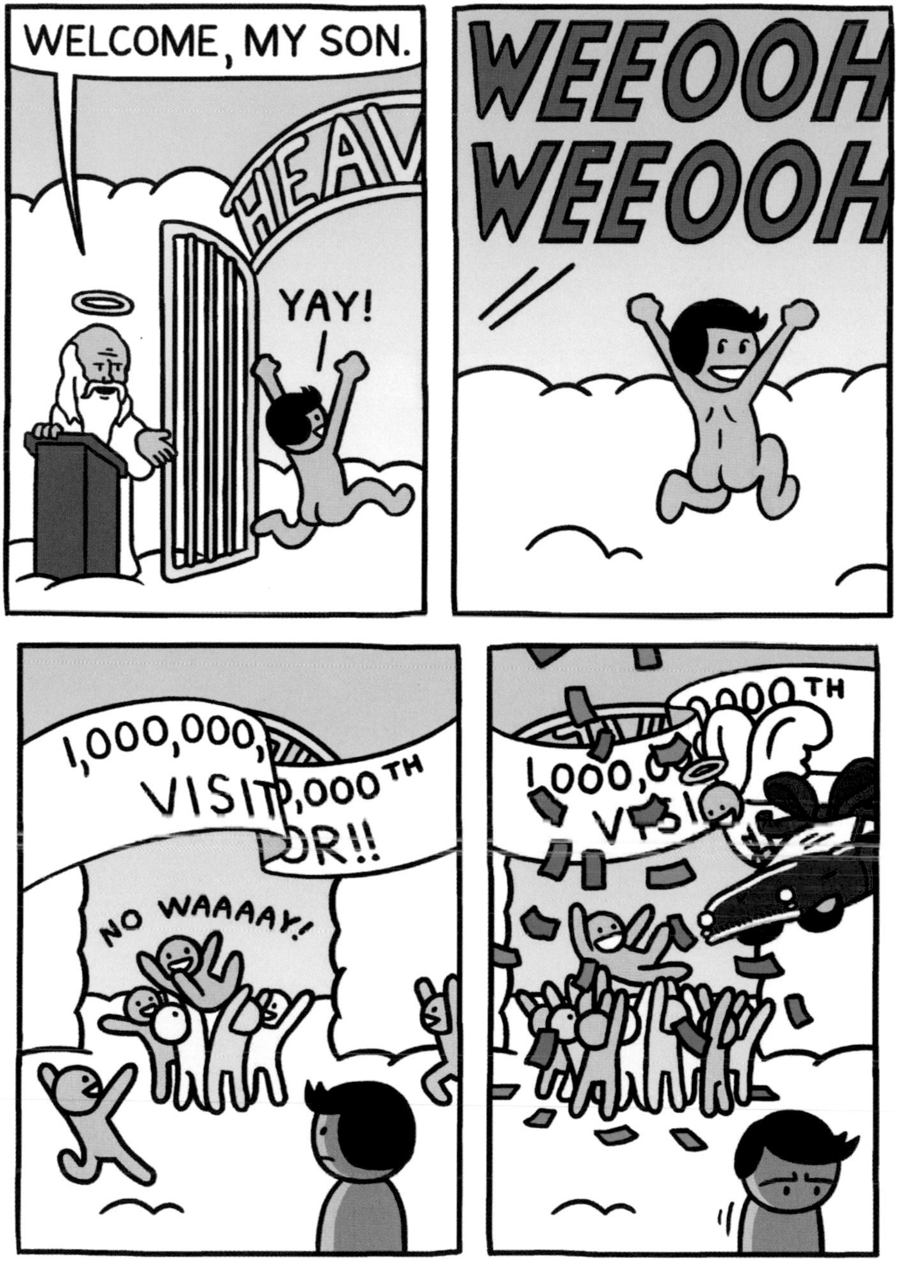
WELCOME, MY SON.
HEAV
YAY!
WEEOOH
WEEOOH
1,000,000,000TH
VISITOR!!
NO WAAAAY!
1,000,0
VISI
000TH

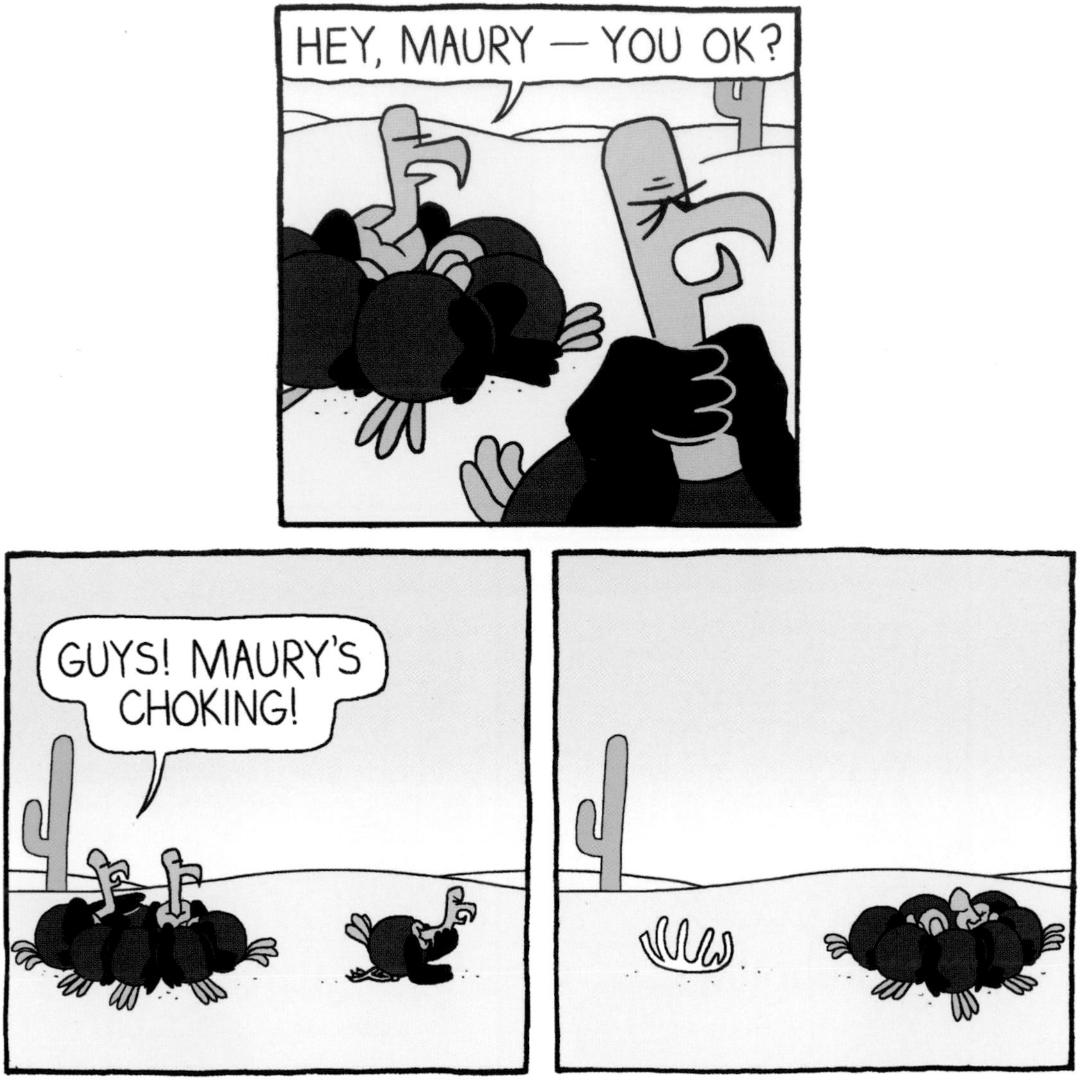
HEY, MAURY — YOU OK?
GUYS! MAURY'S CHOKING!

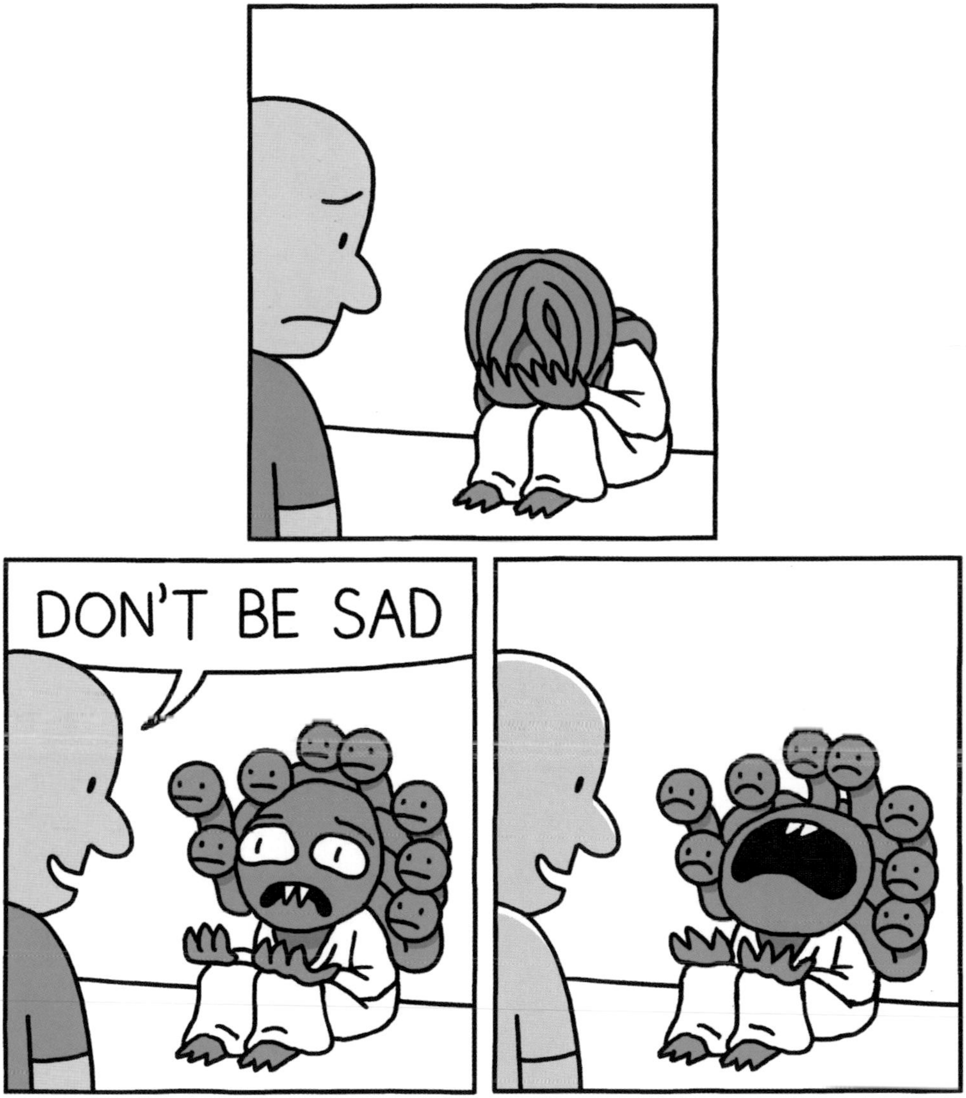
DON'T BE SAD

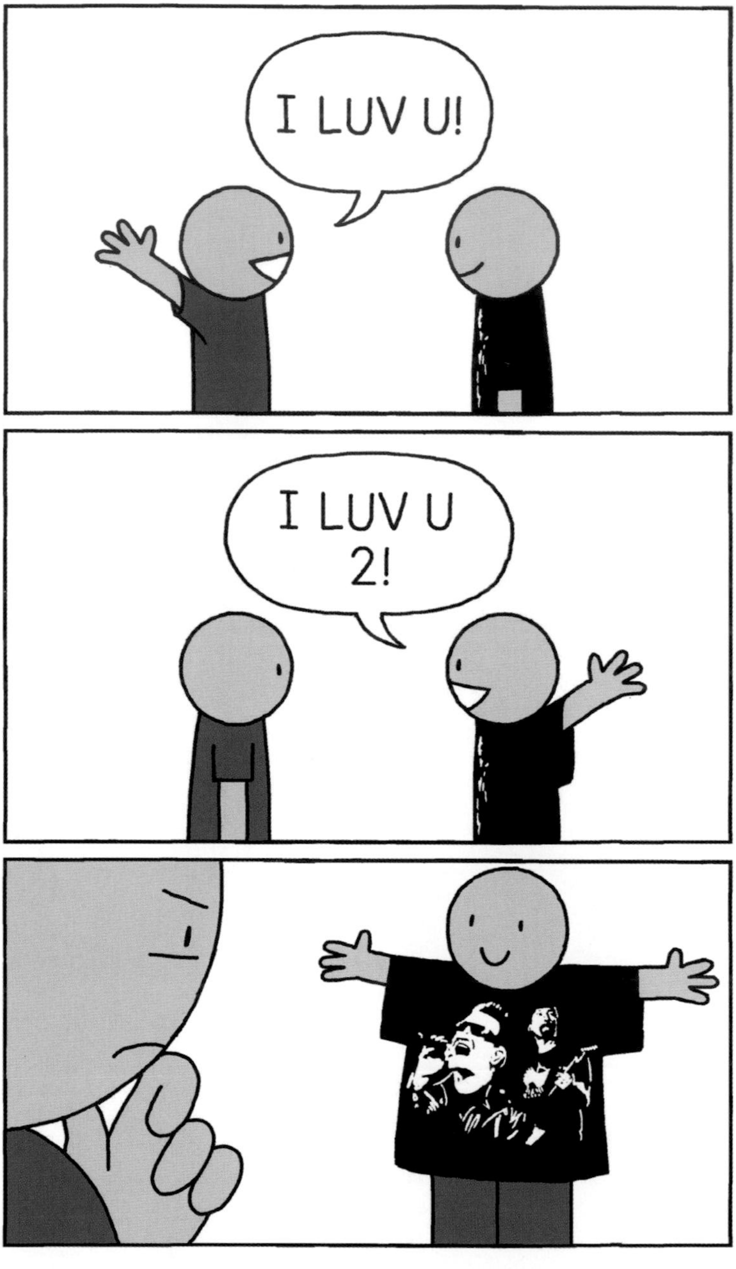
I LUV U!
I LUV U 2!

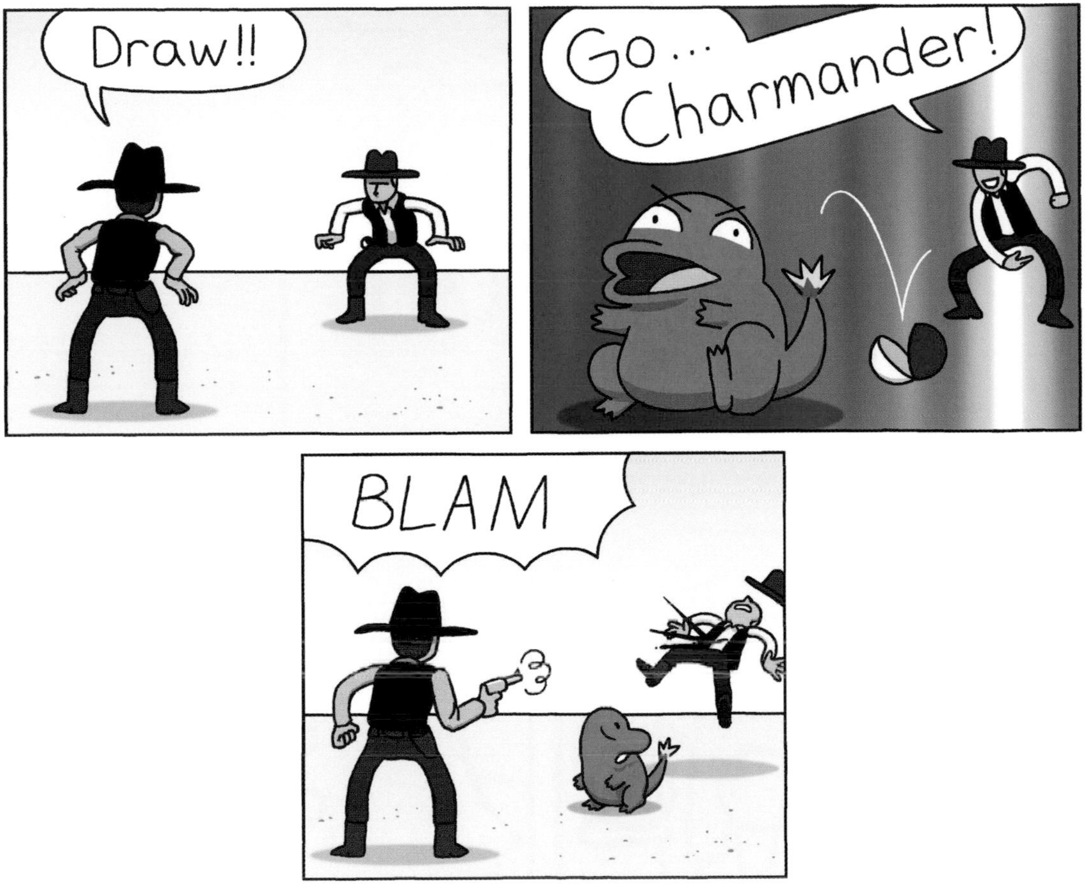
Draw!!
Go... Charmander!
BLAM

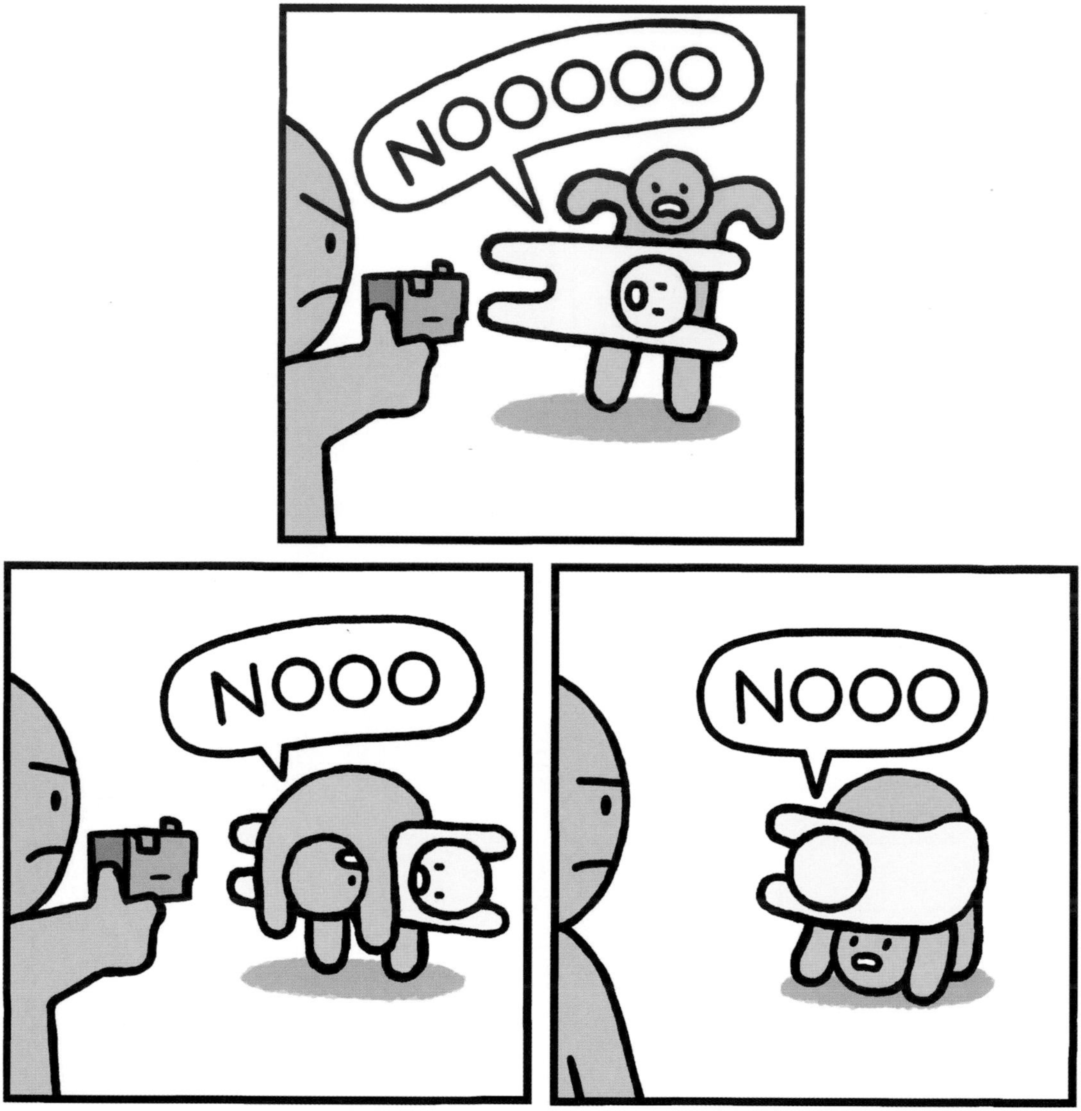
NOOOOO
NOOO
NOOO

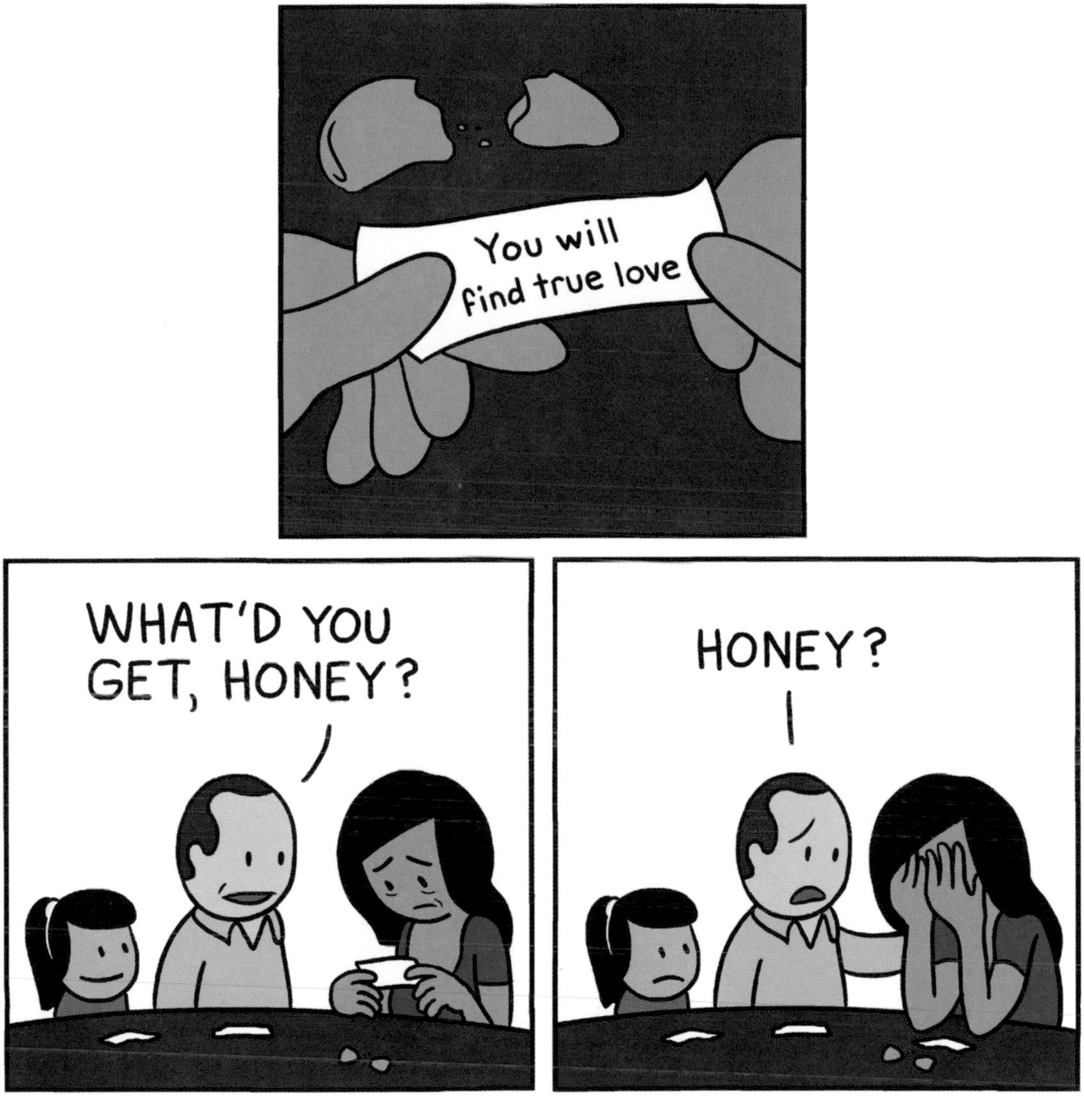
You will
find true love
WHAT'D YOU
GET, HONEY?
HONEY?

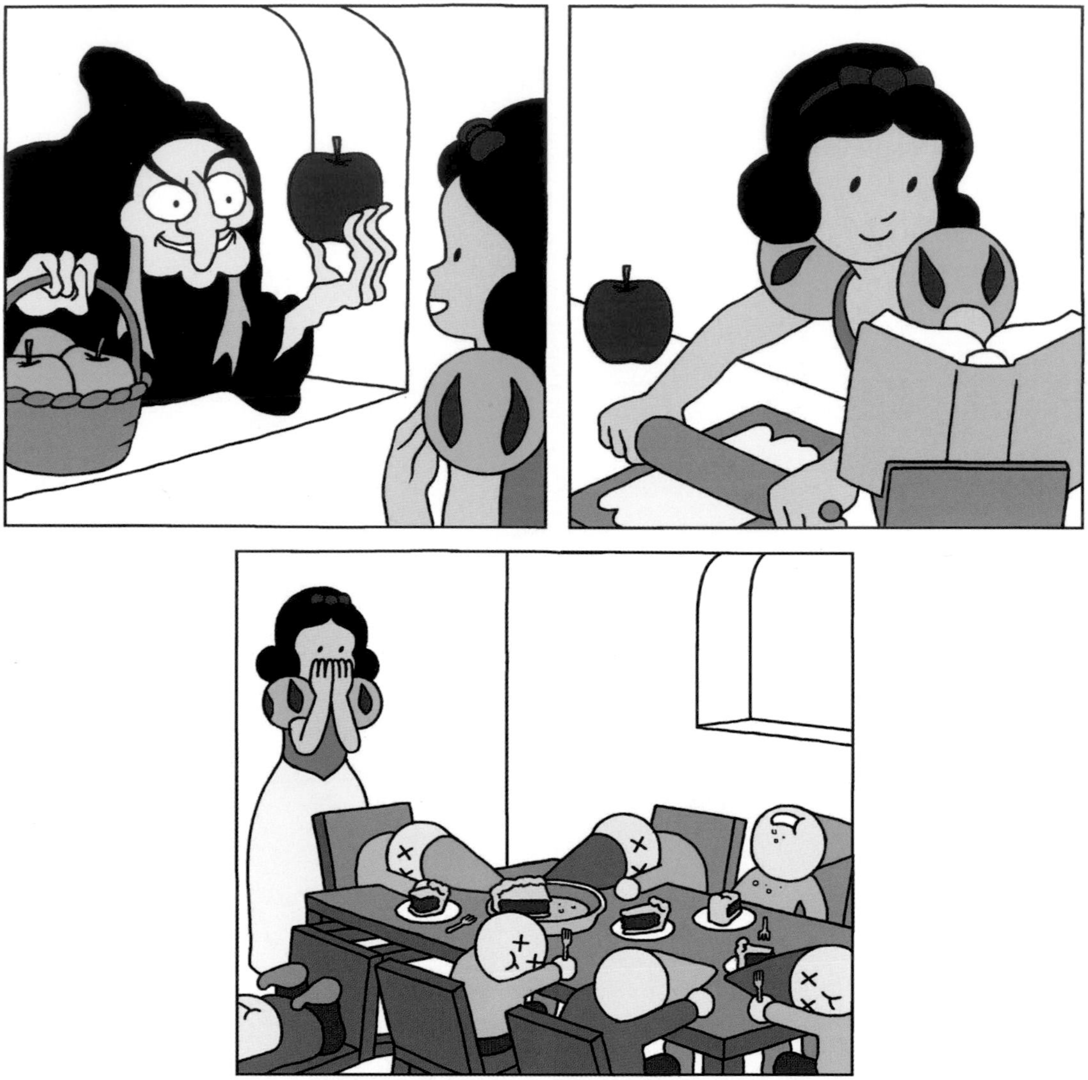

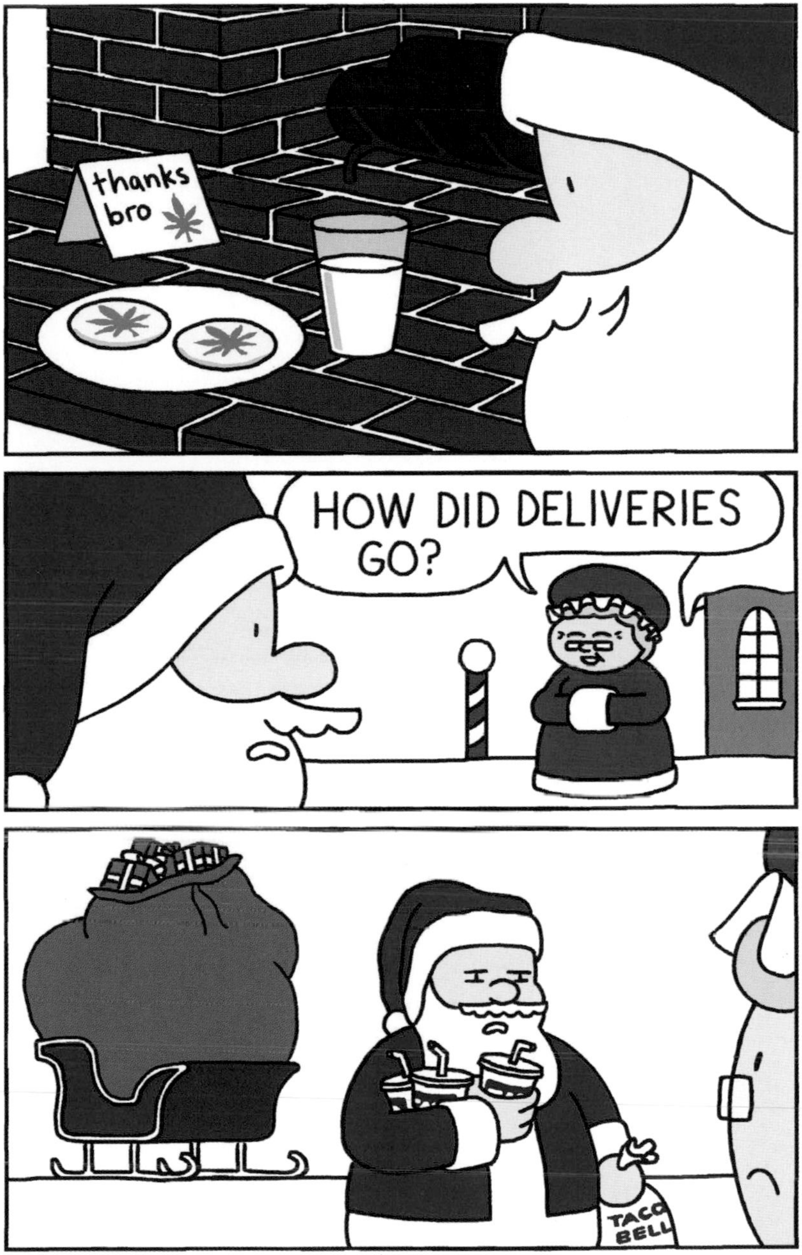
thanks bro
HOW DID DELIVERIES GO?
TACO BELL

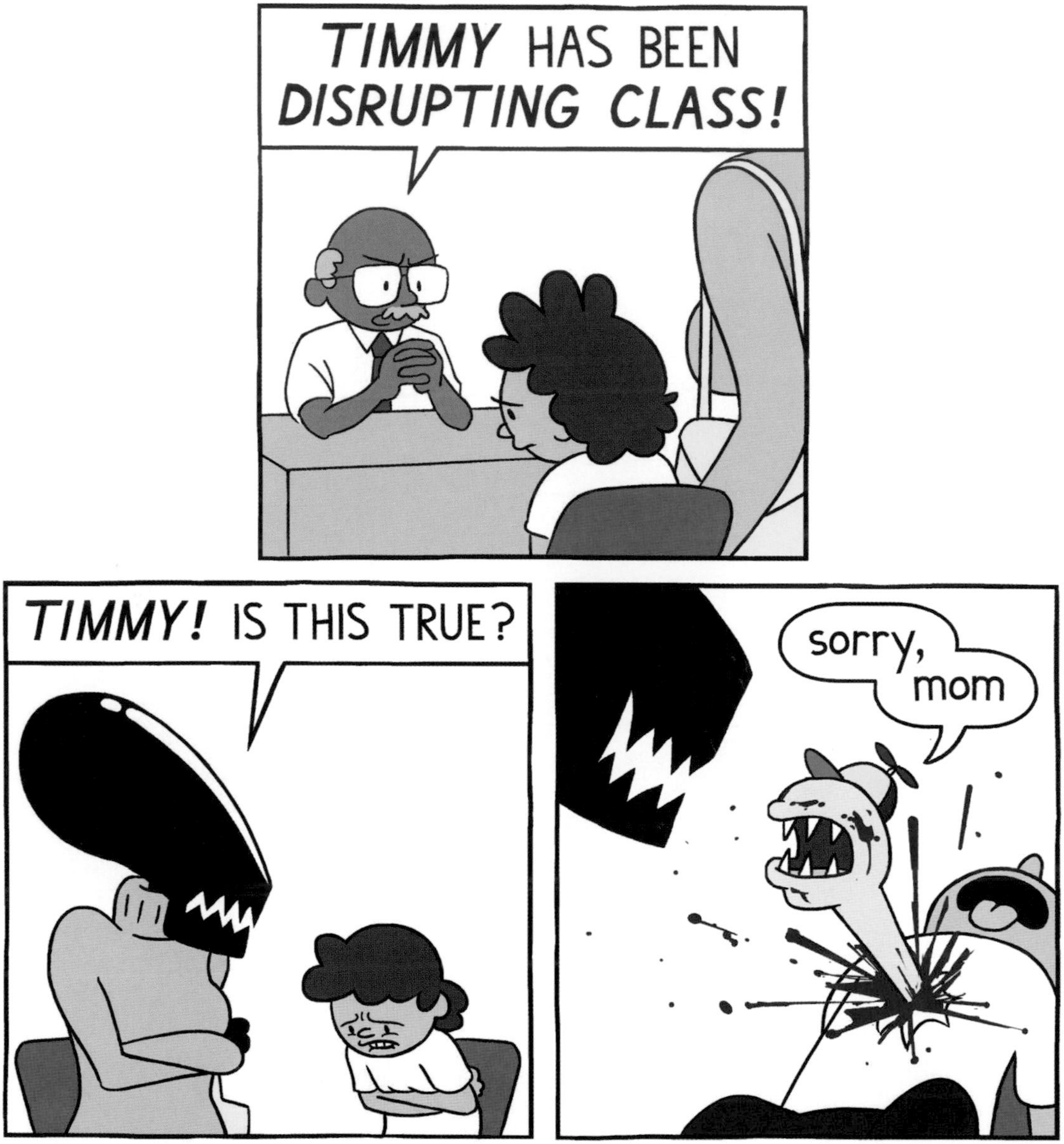

TIMMY HAS BEEN *DISRUPTING CLASS!*
TIMMY! IS THIS TRUE?
sorry, mom

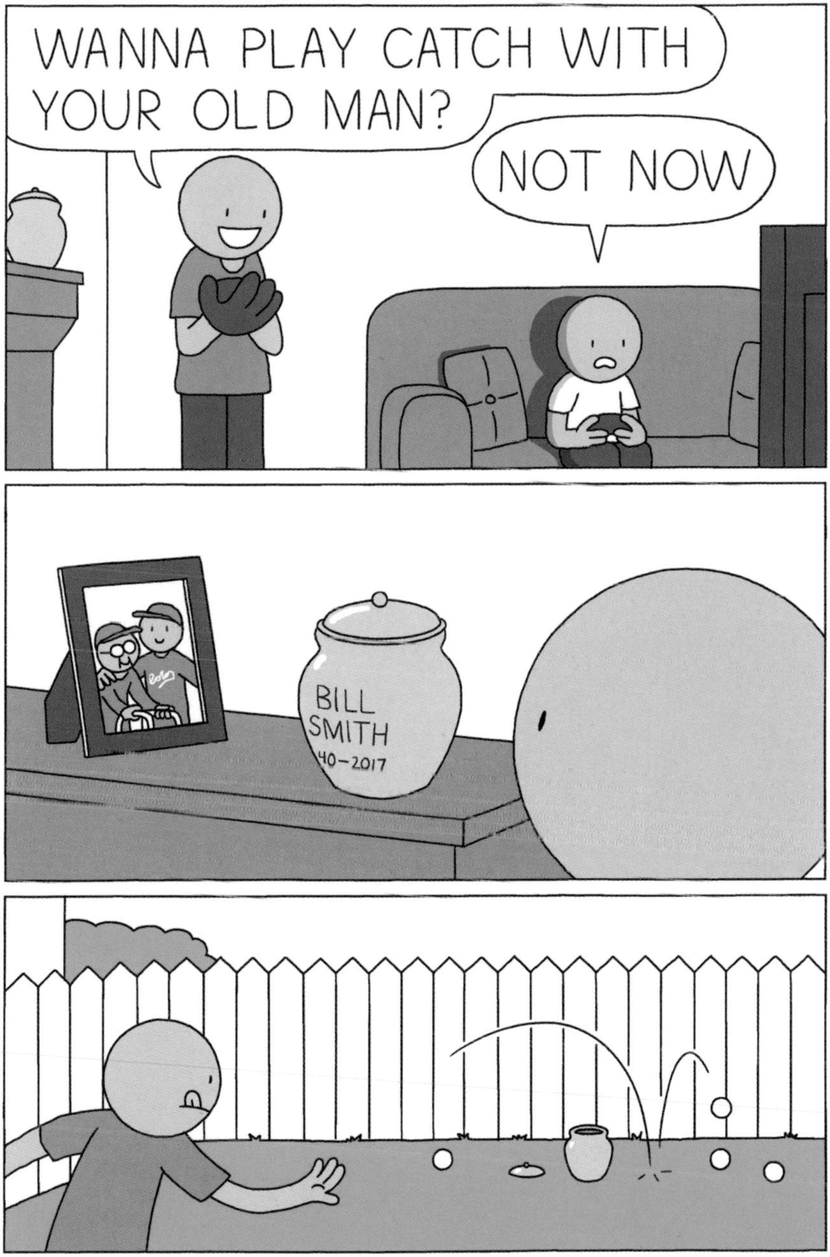
WANNA PLAY CATCH WITH YOUR OLD MAN?
NOT NOW
BILL SMITH
40-2017

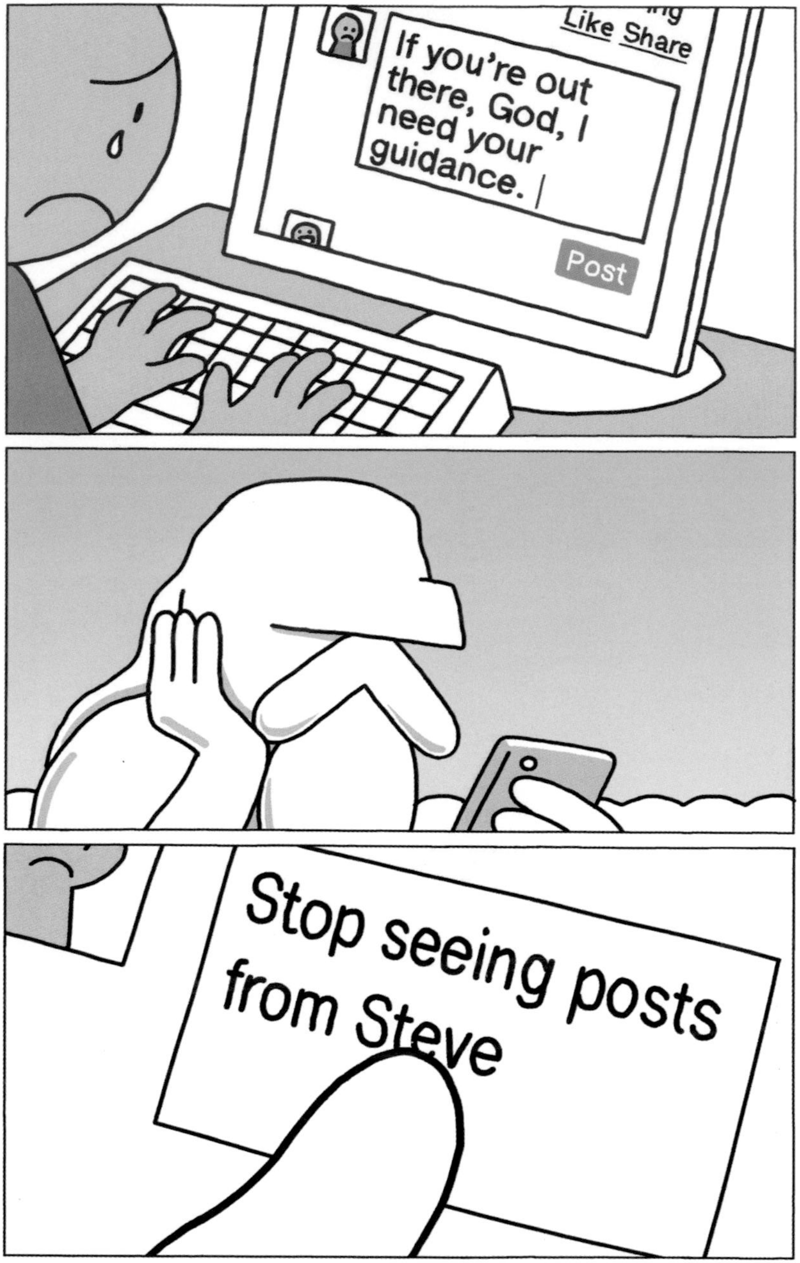
Like Share
If you're out there, God, I need your guidance.
Post
Stop seeing posts from Steve

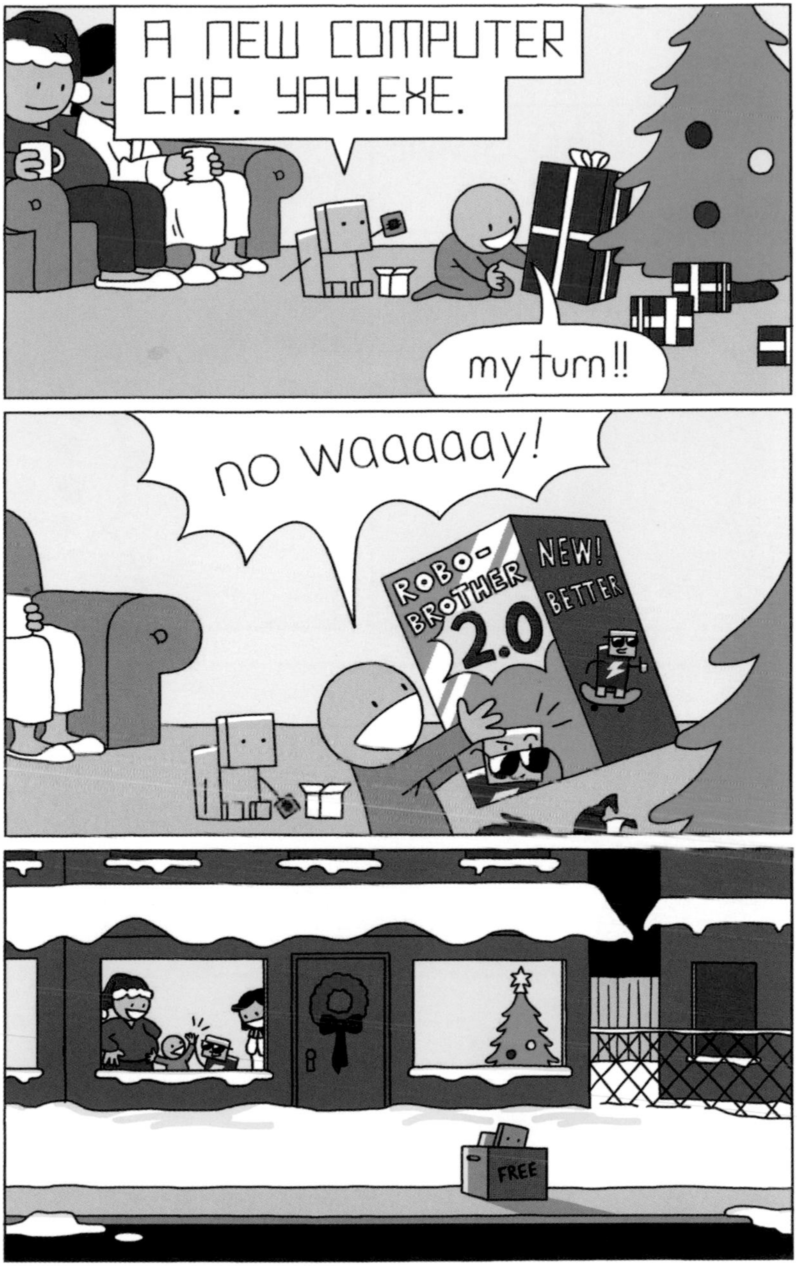
A NEW COMPUTER CHIP. YAY.EXE.
my turn!!
no waaaaay!
ROBO-BROTHER 2.0
NEW! BETTER
FREE

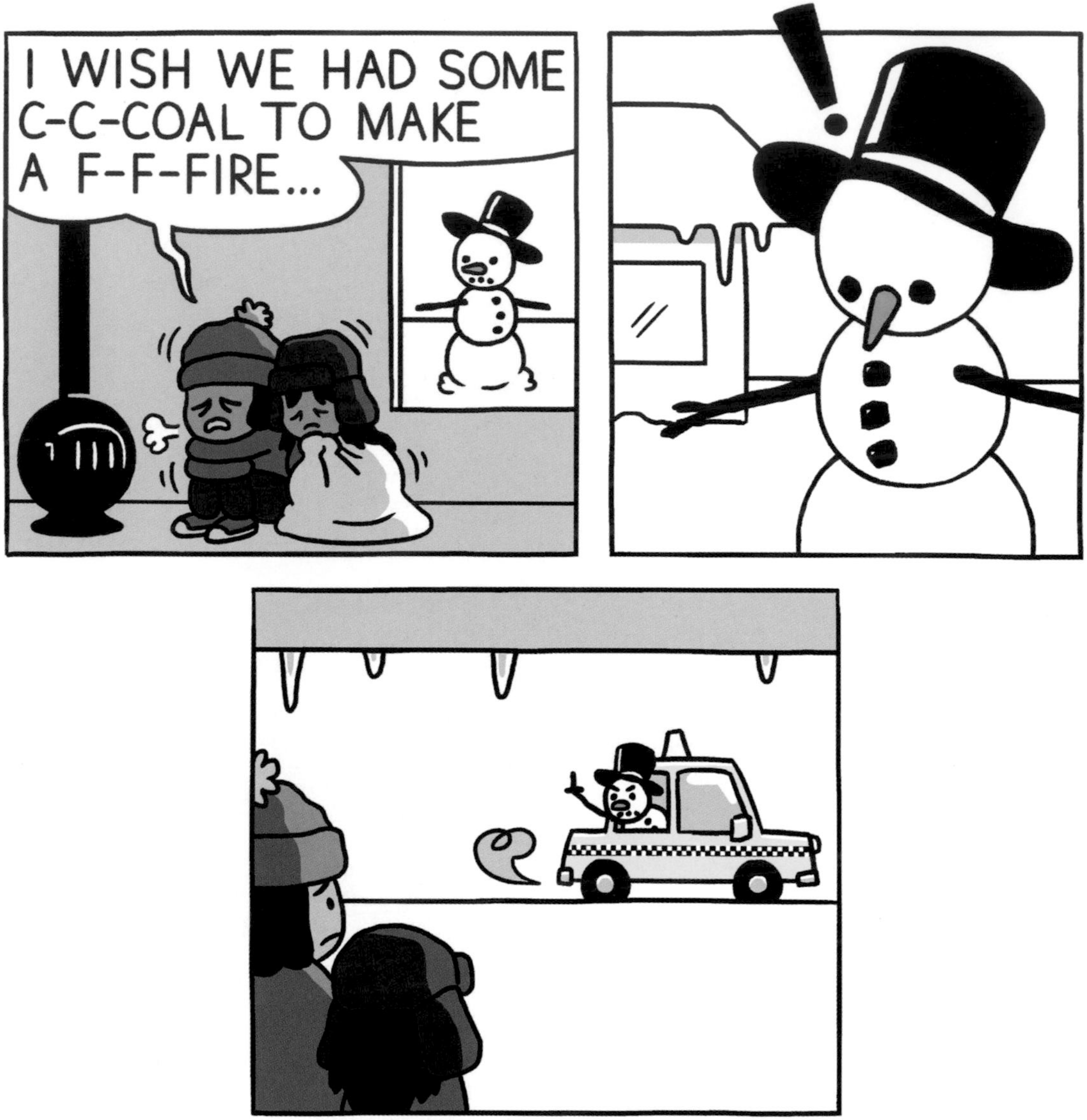
I WISH WE HAD SOME C-C-COAL TO MAKE A F-F-FIRE...
!

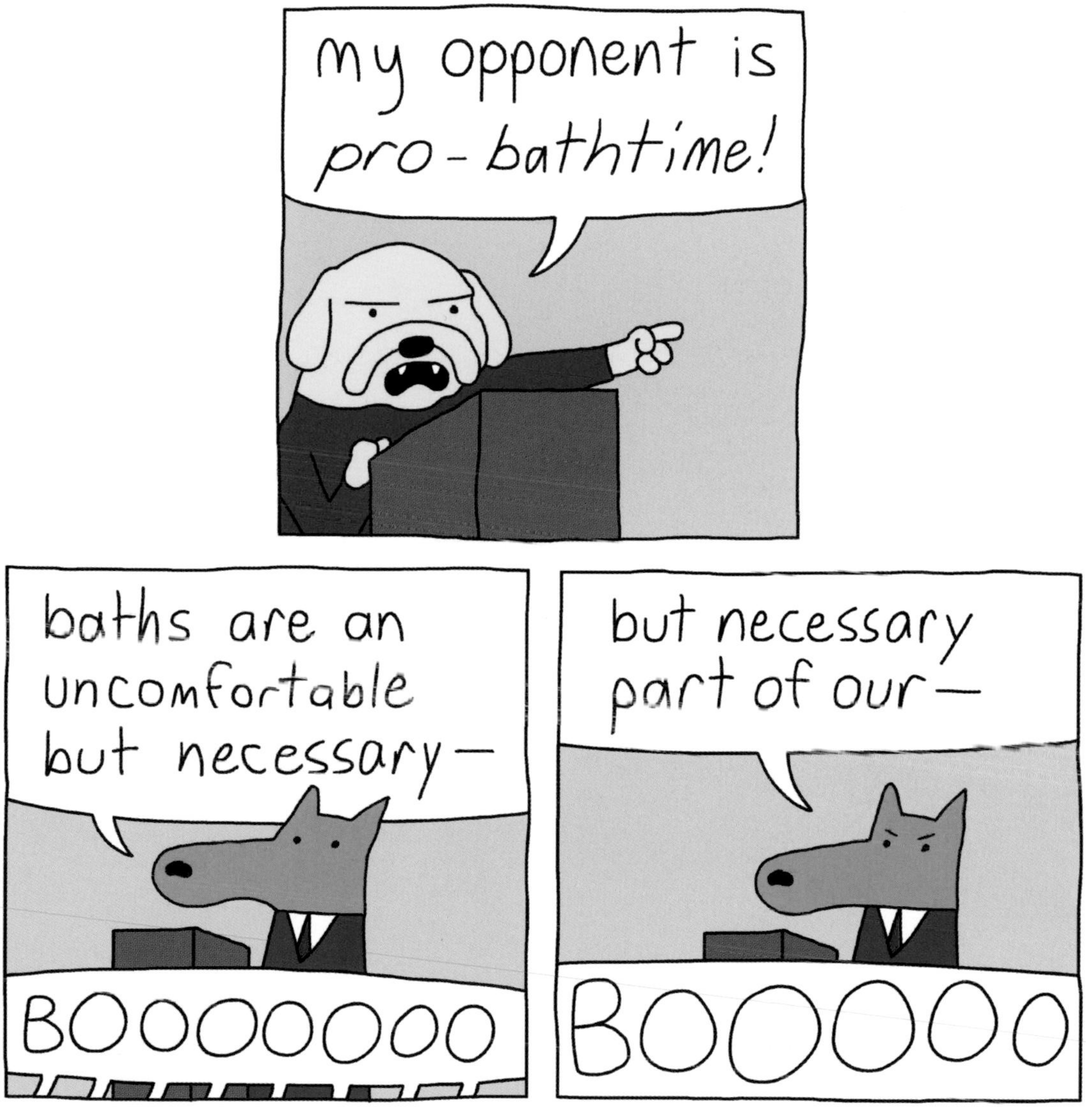
my opponent is
pro-bathtime!
baths are an
uncomfortable
but necessary—
BOOOOOOO
but necessary
part of our—
BOOOOO

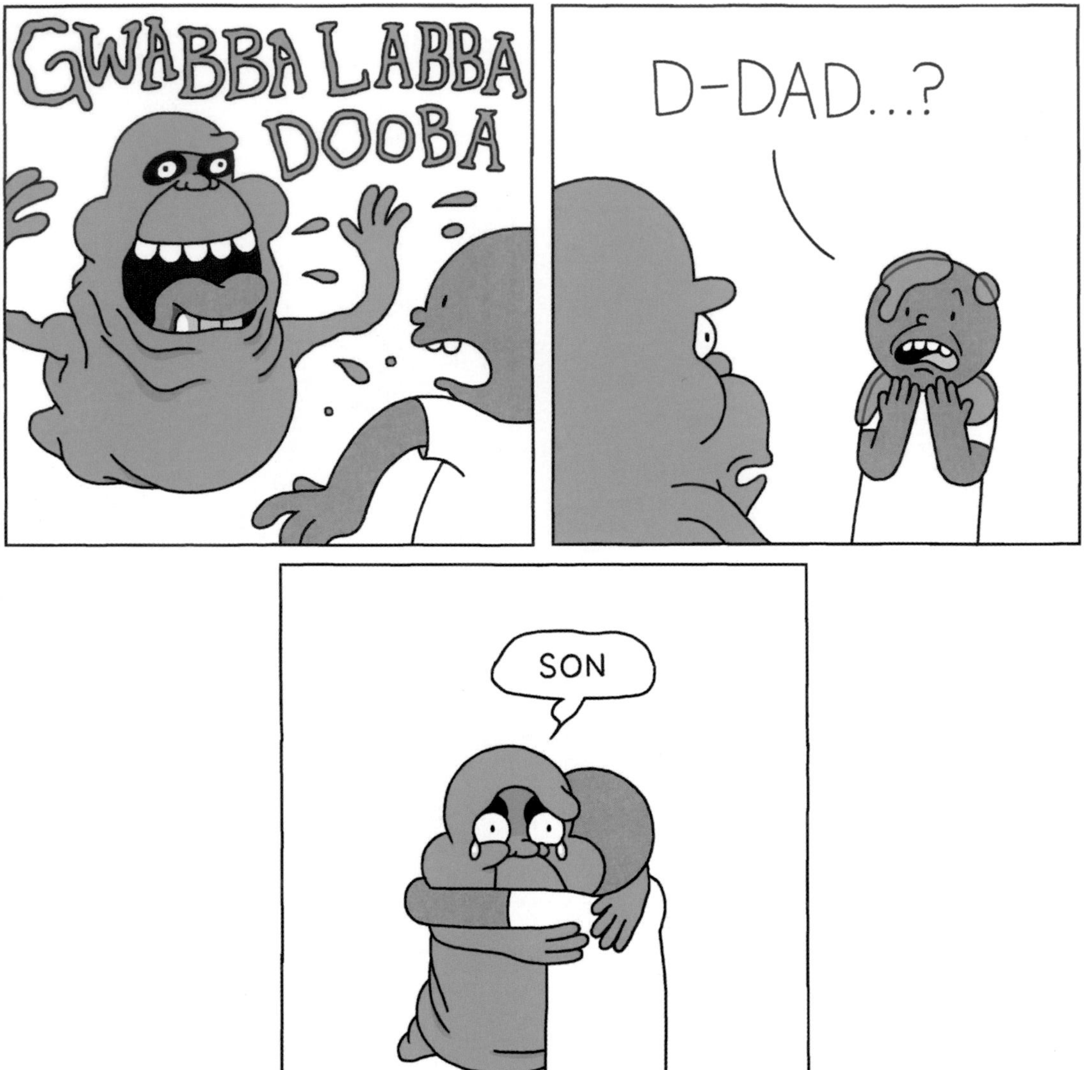
GWABBA LABBA DOOBA
D-DAD...?
SON

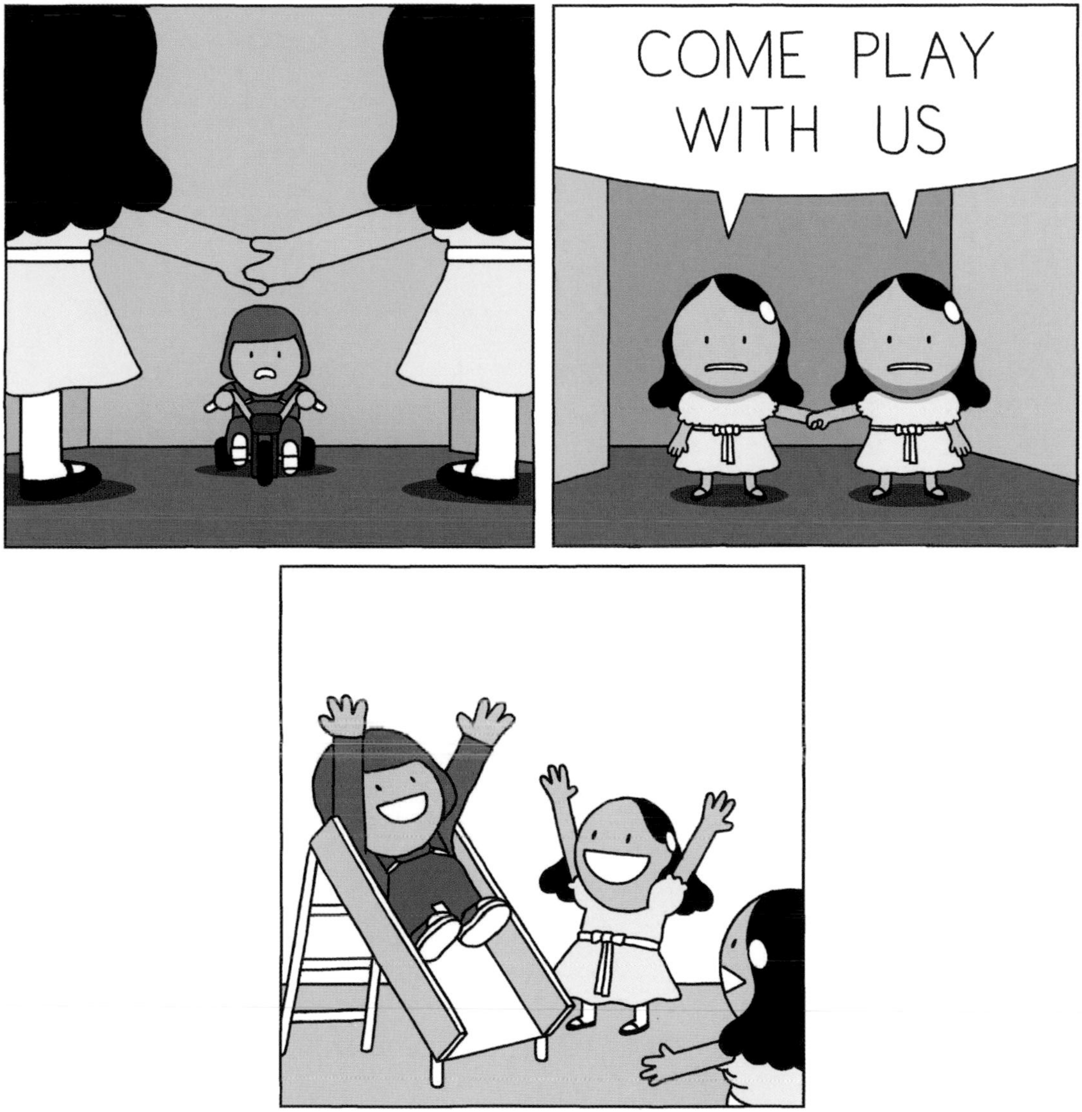
COME PLAY WITH US

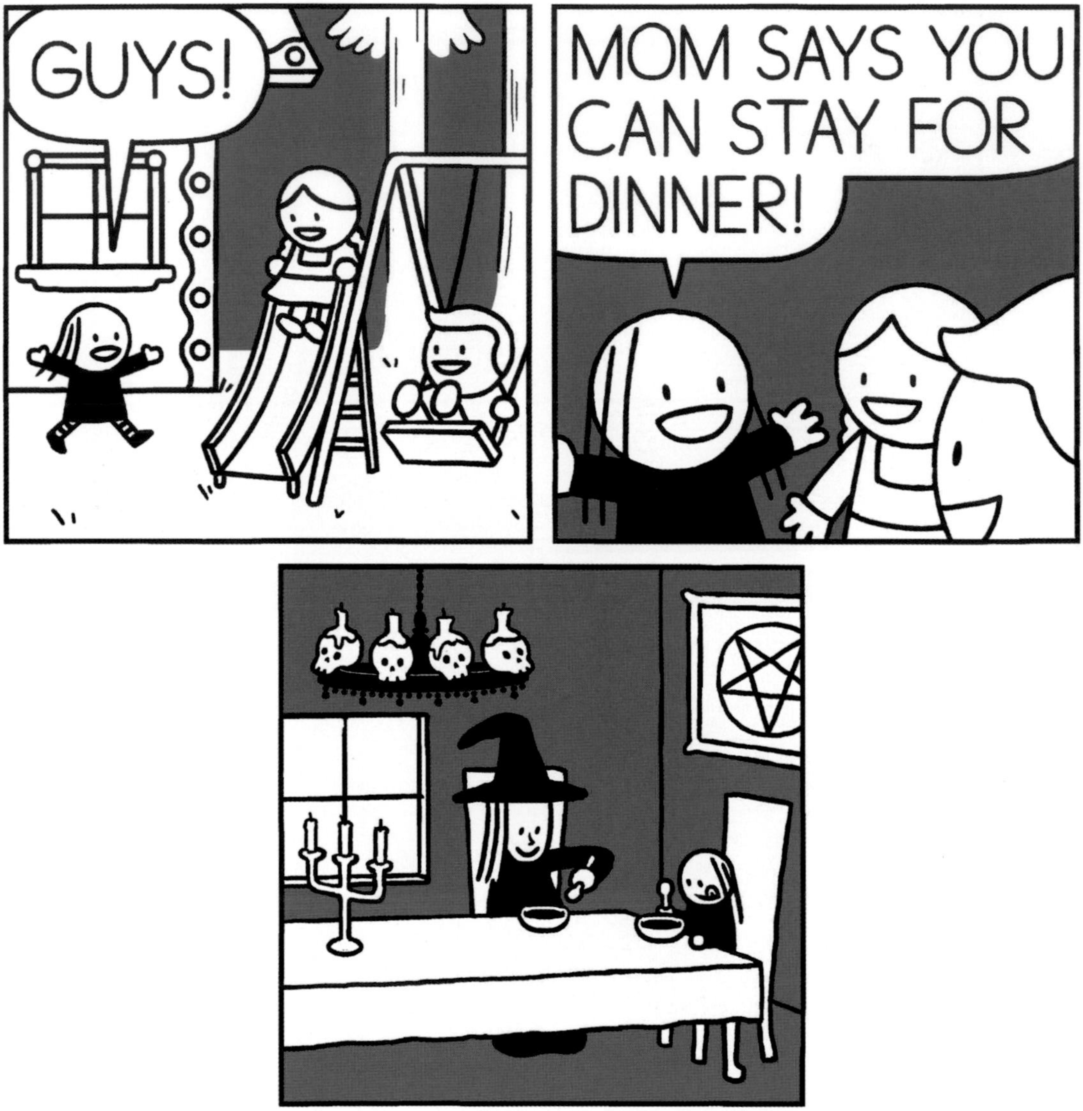
GUYS!
MOM SAYS YOU CAN STAY FOR DINNER!

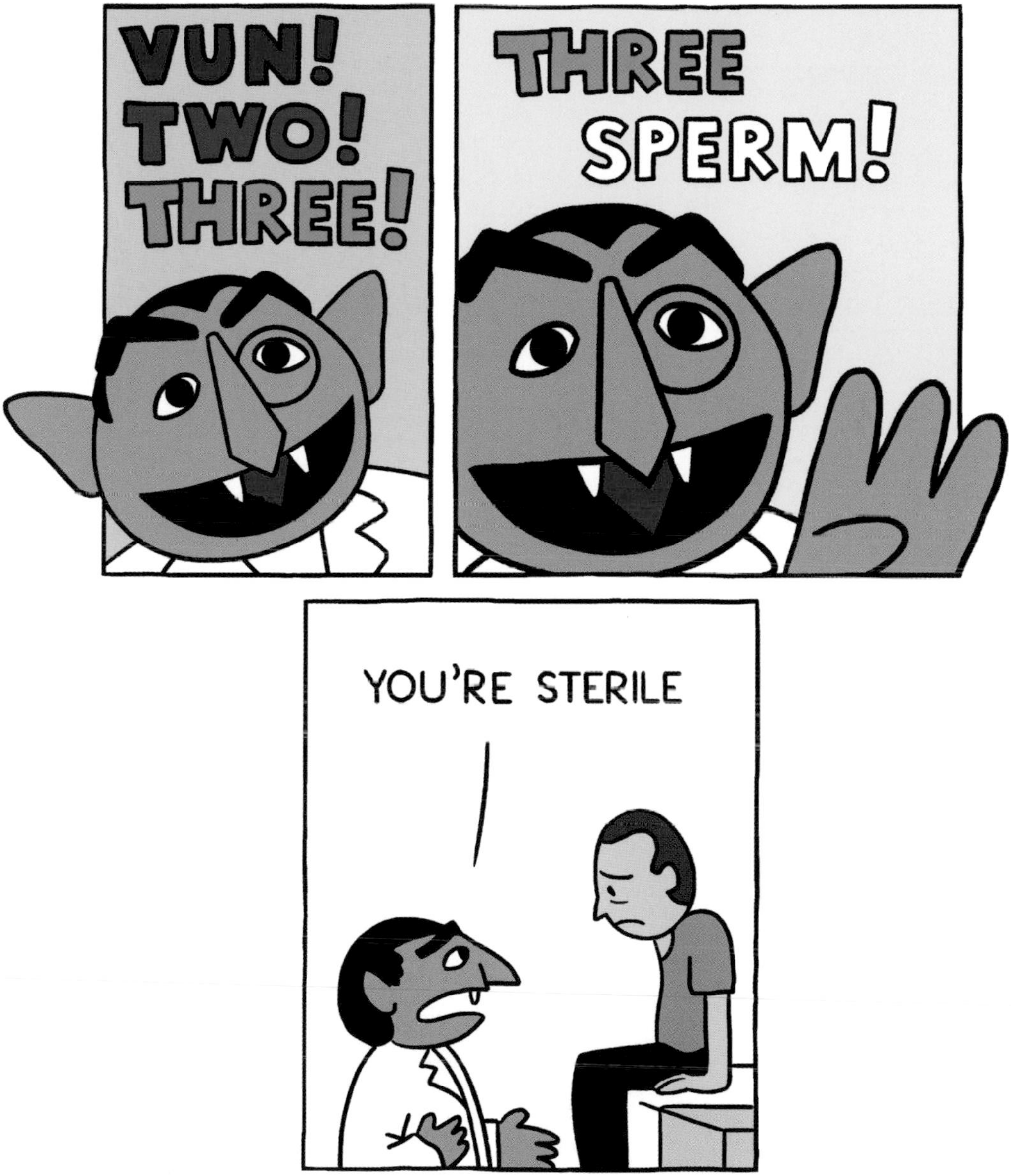
VUN! TWO! THREE!
THREE SPERM!
YOU'RE STERILE

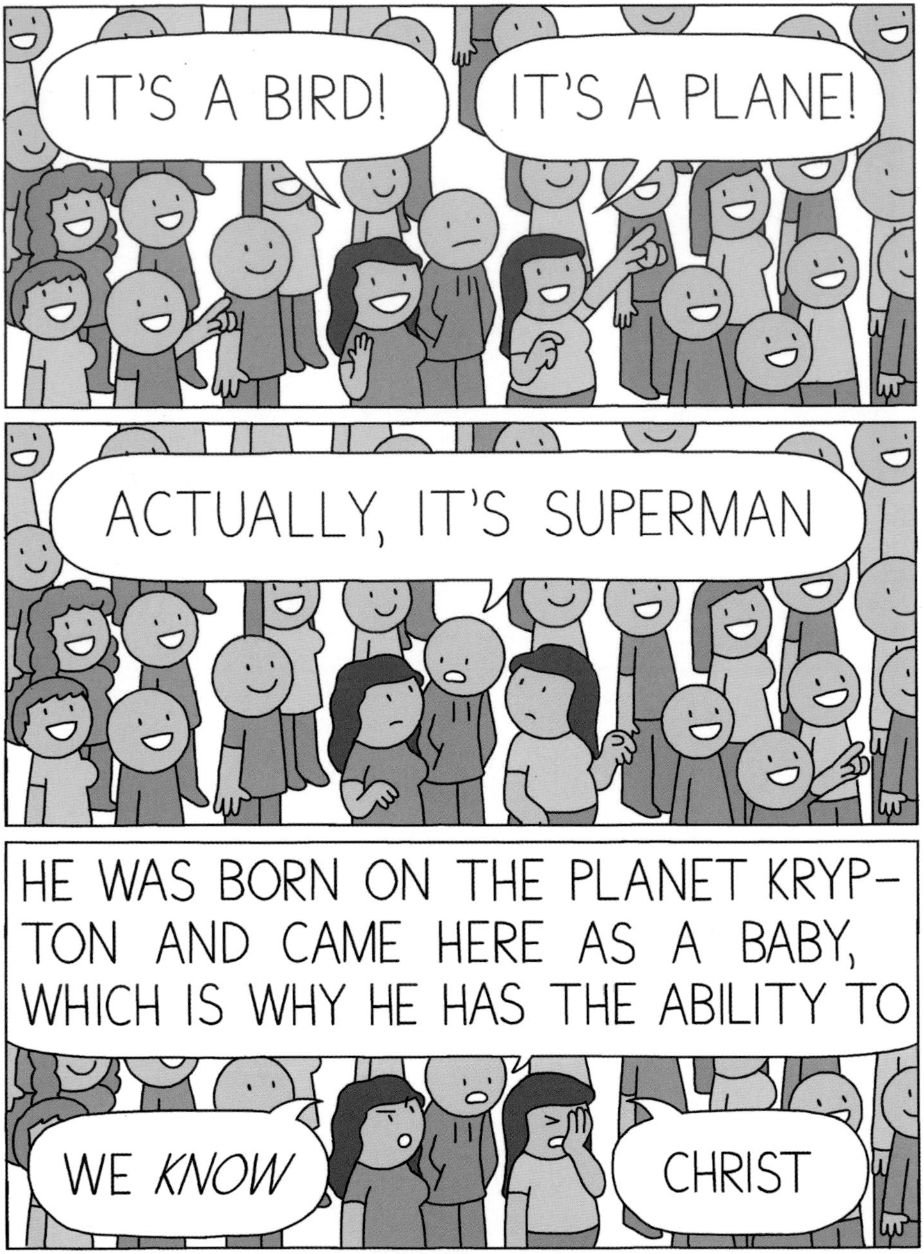
IT'S A BIRD!
IT'S A PLANE!
ACTUALLY, IT'S SUPERMAN
HE WAS BORN ON THE PLANET KRYP-TON AND CAME HERE AS A BABY, WHICH IS WHY HE HAS THE ABILITY TO
WE *KNOW*
CHRIST

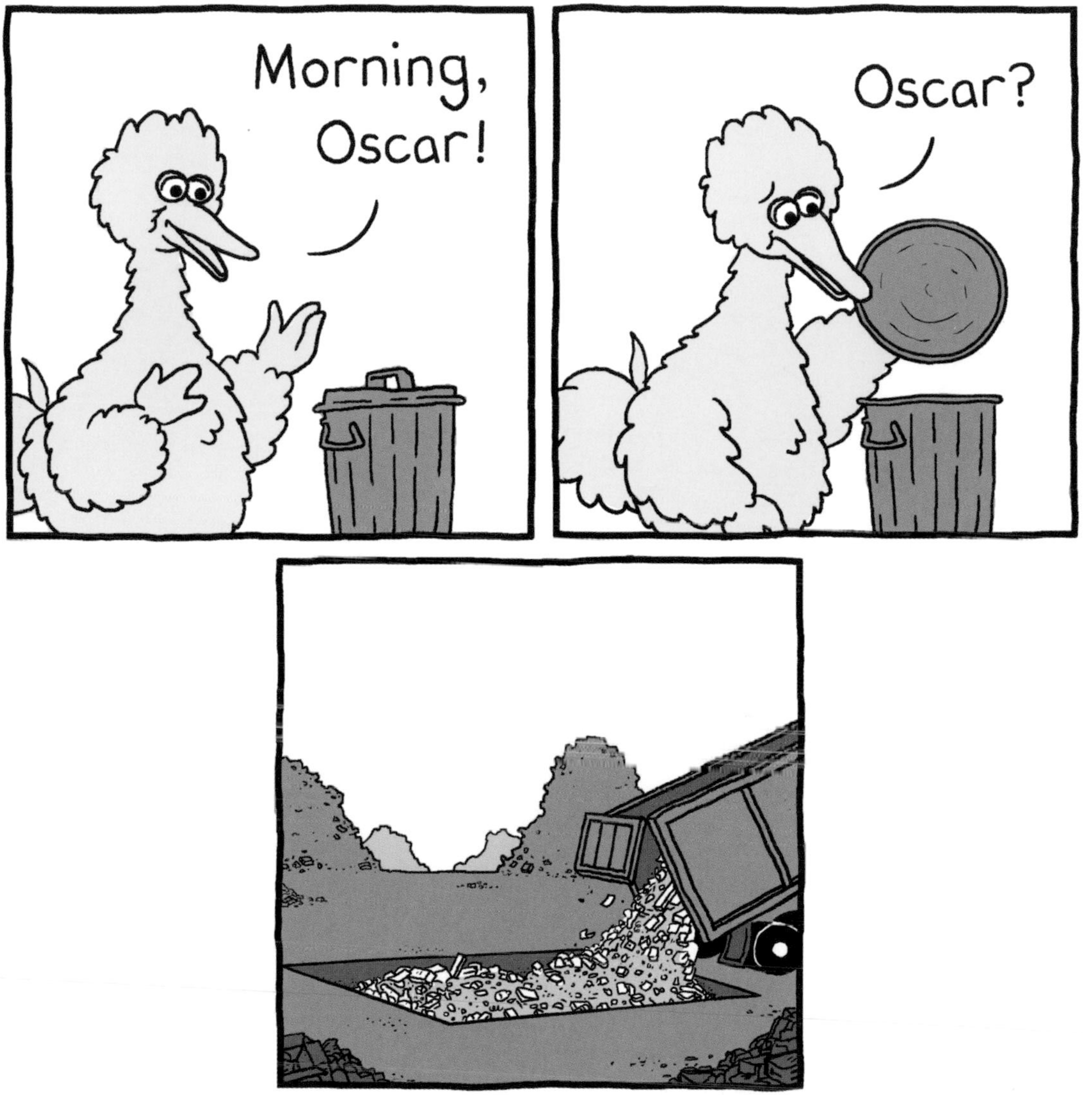
Morning, Oscar!
Oscar?

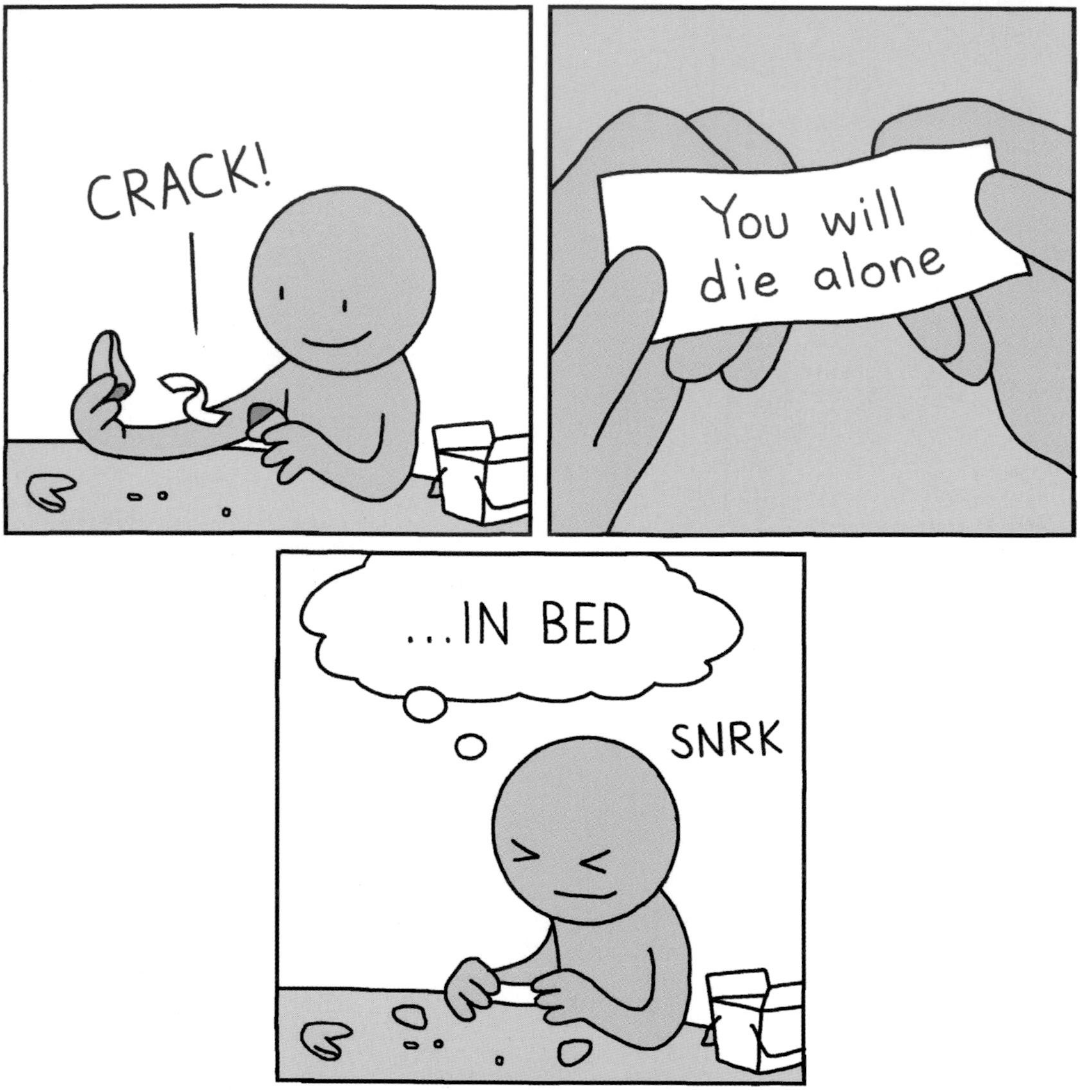
CRACK!
You will die alone
...IN BED
SNRK

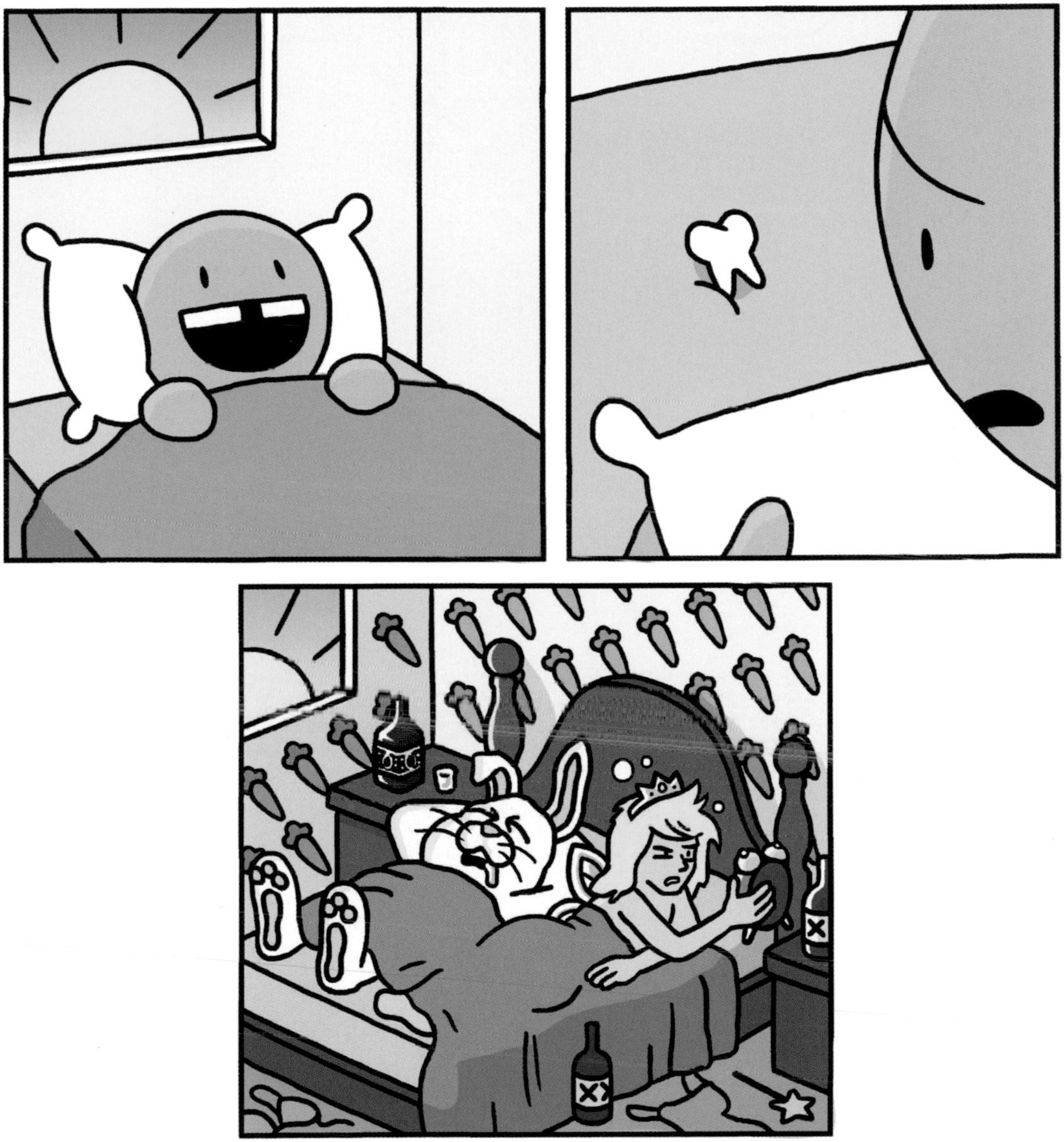

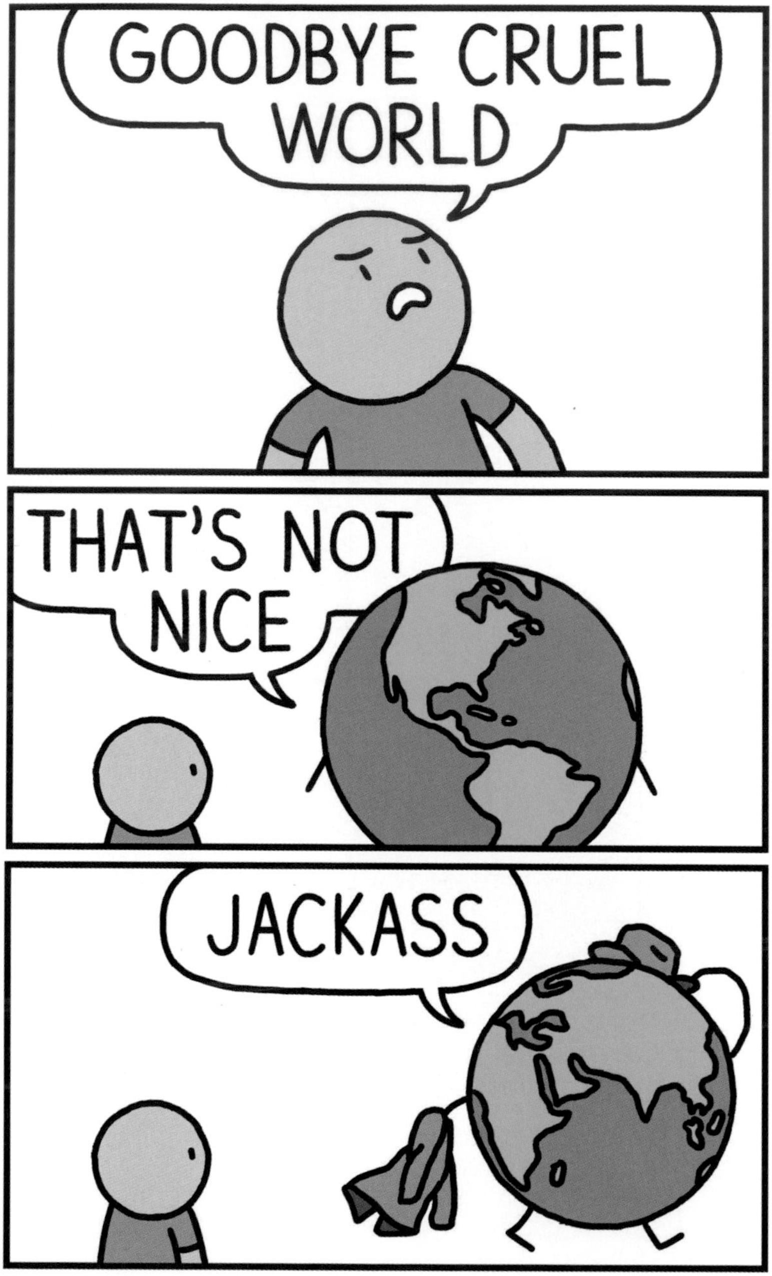
GOODBYE CRUEL WORLD
THAT'S NOT NICE
JACKASS

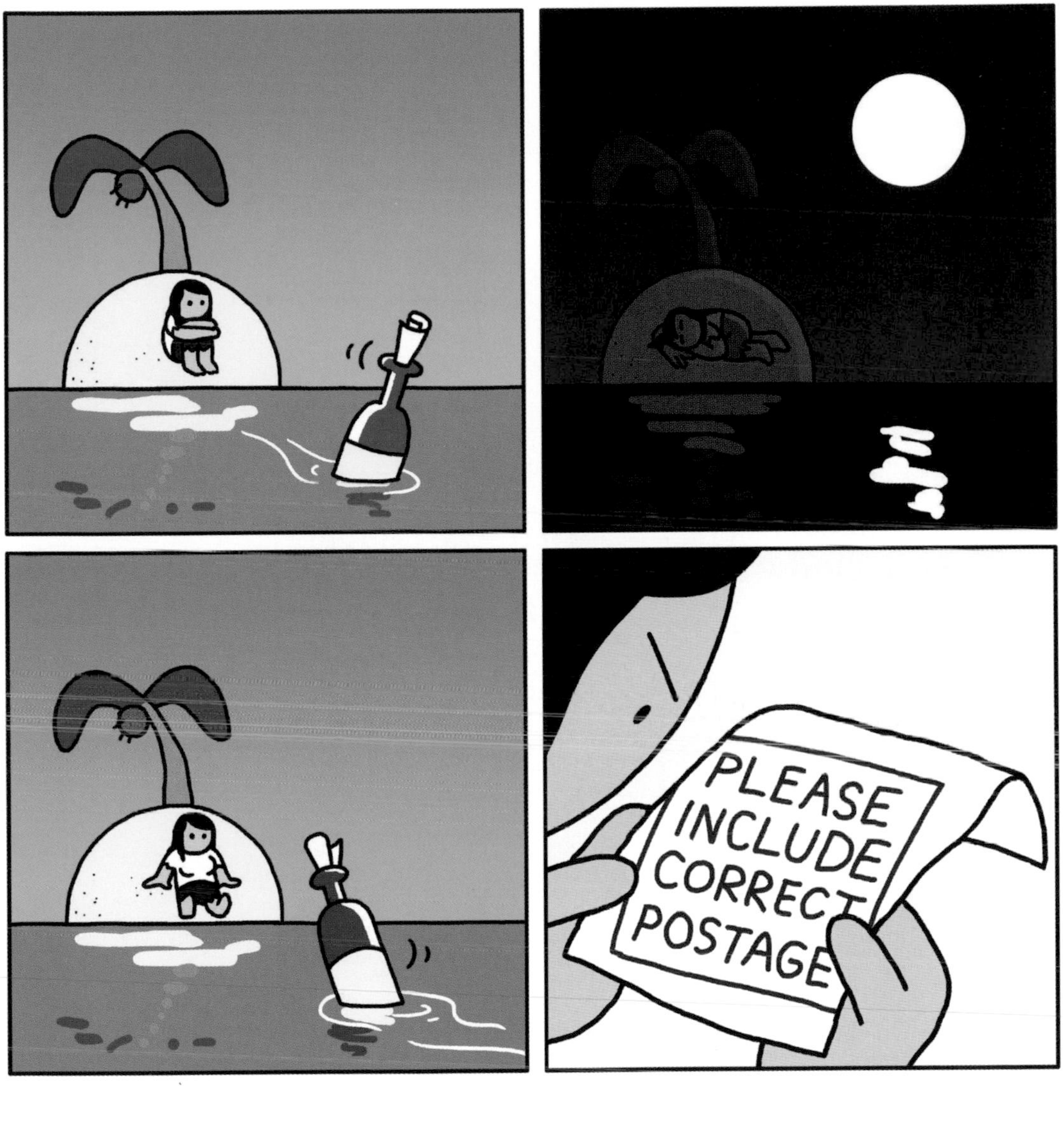
PLEASE INCLUDE CORRECT POSTAGE

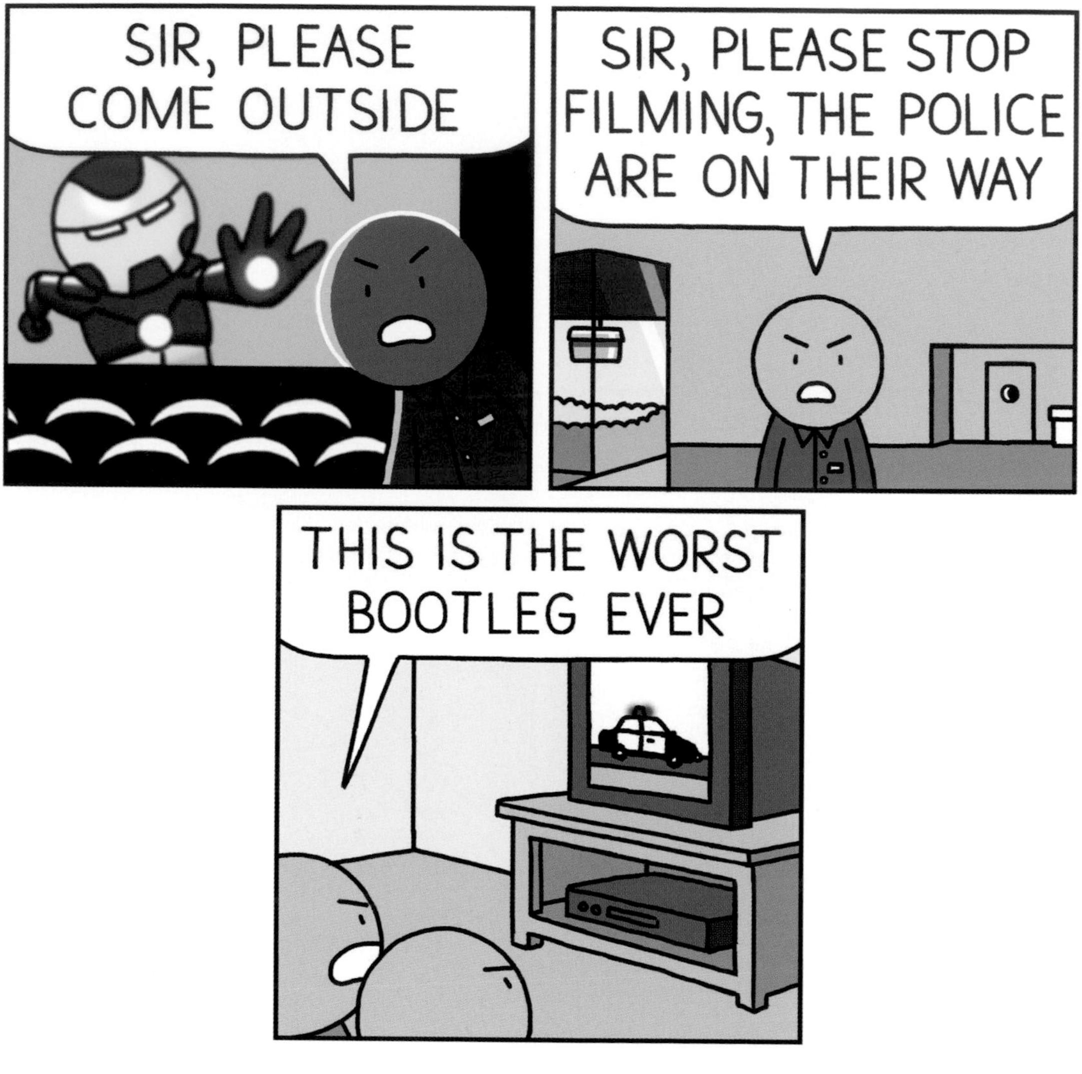
SIR, PLEASE COME OUTSIDE
SIR, PLEASE STOP FILMING, THE POLICE ARE ON THEIR WAY
THIS IS THE WORST BOOTLEG EVER

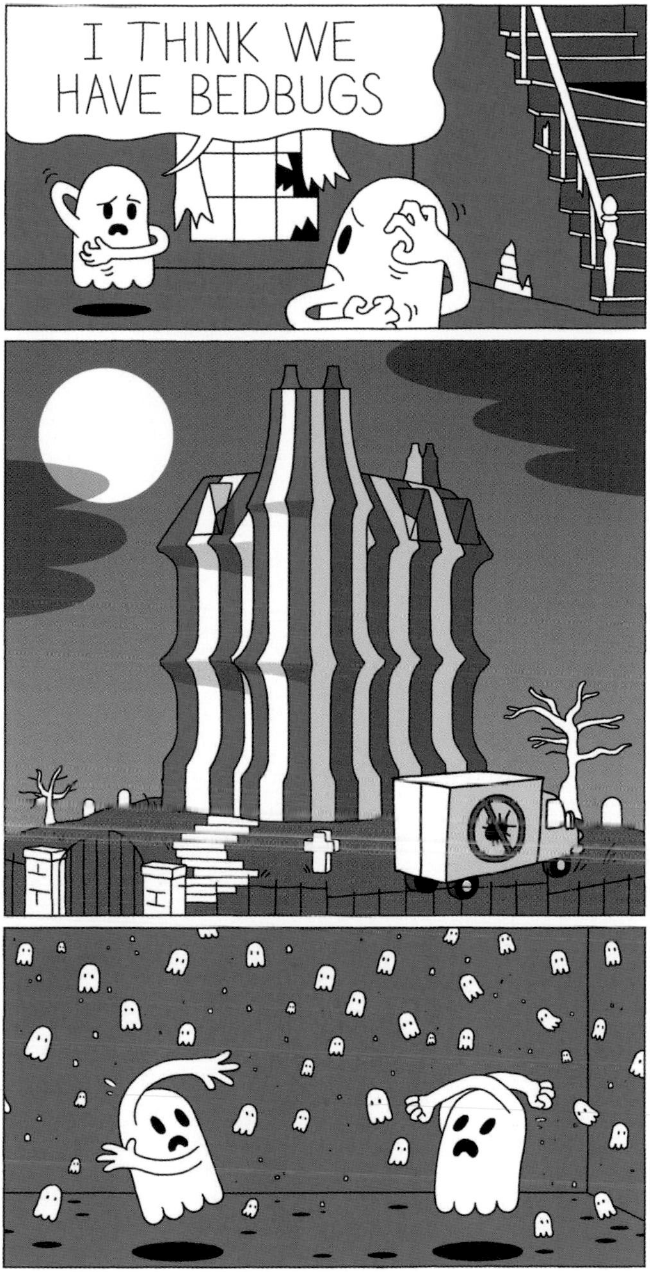
I THINK WE HAVE BEDBUGS

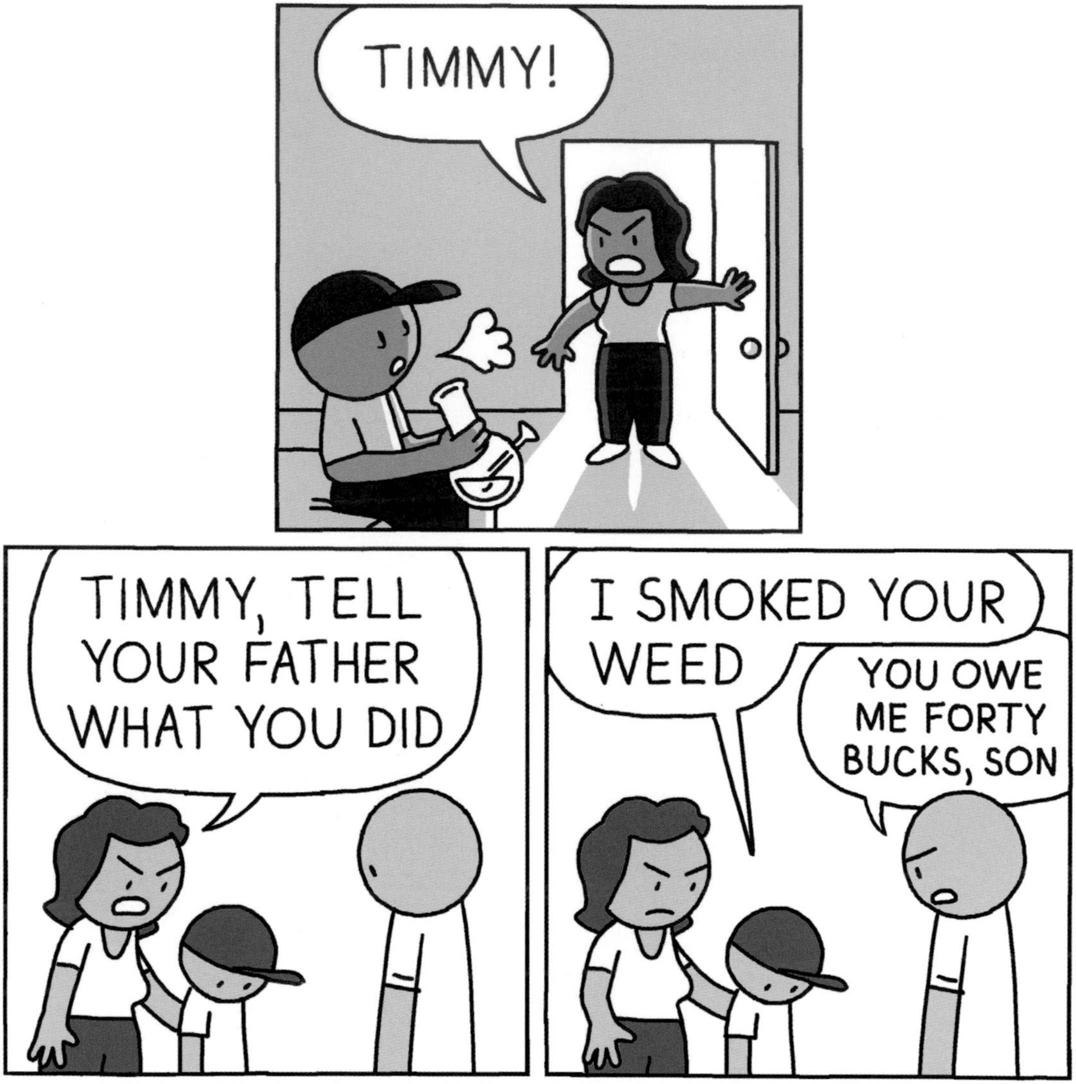
TIMMY!
TIMMY, TELL YOUR FATHER WHAT YOU DID
I SMOKED YOUR WEED
YOU OWE ME FORTY BUCKS, SON

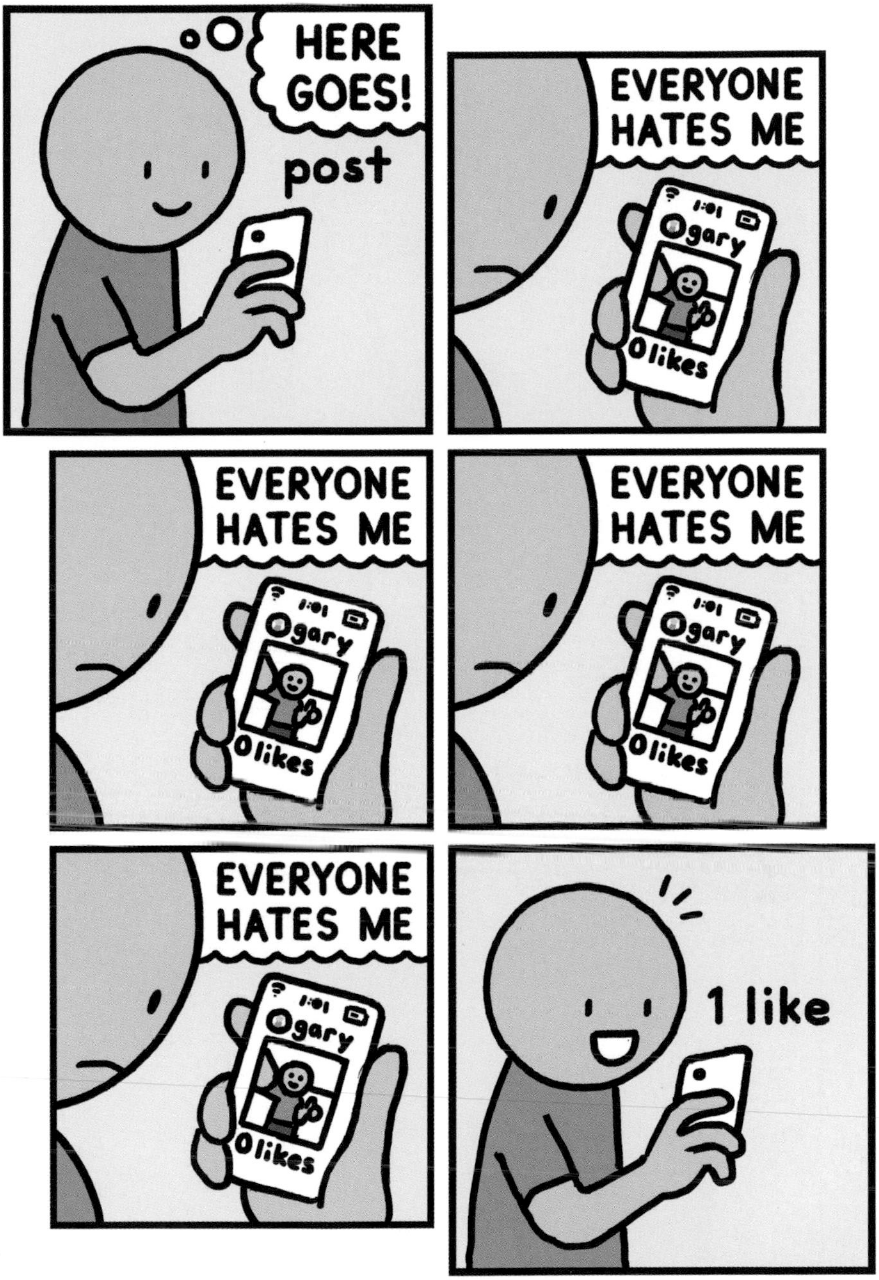
HERE GOES!
post
EVERYONE HATES ME
gary
0 likes
EVERYONE HATES ME
gary
0 likes
EVERYONE HATES ME
gary
0 likes
EVERYONE HATES ME
gary
0 likes
1 like

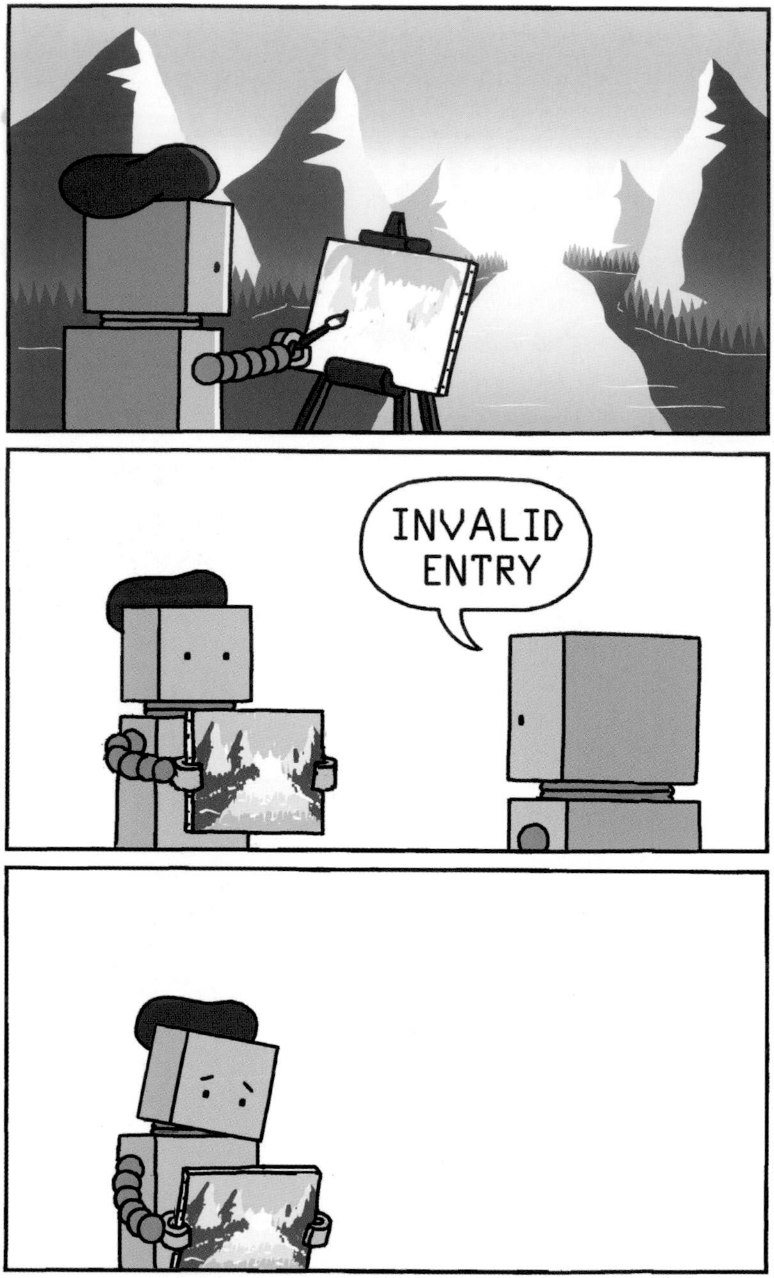
INVALID ENTRY

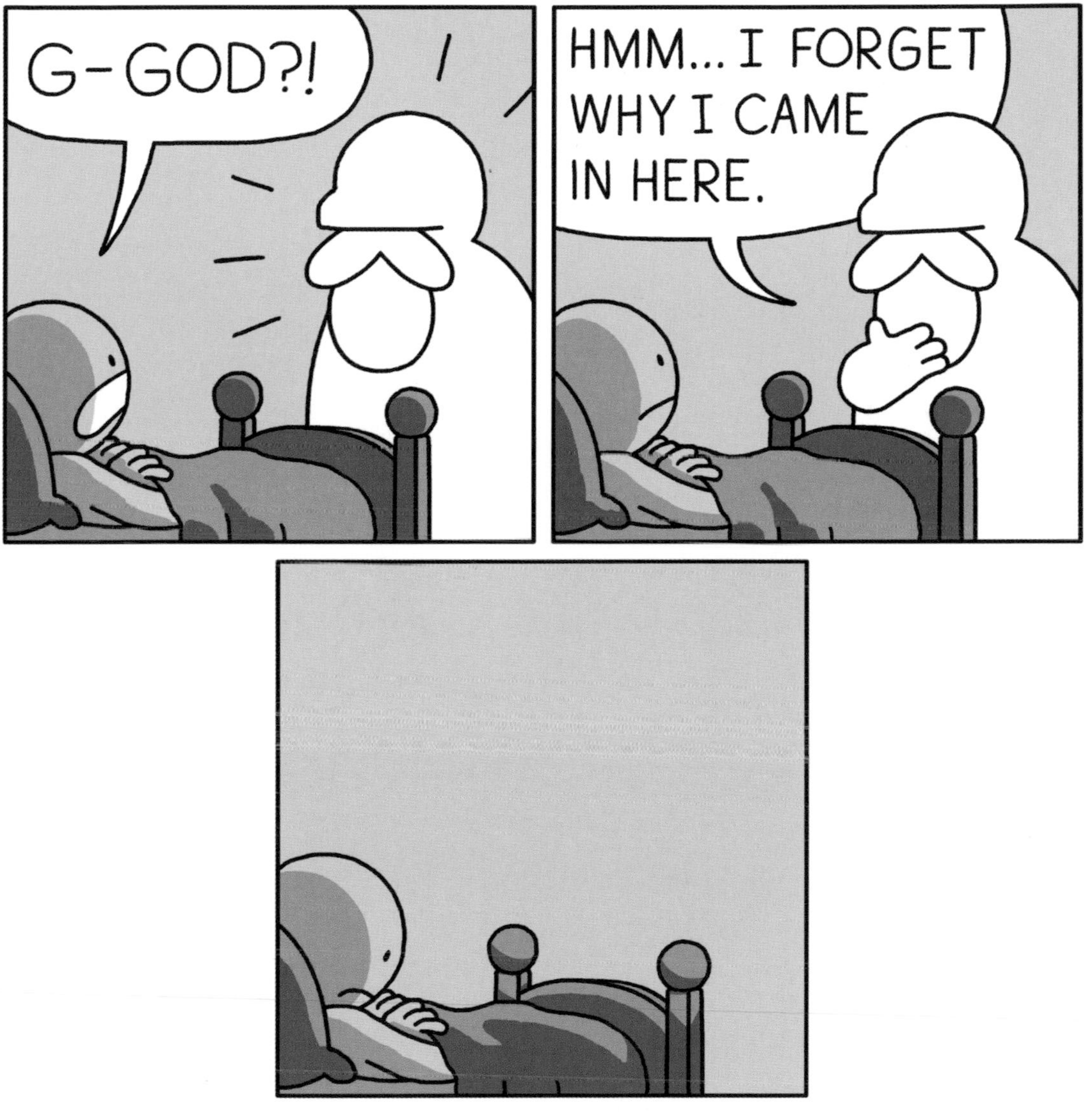
G-GOD?!
HMM... I FORGET WHY I CAME IN HERE.

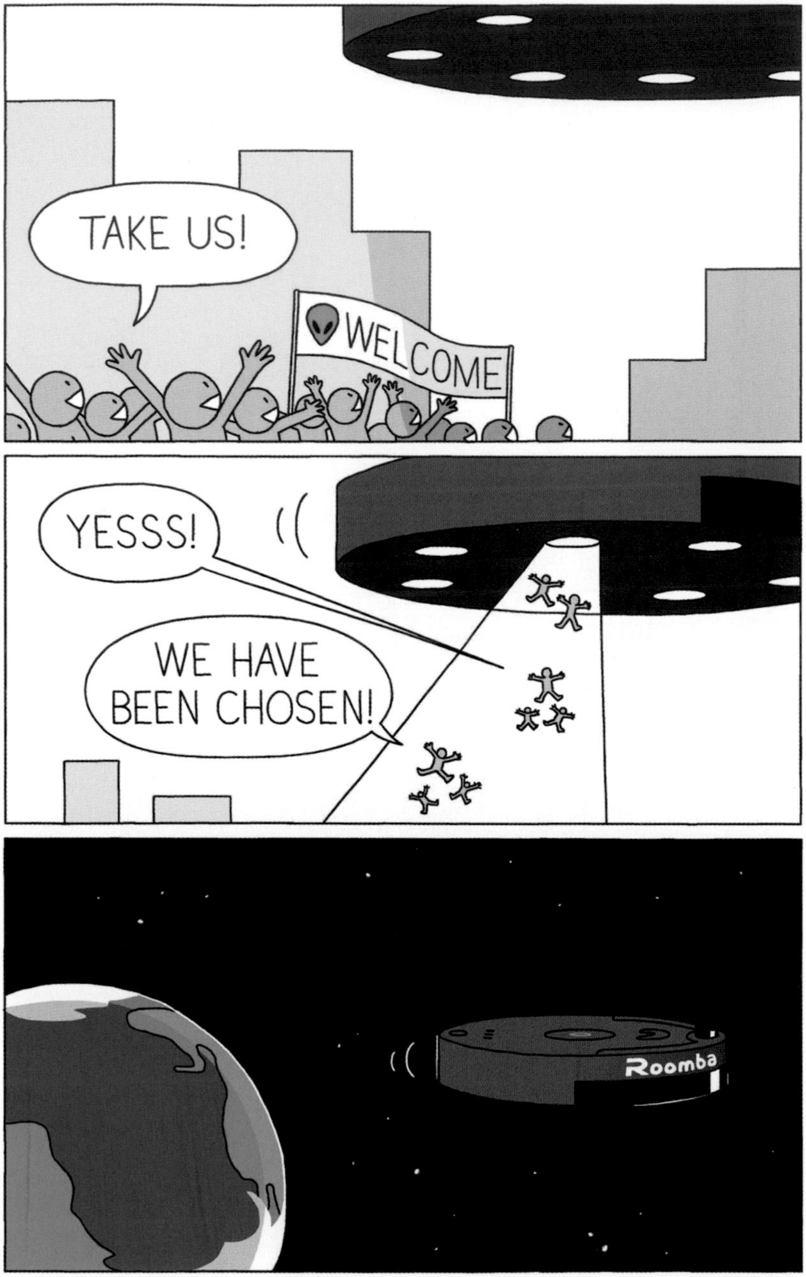
TAKE US!
WELCOME
YESSS!
WE HAVE BEEN CHOSEN!
Roomba

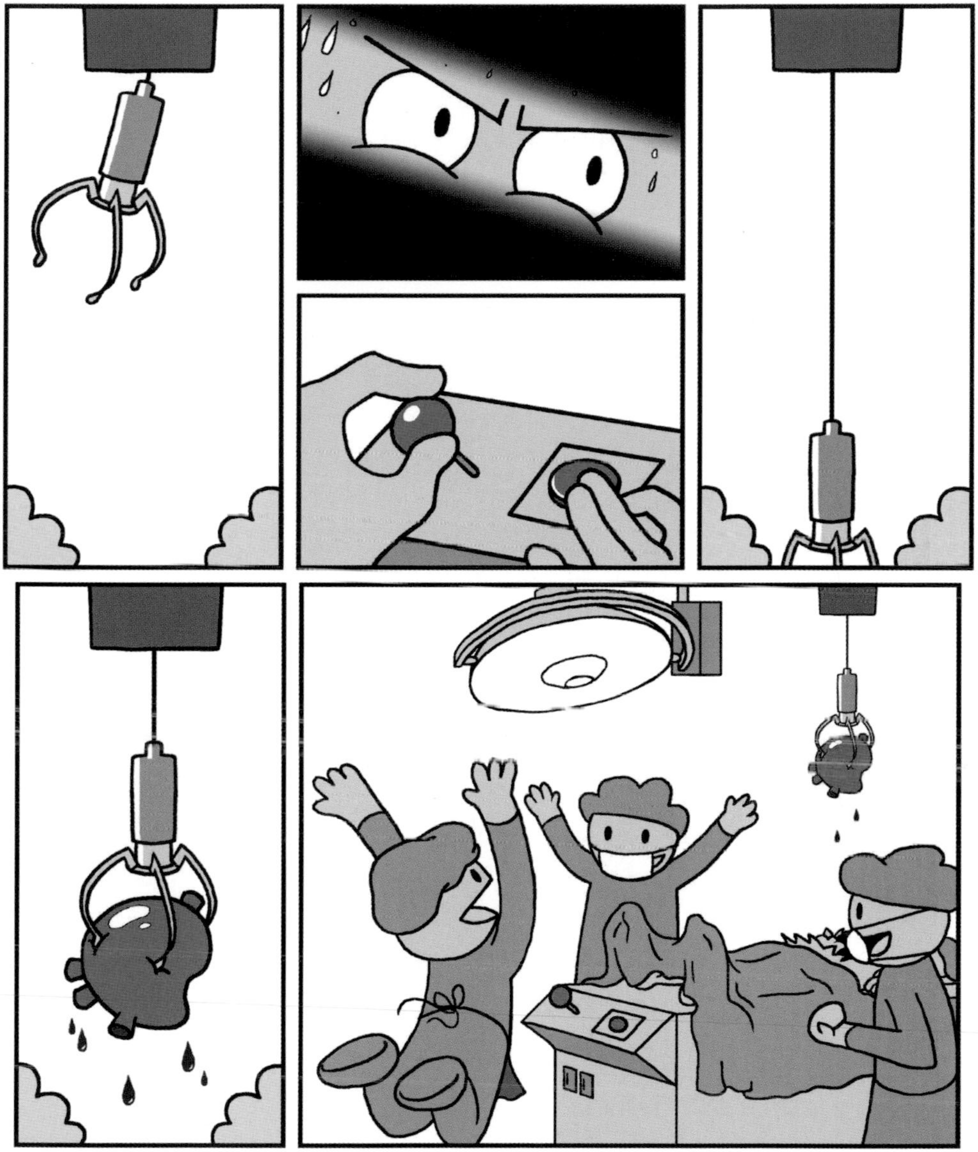

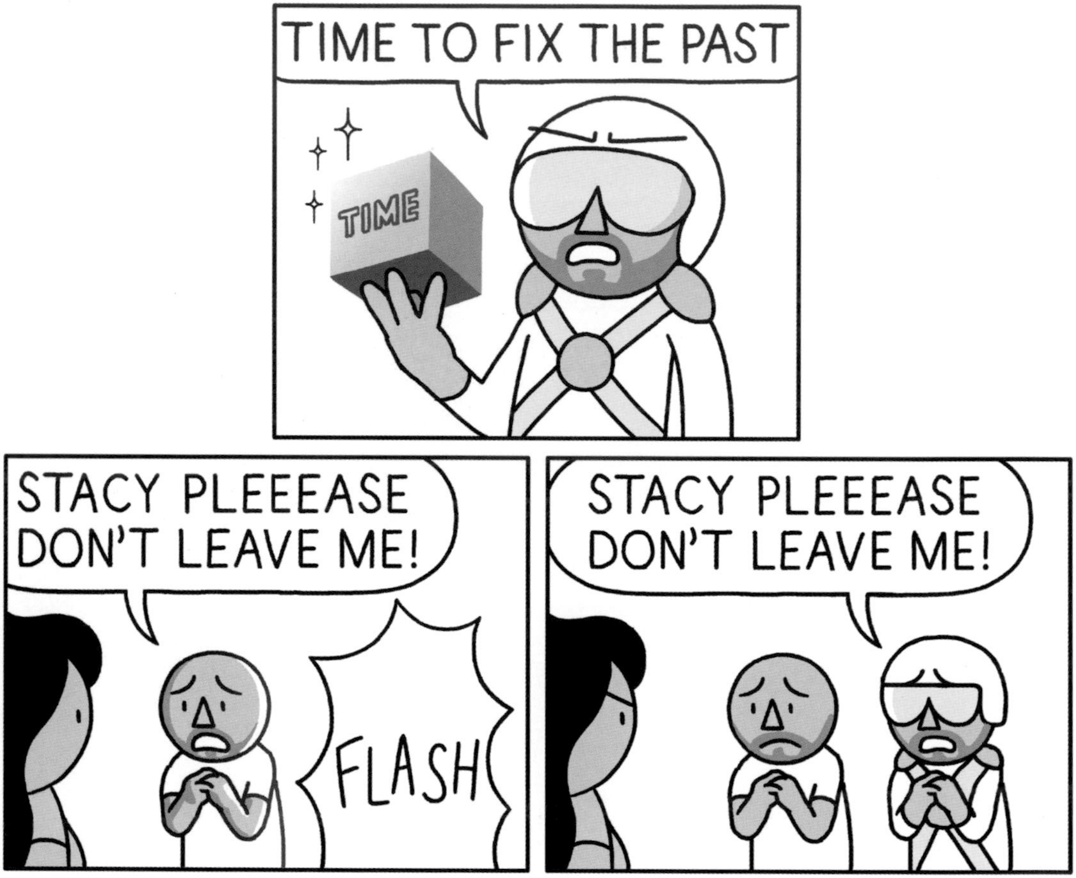
TIME TO FIX THE PAST
TIME
STACY PLEEEASE DON'T LEAVE ME!
FLASH
STACY PLEEEASE DON'T LEAVE ME!

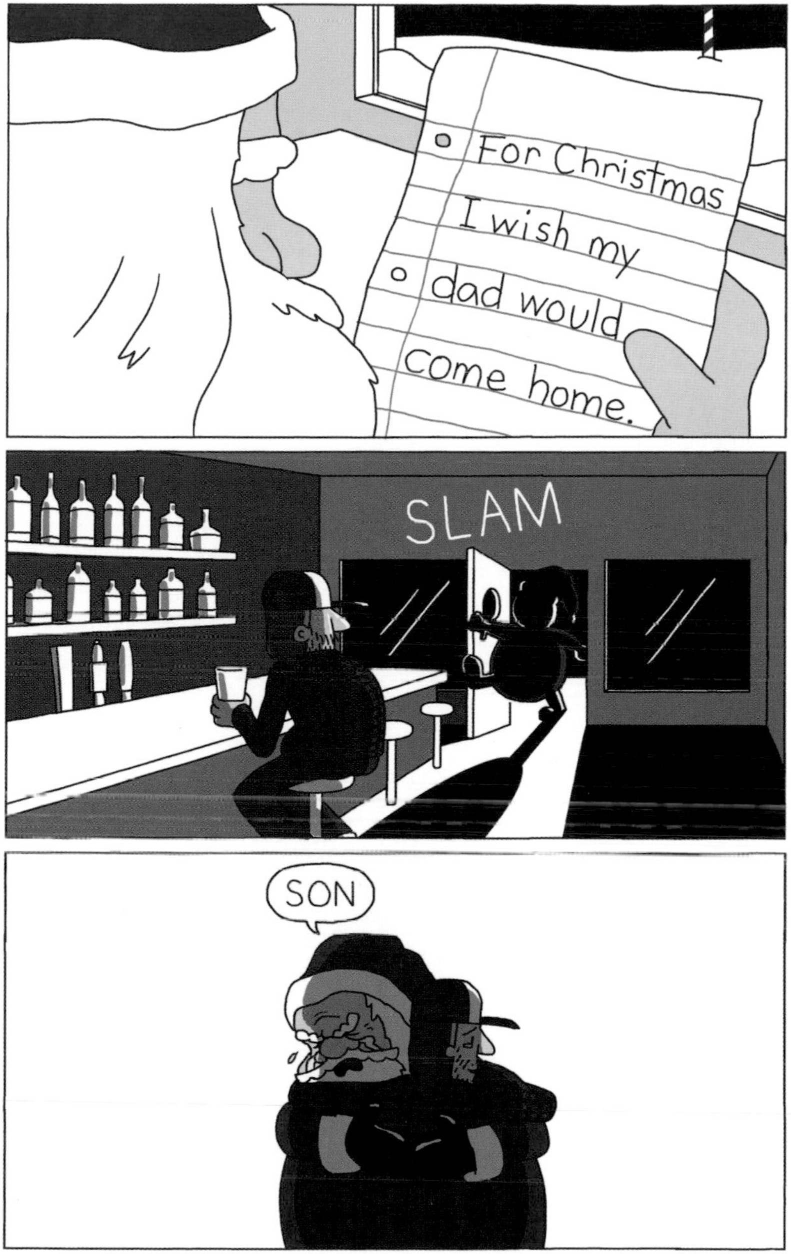
For Christmas I wish my dad would come home.
SLAM
SON

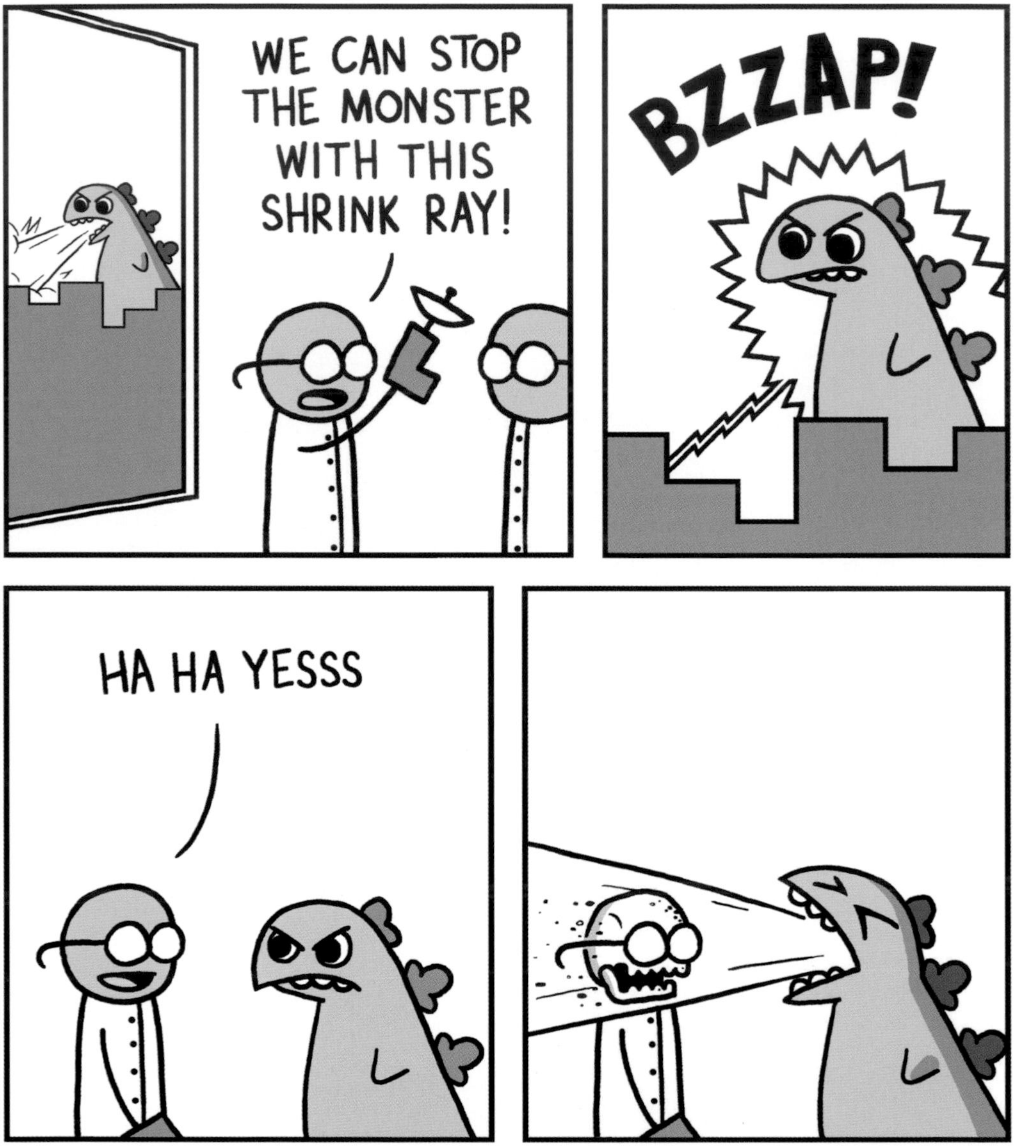
WE CAN STOP THE MONSTER WITH THIS SHRINK RAY!
BZZAP!
HA HA YESSS

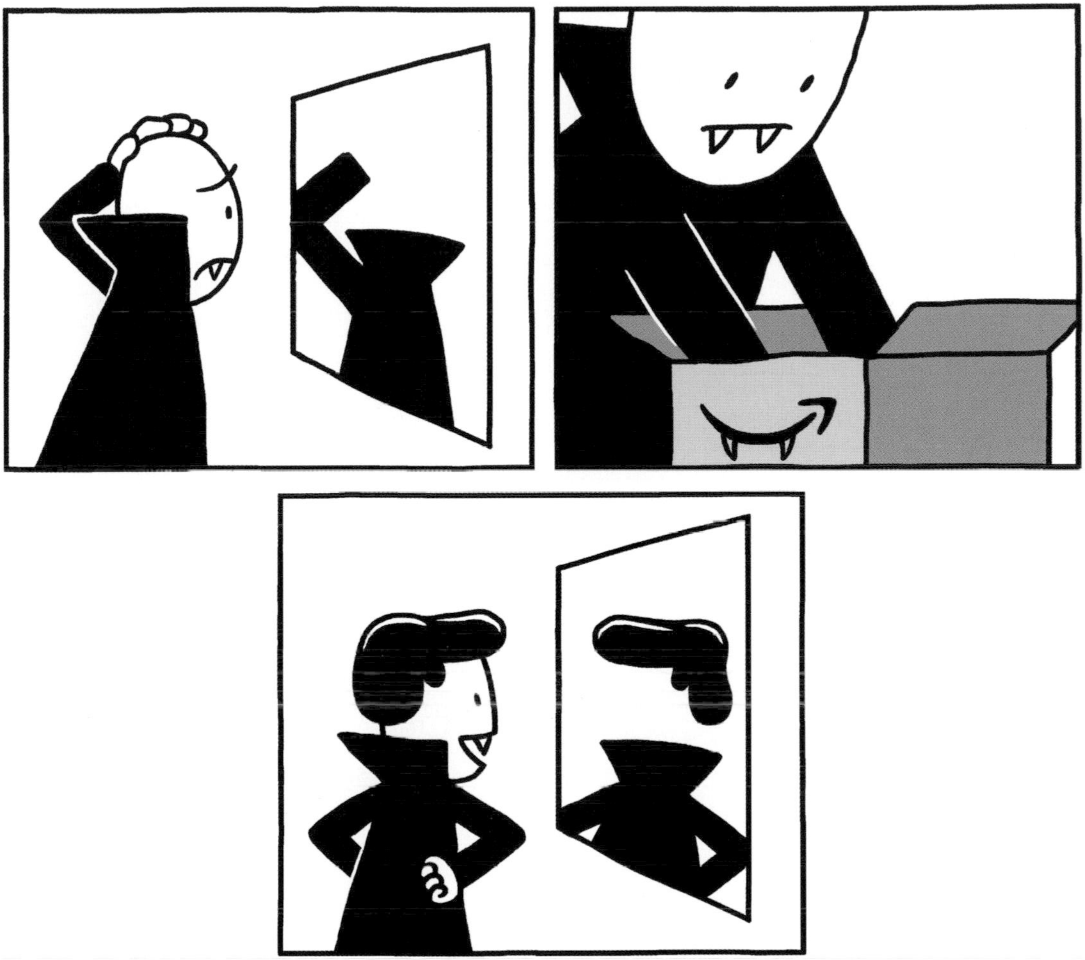

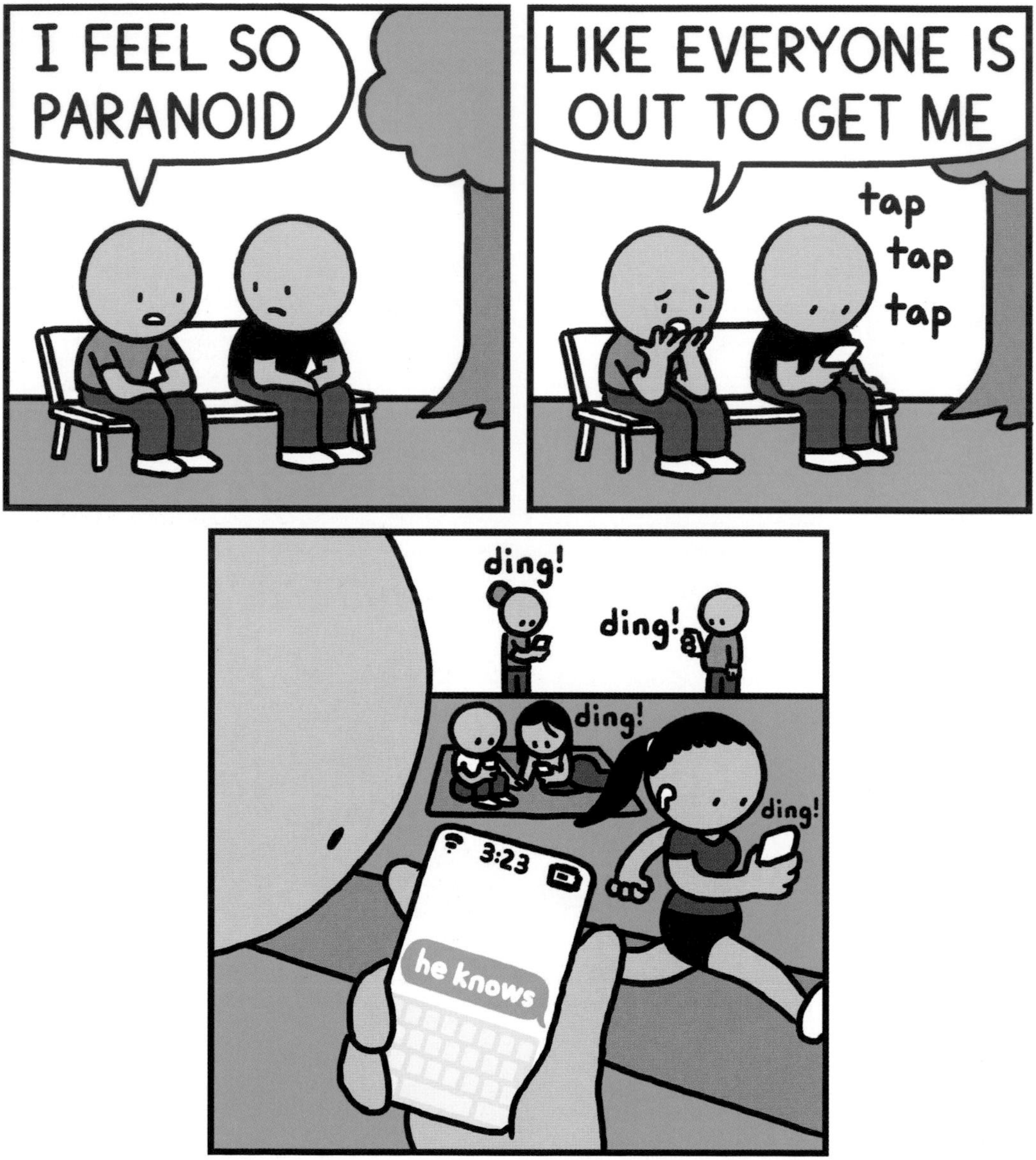

I FEEL SO PARANOID
LIKE EVERYONE IS OUT TO GET ME
tap
tap
tap
ding!
ding!
ding!
ding!
3:23
he knows

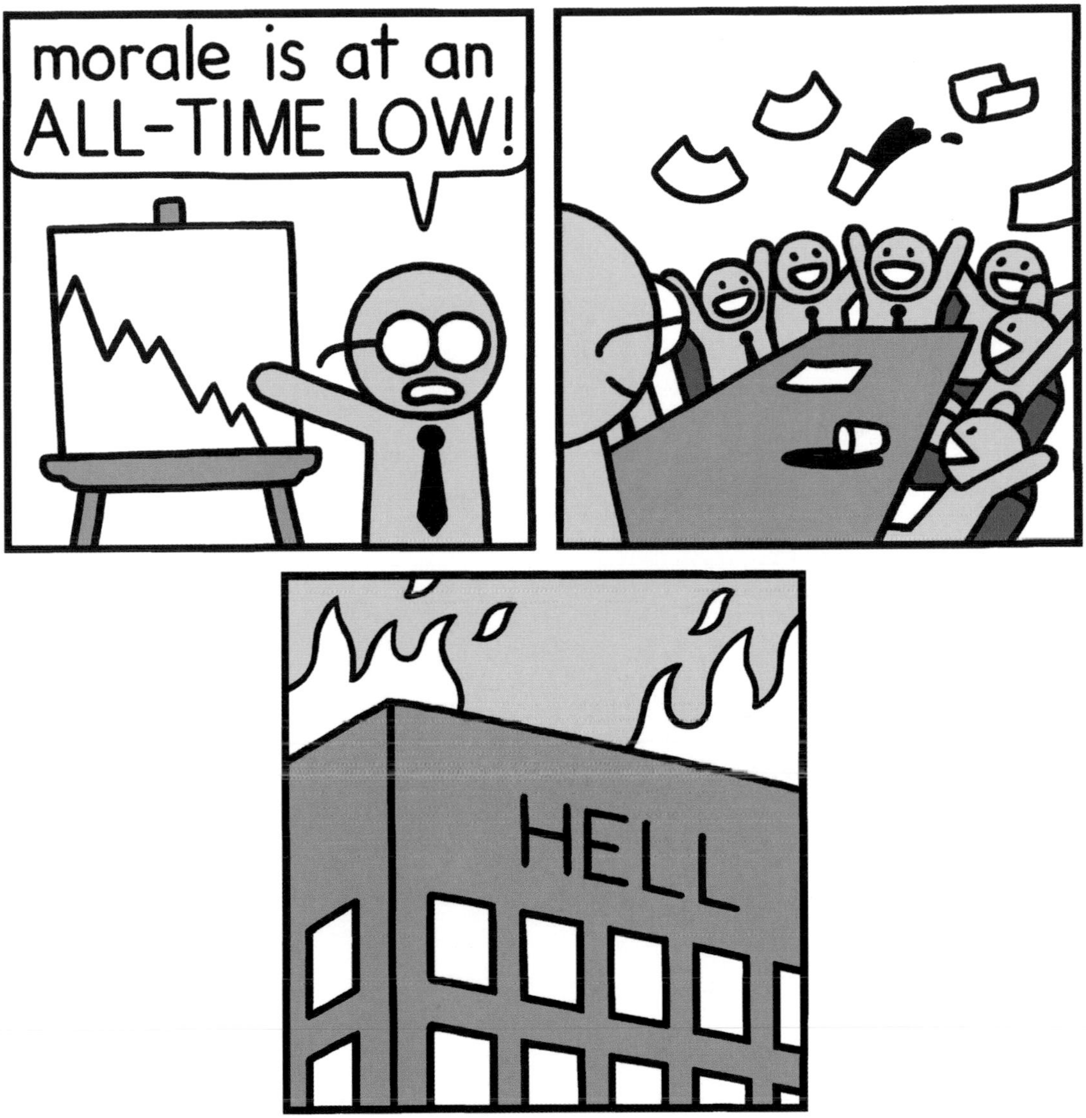
morale is at an ALL-TIME LOW!
HELL

IT'S DANGEROUS TO GO ALONE!
PLEASE STAY
I'M SO LONELY

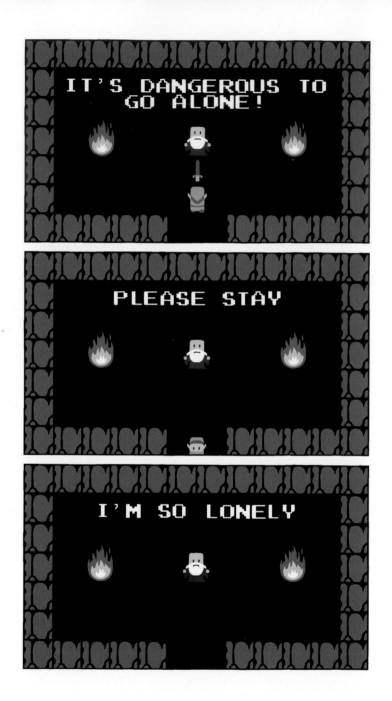

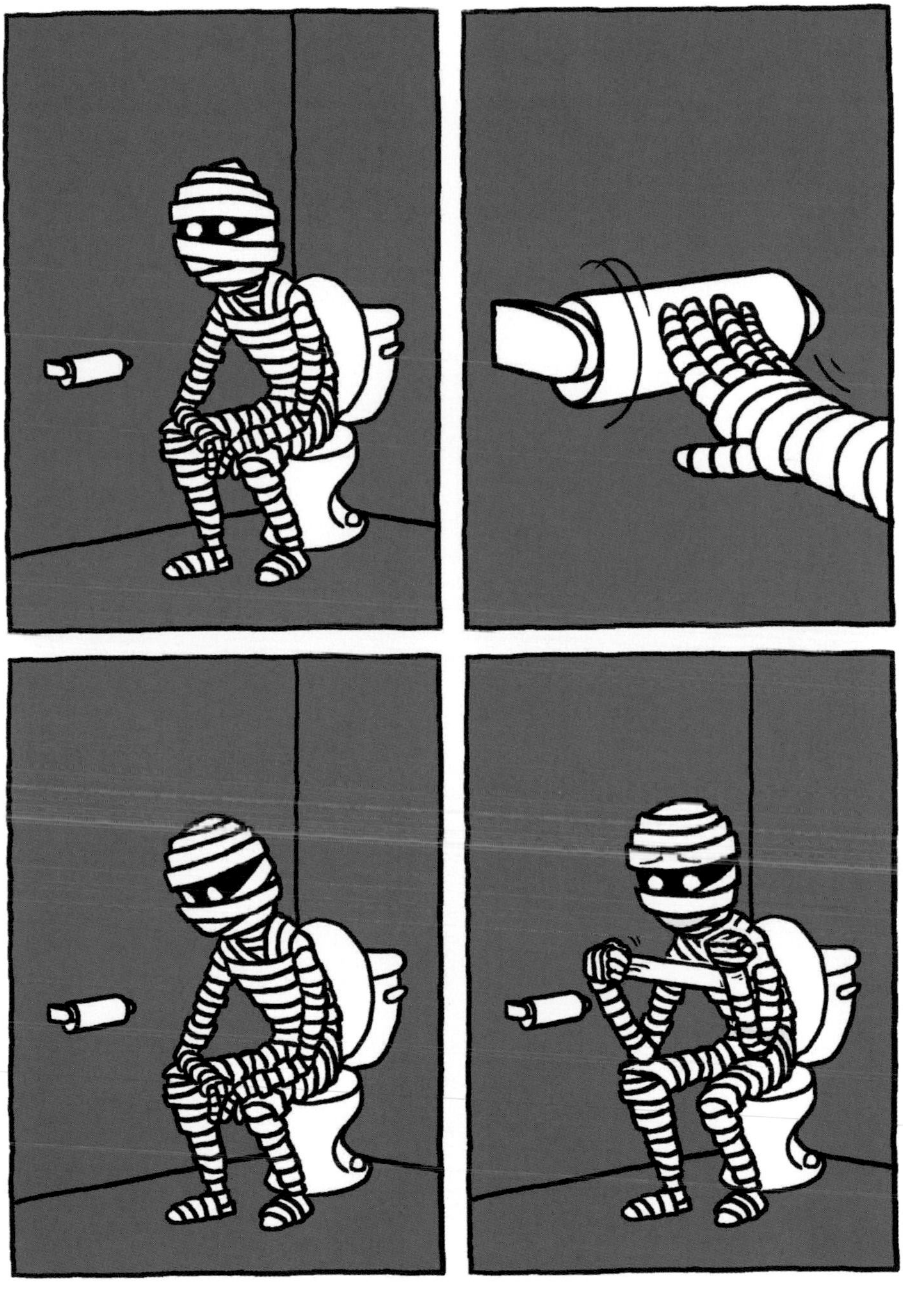

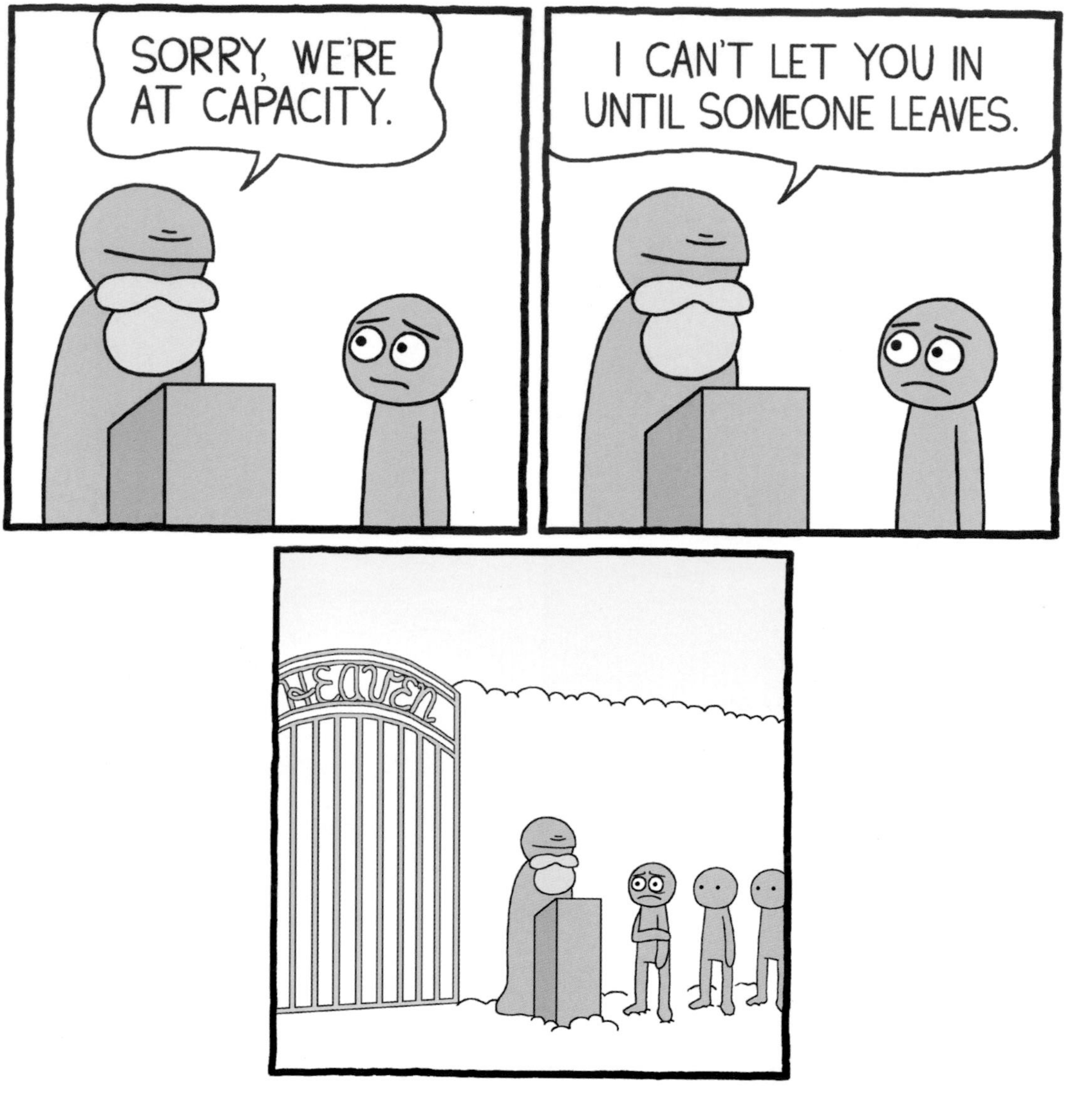
SORRY, WE'RE AT CAPACITY.
I CAN'T LET YOU IN UNTIL SOMEONE LEAVES.
HEAVEN

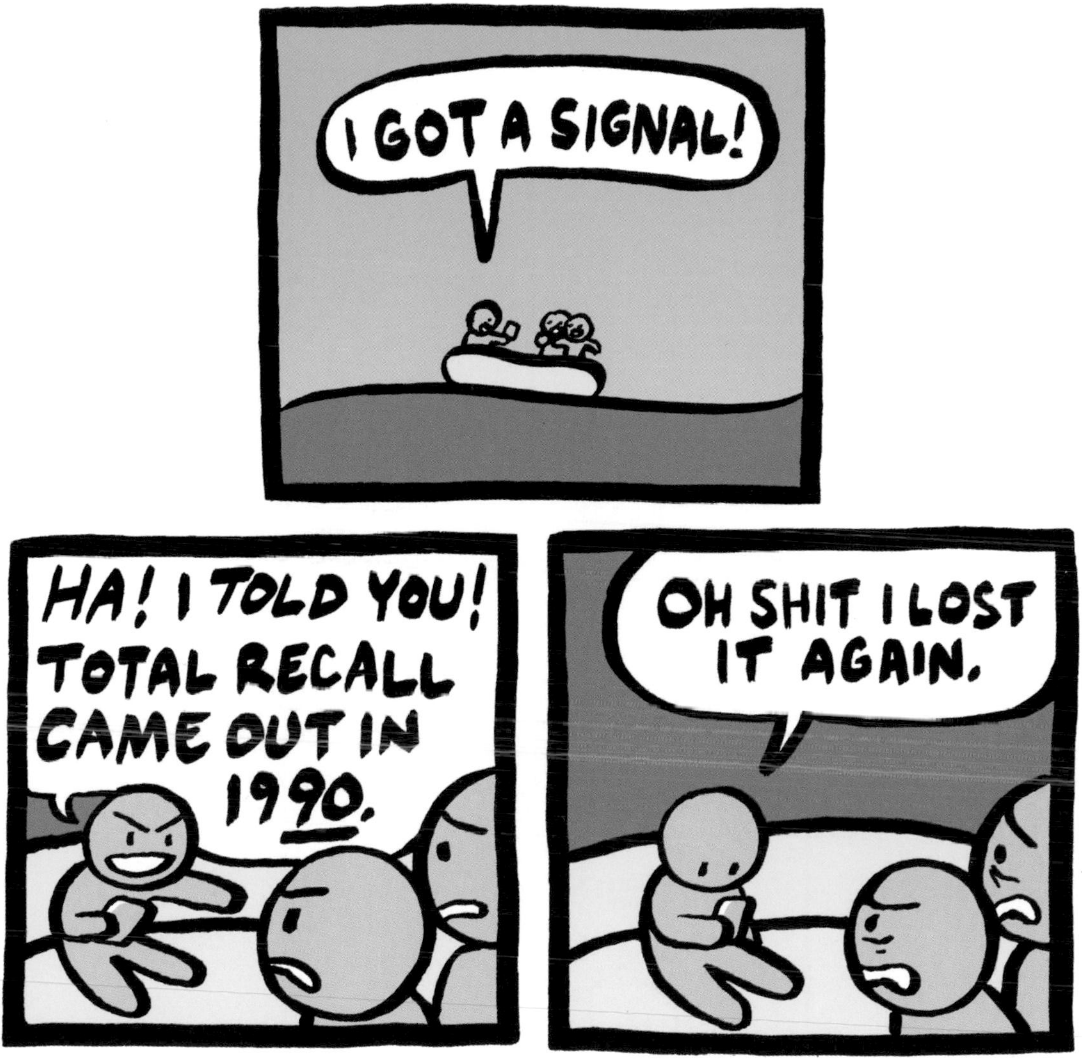
I GOT A SIGNAL!
HA! I TOLD YOU! TOTAL RECALL CAME OUT IN 1990.
OH SHIT I LOST IT AGAIN.

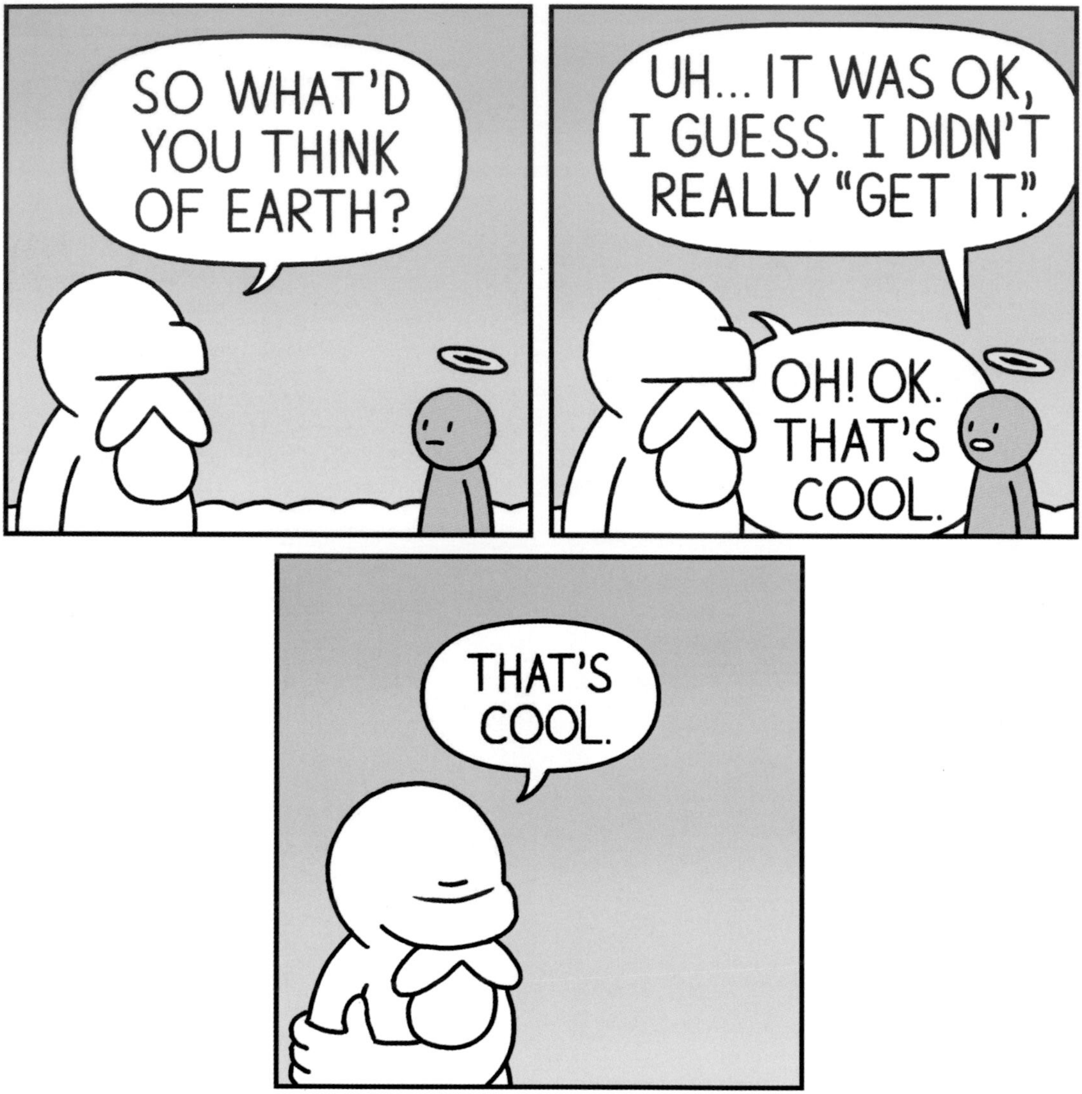
SO WHAT'D YOU THINK OF EARTH?
UH... IT WAS OK, I GUESS. I DIDN'T REALLY "GET IT."
OH! OK. THAT'S COOL.
THAT'S COOL.

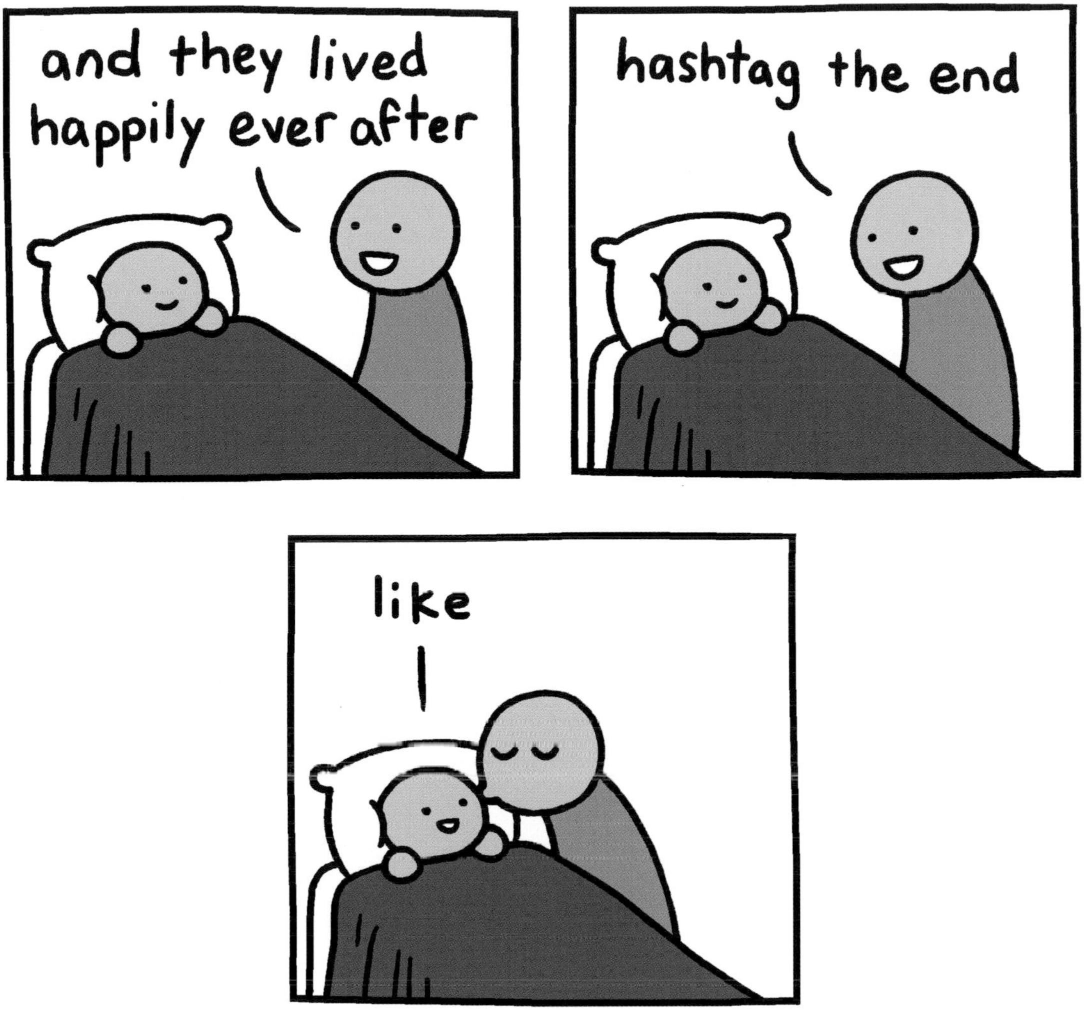
and they lived happily ever after
hashtag the end
like

ACKNOWLEDGMENTS

Thank you, Kelli and Martin Zaehringer, for not ruining my childhood. Thanks, Mom, for writing the joke on page 97.

Thank you, Steve Moore, for *drawing* me into the world of comics (sorry). Without you, I wouldn't have had an *inkling* (sorry) that I could be a cartoonist.

Thank you, Kevin Garvey, for making comics with me every day after school. I hope every aspiring artist finds a partner in crime like you.

Thank you to the members of the *Berkeley Mews* brain trust, whose critiques over the years have been invaluable: Abby and Hannah Zaehringer, Matt DeMartini (who wrote the joke on page 108), Liz Vogt, Andrew Lawrence, and especially Edith Fox (who came up with the idea for the cover art).

Thank you to the good people at Andrews McMeel for their editorial input, creative feedback, and lunch recommendations: John Glynn, Clint Hooker, Shena Wolf, and Lucas Wetzel (who wrote the joke on page 76). Thank you, Spencer Williams and Amy Strassner, for making this book look so pretty.

Thank you to everyone who shared my comics online.

Sorry I ruined your childhood.